D0312515

Praise for
Sacred Treasure—The Cairo Genizah

"How ironic—and fascinating—that one of the greatest discoveries of Jewish texts in history would unfold in a dusty old attic in Egypt! Mark Glickman has written a gripping tale of how the genizah of the Cairo synagogue was uncovered, what the 300,000 documents reveal about Jewish history, and the role of twin sisters from Scotland who made it possible. Writing with descriptive flair, Glickman's book is a page-turner, a fast-paced archaeological mystery, a globe-trotting adventure, and a wonderful story. Highly recommended!"

—**Dr. Ron Wolfson**, Fingerhut Professor of Education, American Jewish University; president, Synagogue 3000; author, *The Seven Questions You're Asked in Heaven: Reviewing and Renewing Your Life on Earth*

"An upbeat, fast-paced adventurer's tale of how the hunt for Jewish documents, one hundred and ten years ago in a corner of Egypt, has shaped our thinking about who we are as Jews. Its quick presentation of what my great-grandfather found is well matched with Glickman's accessible explanations of what the discoveries mean for our world today."

—**Rabbi John S. Schechter**, Congregation B'nai Israel, Basking Ridge, New Jersey

"Shows clearly how genizah documents are very important for Jewish and non-Jewish scholars and researchers in different areas: Jewish history, Islamic history, religions, medicine, languages, biblical and Talmudic studies, etc…. [A] very important book."

—**Dr. Mohamed Hawary**, professor of religious Jewish thought and comparative religions, Ain Shams University, Cairo, Egypt

"Equal to the excitement of Belzoni's adventures along the Nile or Carter's forays into the Valley of Kings is Solomon Schechter's discovery of over a quarter of a million manuscripts hidden in an attic room of an ancient synagogue in Cairo at the turn of the twentieth century. Mark Glickman brings this adventure vibrantly to life, taking the reader on a fascinating journey with him from the bazaars of Cairo to the cloisters of Cambridge, up rickety ladders and through locked vaults, as he tells the story of how these manuscripts were found, where they ended up, and what their enormous significance is today. Glickman's narrative is accessible and engaging, and a great introduction to a complex story of scheming, scholarship, and sensation."

—**Dr. Rebecca J. W. Jefferson**, head of the Price Library of Judaica, University of Florida; former researcher, Taylor-Schechter Genizah Research Unit, Cambridge University

SACRED TREASURE
THE CAIRO
GENIZAH

The Amazing Discoveries
of Forgotten Jewish History in
an Egyptian Synagogue Attic

RABBI MARK GLICKMAN

For People of All Faiths, All Backgrounds
JEWISH LIGHTS Publishing
Woodstock, Vermont

Sacred Treasure—The Cairo Genizah:
The Amazing Discoveries of Forgotten Jewish History in an Egyptian Synagogue Attic

2011 Hardcover Edition, Second Printing
2011 Hardcover Edition, First Printing
© 2011 by Mark Glickman

Library of Congress Cataloging-in-Publication Data
Glickman, Mark.
Sacred treasure—the Cairo genizah : the amazing discoveries of forgotten Jewish history in an Egyptian synagogue attic / Mark Glickman.
p. cm.
Includes bibliographical references and index.
ISBN 978-1-58023-431-3 (hardcover)
1. Judaism—History—Medieval and early modern period, 425-1789—Sources. 2. Cairo Genizah—History. I. Title.
BM180.G56 2010
296.09'02—dc22

2010034260

10 9 8 7 6 5 4 3 2
Manufactured in the United States of America
Jacket Design: Jenny Buono
Jacket Art: A fragment of a schoolhouse primer, copyright University of Cambridge, reproduced by kind permission of the Syndics of Cambridge University Library.
Interior Design: Tim Holtz

Published by Jewish Lights Publishing
A Division of Longhill Partners, Inc.
Sunset Farm Offices, Route 4, P.O. Box 237
Woodstock, VT 05091
Tel: (802) 457-4000   Fax: (802) 457-4004
www.jewishlights.com

For Caron

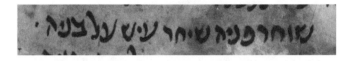

He who has looked into her face has seen the stars.

Joseph Ibn Tzaddik, d. 1149

Contents

"You shall not [destroy the sacred sites, altars, and the name of] Adonai your God."

—DEUTERONOMY 12:4

"The unbroken tablets and the broken tablets were placed in the Ark of the Covenant."

—BABYLONIAN TALMUD, *BERAKHOT* 8B

"Every discovery of an ancient document giving evidence of a bygone world is, if undertaken in the right spirit ... an act of resurrection in miniature."

—RABBI SOLOMON SCHECHTER, NOVEMBER 20, 1902

Solomon Schechter studying Cairo Genizah manuscripts in the Cambridge University Library, summer, 1897.

Prologue

In late December 1896, on a balcony overlooking the main floor of Cairo's Ben Ezra Synagogue, Rabbi Solomon Schechter of Cambridge University climbed a crudely built ladder set against a limestone wall, his eyes fixed on a dark opening above. The opening led to the synagogue's genizah, an attic-like chamber where Cairo's Jews had been depositing texts and documents of every kind for more than eight hundred years.

Schechter had good reason to hope that the Genizah contained a sizable mass of Jewish writings, but as he scaled the ladder, he had no way of knowing that this repository, packed with nearly three hundred thousand documents, represented the largest trove of early and medieval Jewish manuscripts ever discovered. It would transform the world's understanding of medieval Jewry, biblical and Rabbinic literature, medieval Islamic history, and much more. So vast was the collection that nearly a century after Schechter's death in 1915, scholars would still be poring over the contents of the Cairo Genizah and still making discoveries.

Reaching the portal, Schechter held his lantern in the dusty, silo-like space, still unsure as to what riches it contained. In Cambridge, Schechter had recently identified a Genizah manuscript as a page of a long-lost book from biblical times. Would he discover more of its pages in the Genizah? (He would.) Schechter knew that the great twelfth-century rabbi-philosopher Moses Maimonides lived within walking distance of this synagogue. Might the Genizah contain documents from the hand of Maimonides himself? (It did.) Schechter also knew that Cairo was an important cultural and economic hub during the Middle Ages. Did the

Genizah hold important information documenting the lives of
Jews and non-Jews who lived in and traveled through that great
Egyptian metropolis? (More than Schechter could ever imagine.)

Peering into the illuminated chamber, the bearded, red-haired
rabbi beheld an astonishing jumble of texts piled yards high, the
sheer quantity of which must have left him breathless. Schechter
immediately realized that one person—one Cambridge scholar—
would never be able to sift through all this material in ten lifetimes.
It would fall to others, including generations of Cambridge
researchers, to uncover many of the Cairo Genizah's most spectac-
ular documents.

Buried in the Genizah was the last letter to Maimonides from
his brother David, a merchant who was lost at sea on a voyage to
India; the oldest-known Passover Haggadot in the world; the earliest fragment of Rabbinic literature ever discovered; and the clay
seal of the prominent tenth-century sage Rabbi Nehemiah Gaon.
The paper chaos also held the earliest example of Jewish sheet
music—a Hebrew poem set to Gregorian chant during the twelfth
century by a former Italian priest who converted to Judaism during
the Crusades. And much, much more.

In February 2010, more than a century after Solomon
Schechter entered the Genizah and set this massive scholarly project
into motion, I too climbed up to the Genizah portal. Like Schechter,
I am an ordained rabbi, though I serve as leader of two small con-
gregations in Washington State rather than as a Cambridge don.
Like Schechter, I have long had a passion for old Jewish books and
manuscripts, though I cannot lay claim to scholarly achievements
even remotely as extensive as his. Like Schechter—who, according
to some accounts of his life, was forty-six years old when he first
viewed the Genizah—I too was forty-six when I climbed that ladder
in Cairo. I had first heard the Genizah story when I was a rabbinical student in the mid-1980s, and I had been researching it inten-
sively for three years. To see the Genizah chamber for myself, I had
traveled from Seattle to Cairo with my fifteen-year-old son Jacob.
As far as I knew at the time, nobody else pursuing the Genizah's

story had peered into it for nearly a hundred years, and no one had *ever* photographed the interior.

I'll never forget the moment I first looked inside. The room is now empty of documents, but what riches it once held! I imagined page after page after page fluttering down onto the growing pile of manuscripts—letters, Bibles, medical prescriptions, and countless others. Each was a tiny gem; each carried a spark of human memory and wisdom; each was part of the greatest literary treasure ever discovered.

And it was discovered in that very room.

I have countless other memories of this trip with Jacob. Our expedition included stops in Cambridge, England, and New York City to meet Genizah researchers, view additional Genizah-related sites, and see firsthand some of the Genizah's most magnificent discoveries.

It was the experience of a lifetime, and a fitting culmination to my years of research on the story of the Cairo Genizah.

Sacred Words, Sacred Scraps

This is the story of that roomful of sacred scraps—of ripped Torah scrolls, rotted Talmud pages, old business receipts, fallen-away leaves of wisdom books, love letters, friend letters, and large letters of the Hebrew alphabet written in schoolhouse primers. It is the story of a rabbi raised in a Romanian shtetl who moved many of those scraps from the gloomy repository to the bright light of modern scholarship. It is the story of two erudite Scottish sisters whose discovery of a crumbling page of Hebrew text spurred that rabbi toward his find. It is the story of conservationists who preserve the texts, scholars who study them, technicians who digitize them, philanthropists who support this painstaking work, and curious readers around the world who can now peruse these ancient treasures online.

Most important, it is the story of countless Jews from many lands and centuries who somehow left a bit of themselves in those old documents. For in those sacred scraps we see reflections of the lives of millions. We read of their daily activities and encounter their sages' wisdom. We see what stirred their souls, what they loved and what they feared, what set their hearts soaring, and also what angered them. They wrote to one another, for one another, and about one another. They composed poetry, recorded business transactions, and signed legal deeds. They transcribed scripture; they wrote philosophies, theologies, and commentaries on sacred text; and sometimes they just doodled. They believed that the words and images they had inscribed were so sacred that they never threw them away. Instead, they stashed the documents in a synagogue chamber. Perhaps forever.

Built in the ninth century or earlier, then destroyed and rebuilt during the eleventh century, the Ben Ezra Synagogue was home to a Jewish community that thrived and flourished for centuries. Not only did its members excel in scholarly, artistic, and business endeavors, but the community was also a center of artistic, commercial, and intellectual life for Jews and non-Jews throughout North Africa, the Middle East, and beyond.

Historically, Judaism has viewed any document containing Hebrew as sacred, and Jewish law forbids the disposal of sacred documents. As the renowned Rabbi Moshe ben Maimon—Maimonides—wrote in thirteenth-century Cairo: "It is forbidden to destroy any sacred writing or its commentary or its interpretation."[1]

Words, in Judaism, carry sacred power. Especially Hebrew words. And even more especially, the words of Torah. The Jewish mystical tradition teaches that the letters of the Torah were fire—black fire inscribed on white fire. They are to be handled only with great care.

So what are Jews to do when their Hebrew books and papers become damaged, destroyed, or simply out-of-date? One option is to bury them in a Jewish cemetery, customarily near the grave of a scholar. The other (often more convenient) option is to designate a room, usually an attic or a cellar in the synagogue, as a genizah—a repository for damaged sacred documents.

Originally, the only documents placed in genizahs were those bearing one of the many names of God that appear in sacred

Jewish literature; those documents are called *shemot*, "names." But over the years, the genizah requirement broadened. Eventually, not only documents including the name of God, but *any* document with *any* Hebrew on it also went into a genizah. If you used a Hebrew name on a business receipt, or quoted the Bible in a letter to your mother, or wrote a secular poem containing some Hebrew words, Jewish law and custom called upon you to put it into a genizah rather than a trash can when you were done with it.

Still later, the genizah requirement broadened even further. Jews began depositing in their genizahs any paper even remotely related to their Jewish lives. Many such documents were in Hebrew, but others, especially in the Cairo Genizah, were in Arabic, Persian, Yiddish, and at least one language yet to be identified.

So, from the tenth through the nineteenth centuries, in that tall, narrow, dark chamber, there grew an astounding pile of tattered old documents. The texts were unusable, but in a literal sense, they were also indispensable. And into the Genizah they went—one torn page, one tattered parchment, one scrap at a time. For nearly a thousand years.

Then one day in 1896, Solomon Schechter's lantern illumined the Genizah, and from the dusty recesses of the ancient chamber, the light of the old letters began to shine once again.

Treasures in the Synagogue Attic

In 1025, the first papers of the Cairo Genizah fluttered to its floor. We don't know what they were—loose pages of decrepit prayer books, a bundle of old letters, or perhaps some unneeded business records. Whatever their identity, they began a steady stream of texts flowing into that unlit room for centuries. Many of the documents were composed locally in or around Cairo. But others had traveled great distances. Some came by camelback from the west, in caravans from Algeria, Tunisia, or Morocco. Others arrived on ships from Europe or trade routes between Africa and India. And some came from Babylonia in the north, often by way of the Land of Israel.

From all of these places and others, the documents flowed to Cairo. The Egyptian capital, whose name means "Triumphant," was not the world's largest Jewish community back then—Baghdad and Cordoba were larger. Nor was Cairo considered sacred, like Jerusalem. It was, however, a major crossroads of medieval Arabia where Jewish life thrived. Its Jews were active in Egyptian commercial life, had Egyptian friends and business associates, and sometimes even held high-ranking government positions.

The Narrow Place

Egypt was, of course, an odd place for Jewish life to flourish. Many centuries earlier, the Egyptians had enslaved the Israelites, oppressing them with hard labor. Jewish legend minces no words in describing the Egyptians' cruelty: they deprived the Israelites of straw to make bricks and flogged their foremen when the work teams came up short; they punished workers who produced too little by killing one of their children; when a baby fell into a vat of mortar, the taskmasters refused to allow the Israelites to save it, sealing the child's body forever inside a brick. The Hebrew word for Egypt is *mitzrayim*, meaning "the narrow place," the place of constriction.

And yet, Jewish tradition is not complete in its vilification of Egypt. Abraham, the first Jew, traveled there with his wife, Sarah. In Egypt, Joseph rose to great heights of power and saved his brothers from famine. Jacob, on his way to Egypt to be reunited with his beloved son Joseph, feared that God would be angry at him for willingly going into exile. But God reassured Jacob, saying, "Do not be afraid to go down to Egypt, for there I will make you into a great people" (Genesis 46:3).

Indeed, it was in Egypt that the ragtag clan of Israelites first became a "people," and Pharaoh was the first to notice it. "Behold," he said, "the people of the children of Israel are too numerous and mighty for us" (Exodus 1:9). The realization frightened Pharaoh into enslaving the Israelites, and it was in the crucible of Egyptian suffering that they forged their identity into a nation.

In Jewish memory, then, Egypt is a land of both enormous torment and invaluable national growth. And it was from that place of narrowness and constriction that Jews first ventured toward vast horizons in pursuit of their shared destiny.

Return to Egypt

After they left Egypt, God forbade the Israelites from turning back: "You shall not return this way ever again" (Deuteronomy 17:16). But they returned anyway, those wandering Jews. Legend has it that the prophet Elijah (ninth century BCE) visited Egypt and revealed himself at a spot that would later become the site of a Cairo synagogue. Later, it is said, the prophet Jeremiah (sixth century BCE) mourned the destruction of the Temple in Jerusalem at the very same spot. Decades later, the Temple was rebuilt, partly under the leadership of Ezra the Scribe. Legend has it that he, too, journeyed to Egypt, where he penned a Torah scroll for the Jews who lived there.

The first permanent, post-Pharaoh Jewish community in Egypt appears with the dedication in 332 BCE of Alexandria, built in northern Egypt where the Nile meets the Mediterranean. There are reports of Jews present at that ceremony, and there is evidence that within a few years of its founding Alexandria had become home to a sizable Jewish population.

In the seventh century CE, Arab armies conquered Egypt and established the national capital at their encampment along the eastern bank of the Nile, at the border between the ancient kingdoms of Upper and Lower Egypt. They called their capital Fustat—tent city. By the ninth century, an estimated 120,000 people lived in Fustat; by 1168, that number had grown to 200,000.

Fustat remained the capital until the tenth century, when an invading Arab army from Tunisia called the Fatimids conquered Egypt and moved the capital to Fustat's northern suburb, a city called Al-Qahira—Cairo. In time, Cairo would grow large enough to engulf Fustat, but the two cities existed side by side for many centuries, and a sizable Jewish community remained in Fustat even after the capital moved to Cairo.

The Ben Ezra Synagogue and the Cairo Genizah

Among the earliest references to Jews in Fustat is a Christian document indicating that in 882, a patriarch of the Coptic Church—an Egyptian Christian denomination—needed to sell a church there to pay a tribute to Ahmed ibn Tulun, the ruler of Egypt. He sold a former Greek Orthodox church and the land around it to the Jewish community, who turned it into a synagogue.

By then, there were three distinct groups of Jews in Cairo: the "Babylonians" or "Iraqis," who were allied with the Rabbinic sages of Baghdad; the Palestinians, who were connected with the Rabbinic sages of the Land of Israel; and the Karaites, a group that rejected the authority of the Rabbis and were allied with no Rabbinic sages whatsoever.

For many years, scholars believed that the church sold to the Jews by the Coptic patriarch in 882 later became the Ben Ezra Synagogue, which housed the Cairo Genizah. But the Ben Ezra belonged to the Palestinians, and it turns out that the Jews to whom the patriarch sold his church were newly arrived immigrants from Iraq—Babylonian Jews. Other documents indicate that the original Ben Ezra Synagogue was pre-Islamic, though we don't know exactly when it was built. At any rate, the Ben Ezra Synagogue was established prior to 822 and might date back much farther than that. Sometime around 1012, the caliph Al-Hakim ordered the destruction of all Jewish and Christian houses of worship in Egypt. The Ben Ezra Synagogue was duly demolished, its bricks and timber sold as scrap. Soon afterward, however, the environment in Egypt changed, and the Palestinian Jews of Cairo received permission to rebuild their synagogue. Visitors during the Middle Ages report an inscription above its entryway indicating that the building was rededicated and reopened in 1025.

The newly redesigned building included a genizah. This genizah was larger than most—two stories high, more silo than attic—with a rooftop opening accessible from above. With so much room inside, the synagogue caretakers could avoid moving its contents to the cemetery several miles away. This genizah had plenty of room. With luck, it would last for many centuries.

The oldest known *dated* document in the Cairo Genizah is a fragment from a ninth-century *ketubah*—a Jewish marriage certificate—that predates the Genizah by about 155 years. It is small piece of paper, 5½ inches wide, 3½ inches high. In keeping with custom, the scribe who penned the *ketubah* recorded the date— Friday, the seventeenth of Tishri, Seleucid year 1183 (October 6, 871)—and other details. Partway through, however, the scribe realized that he had made a mistake. The seventeenth of Tishri that year was a *Saturday*, not a Friday as he had written. Not only was it an error, but if anyone caught it later, it might look as if he had been trying to cover up a wedding that had taken place on Shabbat, which Jewish law forbids. The scribe put aside his partially written *ketubah* and began again from scratch. The mistaken document would need to go into a genizah.[1]

The oldest dated document in the Cairo Genizah

The Genizah's Ancient Origins

Jews have saved unusable scraps of text since ancient times. The practice dates back to the very first Jewish text of all: the tablets that Moses received on Mount Sinai. Jewish legend teaches that Moses engraved the entire Torah onto those tablets and that those rock pages were God's greatest gift to the Jewish people before or since. After engraving the text, Moses lugged the tablets down the mountainside, only to discover the Israelites worshiping a golden calf instead of God. Perhaps in anger, perhaps to prevent his people from being held accountable to the laws, Moses smashed the tablets on the ground. Later, after the situation calmed and cooler minds prevailed, Moses returned to the mountaintop to get a second set of tablets.

The tablets were placed in an ornate box, the Ark of the Covenant, and it was said that any army carrying that Ark into battle would be invincible. When Jews built the First Temple under King Solomon's leadership in Jerusalem in 960 BCE, they placed the Ark in its innermost sanctuary, the Holy of Holies. Nobody but the High Priest ever entered that sanctuary, and even he only ventured inside once a year, on Yom Kippur, the Day of Atonement.

Jews have studied the Temple rituals and the story of the Ark in detail for centuries, and one detail about the Ark puzzled a fourth-century sage from Babylonia, Rabbi Joseph. What, he wondered, was *really* in that box? Did it hold only the second, unbroken set of tablets, or did it also hold the shards of the first set—the ones that Moses smashed? His answer was clear: "Rabbi Joseph taught ... that both the [unbroken] tablets and the fragments of the [broken] tablets were deposited in the Ark."[2]

The Ark of the Covenant, in other words, was the world's first genizah.

The Power of Language

Judaism considers language—the spoken and written word—to be a tool that is both sacred and powerful. In one of the most widely acclaimed of all divine acts, the book of Genesis tells us that God created the world through a linguistic act: "And God said, 'Let there be light!" As a result of the magical and creative power of God's spoken word, scripture hastens to add, "there was light" (Genesis 1:3). God also created humanity through an utterance: "Let us make man in our image" (Genesis 1:26). Among the most significant passages in the Torah is the Ten Commandments—in Hebrew, *Aseret Hadibrot,* "the Ten Utterances." At the very heart of Judaism, then, is the Utterance, and from its very inception, Judaism has seen in language the power to create, the essence of humanity, and the commanding voice of God.

Of all the world's languages, Judaism sees Hebrew as the holiest of all. It is *lashon hakodesh*, "the sacred tongue"—so holy that some Jews have insisted on speaking it whenever possible, and so holy that others reserve it for special settings. In ancient days, Hebrew was spoken by Jews in the Land of Israel. When Jews moved to other lands and spoke other languages, it became a rarefied parlance of prayer and study, too sacred for everyday use. But in modern times, the ancient language was reborn in the State of Israel, and some Jews saw it as indispensable for the redemption of the Jewish people. Others argued that using Hebrew in schoolyards, department stores, and restaurants was nothing short of sacrilege. Both perspectives share a reverence for Hebrew as the ancient, hallowed language of the Jewish people.

Of all Hebrew words, the holiest to Jews are the words of Torah and other sacred texts. Judaism sees the Torah not as a book that is *full* of wisdom, but a book that is the *very embodiment* of wisdom itself. Judaism teaches that at Mount Sinai, God gave Moses not only the words of the Five Books of Moses—what we call "Written Torah"—but also a vast amount of additional material. These additional words, Jewish tradition teaches, were passed down through the ages by word of mouth as "Oral Torah," and eventually they, too, began to be written down in the Talmud, Rabbinic commentaries, law codes, and other sacred texts. According to Jewish tradition, they are all revelations of God's wisdom.

As a result, Jews see each word of Torah—each word of the enormous library of sacred Jewish literature—as packed with meaning. Through the centuries, Jews have studied and dissected these words, striving to wring as much truth and wisdom from them as possible. Jewish law calls upon Jews to study the words of Torah, to recite them in worship, to read them regularly in the synagogue. Before studying, Jews praise God: "Blessed are You, O Eternal our God, Ruler of the Universe, who has sanctified us with commandments, and commanded us to engage in the words of Torah." In Judaism, relating to these ancient words is a holy act.

The Torah's Most Sacred Words of All

In the Torah, the holiest word of all is the name of God. The Torah sometimes refers to God as *El* or *Elohim*, derived from an ancient word for judge, but many scholars see this as a divine title or job description rather than as a private name. God's intimate name, God's "first name," is a word so sacred that we never pronounce it. As mortals, we are not on a first-name basis with God.

God's secret name is the Tetragrammaton, the ineffable four-letter word spelled with the Hebrew letters corresponding to *YHVH*. The Hebrew alphabet is all consonants; its vowels are usually dots and dashes beneath the letters, and the vowels don't appear in Torah scrolls. There are book editions of the Torah that do include the vowels, but the pronunciation of God's secret name is shrouded in mystery, and modern readers use a replacement: *Adonai*, "Sovereign." Indeed, the only person who ever knew how to pronounce God's name was the High Priest. It was the word he uttered during his annual Yom Kippur visit to the Holy of Holies as he atoned on behalf of himself, his family, and all Jews everywhere. If an impure thought entered his mind as he uttered God's name, the world would come to an end.

One word. It is imbued with power and danger; it is shrouded in mystery. As God's name, it can transform a people; misused, it can lead to utter catastrophe.

Storing the Sacred and the Forbidden

Nowadays, the word *genizah* refers to a repository for damaged or destroyed Jewish documents, but this wasn't always the case. *Genizah* derives from the Persian *ganj*, meaning "treasury" or "storehouse." In the Bible, the term appears in the books of Esther and Ezra referring to the rooms holding royal treasuries.

By the sixth century CE, however, the term had taken on several more specific meanings. For example, the Talmud refers to a genizah as a storage place for sacred objects that had become unusable. The Talmud's oldest section, the Mishnah (codified around 200 CE), teaches:

> Articles used for fulfilling religious obligations may be thrown out. But articles used for sacred purposes need a genizah. What are "articles used for fulfilling religious obligations"? Sukkah,* lulav,† shofar,‡ and fringes (tzitzit).§ What are "articles used for sacred purposes"? Torah scrolls, tefillin,** and mezuzahs,†† as well as Torah scroll cases, tefillin straps, and their cases.[3]

It is important to note that not just any damaged or destroyed religious items were stored in such a genizah—the genizah was only for items used in the most sacred of activities. Those items, at least in this mishnah, happen to be texts and their accessories.

Elsewhere, the Mishnah understood *genizah* differently. This definition appears in a discussion about a religious conundrum. On Shabbat—the Sabbath day—Jewish law forbids many routine activities, such as lighting or extinguishing fires. Apparently, the original intent of this prohibition was to disallow cooking, burnt offerings in the Temple, and other fire-related activities on Shabbat. But, of course, there must be exceptions to this rule.

---

* A decorated, open-air booth in which Jews are to live during the autumn festival of Sukkot.

† A palm branch held with sprigs of willow and myrtle, which Jews wave during the Sukkot festival.

‡ A ram's horn blown in synagogues on Rosh Hashanah, the Jewish New Year.

§ The Torah calls for Jews to tie fringes to the corners of their four-cornered garments.

** Small black boxes containing sacred texts written on parchment. They are worn by many traditional Jews during worship—one on the forehead, and one on the upper arm—and are held to the body with narrow leather straps.

†† Small containers hung on the doorposts of Jewish homes. Inside them are parchments bearing handwritten Hebrew prayers.

What if you are freezing to death on Shabbat—literally—and you need a fire to stay warm and survive? In such an extreme situation, is it okay to light a fire? What if your house is burning down on Shabbat? Are you allowed to put the fire out *then*? And what if your synagogue is on fire? Are Jews permitted to douse the flames to save their sacred texts? And if the answer is yes, then exactly which texts count as sacred?

The Rabbis, of course, had an opinion regarding these questions:

> One may [transgress the rules of Shabbat to] save all sacred writings from a fire, whether or not they are the kind of writings that we read [in the synagogue on Shabbat]. Sacred writings in any language need a genizah…. One may save the book jacket with the book, and a tefillin case with the tefillin, even if it has money in it.[4]

To the ancient Rabbis, the genizah was not only a place for damaged goods, but also a place of safety—a place to shield imperiled sacred items from destruction. And the requirement to use it was of paramount importance, trumping even the laws of Shabbat.

Sacred text, in other words, is like a person. Like a person, it is of immeasurable sanctity. Its complexity invites our respect and attention. It has profound truths to teach. And like a person, we can never fully understand it. For centuries, Jews have honored their sages by burying Torah scrolls and other sacred texts in or near their graves. We honor the person for living the text.

Genizahs weren't only for holding sacred objects; Jews also used them to hide forbidden items. Long ago, before there was a Bible, before there was a standardized ritual in Jerusalem's Temple, the Middle East was rife with stories and legal traditions of all kinds. There were law codes, creation myths, and epic tales passed down through the generations by word of mouth. In time, Jews compiled many of these stories and laws into what we now know as the Bible. They had a lot of material to choose from, so some books made the cut, and others didn't.

The books that didn't get included in the Bible were considered too heretical, too shallow, or unfit for some other reason. And when ancient Jews rejected these books, they rejected them with gusto! Not only were certain books not included in the biblical canon, but they were also forbidden from Jewish homes and from being held by Jewish hands. When later rabbis codified the rules about these rejected books, they decreed that reading or even owning them was a horrible sin. They were "hidden books"—*apocrypha*, in Greek—and Rabbi Akiba proclaimed that a Jew who reads them will not earn a place in the world to come.

And where were these hidden books to be hidden? In a genizah.

Nevertheless, most books in genizahs were those that had become damaged or unusable. Solomon Schechter wrote, "[The act of preserving damaged] books … means much the same thing as burial means in the case of men. When the spirit is gone, we put the corpse out of sight to protect it from abuse. In like manner, when the writing is worn out, we hide the book to preserve it from profanation."[5] Indeed, in the beginning, as mentioned, Jews buried their unusable texts in local cemeteries, often near the graves of great scholars. But as more and more books came to be written down, schlepping piles of torn and tattered tomes out to the cemetery became increasingly impractical. As the volume of texts grew, the volume of worn-out or damaged texts grew, as well. With so many needing proper disposal and with the cemetery so far away, what were the Jews of Cairo to do? The really big genizah in the Ben Ezra Synagogue solved that growing problem. It meant that they wouldn't have to worry about their tattered books and papers for a long, long time.

Most genizahs have long been lost to history. Sometimes Jews fleeing from persecution or leaving home for other reasons simply abandoned their synagogues and genizahs. Sometimes—due either to accidents or to acts of hatred—synagogues burned to the ground along with their genizahs. Mold, insects, and vermin also feasted on the old words as they stewed through the years in the damp and the dark.

Genizahs, therefore, rarely survive for very long. For a genizah to last, it would need a Jewish community healthy enough to stay in one place, secure enough to escape attack, dry enough to avoid the ravages of water, mold, and worms, and lucky enough to avoid accidental destruction. For all of these genizah-friendly factors to converge in a single community would have been a very rare occurrence indeed.

Rare. But not impossible.

1

The Genizah Moment

In the 1890s the Cairo Genizah came out of the shadows. For centuries, only the caretakers of the Ben Ezra Synagogue and perhaps a few other Cairo Jews had seen the cluttered chamber. Everyone could have surmised that the Genizah was there, just as they knew that the synagogue rested on a foundation and that there were rafters inside its walls. But nobody cared.

Similarly unnoticed were the Jews of Cairo themselves, and for that matter, all Jews in the Middle East. Everyone knew they were there, but few outsiders paid much attention. Jews in industrializing Europe and America gave little thought to their fellow Jews in places like Egypt. In the West, many Jews saw their religion as one of rationalism and enlightenment—the epitome of modern European ideals. To them, the dark-skinned, turbaned Jews of the Middle East didn't fit their image of what Jews were supposed to be.

It mattered little that these Gilded-Age European Jews knew that there had long been Jews living in the Middle East. The Bible itself teaches that Judaism began in modern-day Turkey, in a place called Haran. There God first spoke to Abraham, telling him that his offspring would one day be a great nation. "Go forth," God said, "to the land that I will show you" (Genesis 12:1).

Many years later, during a horrible famine in the land God promised to Abraham, his seventy male descendants went with their families to Egypt in search of food. They set down roots in Egypt, only to be enslaved by Pharaoh when their numbers grew. Then, under Moses's leadership, they left Egypt, wandered through the Sinai for forty years, conquered their ancestral homeland, and set down roots anew. In 1000 BCE, under King David, they established their national capital in Jerusalem, and under David's son Solomon, they built a magnificent Temple in Jerusalem.

That Temple stood for about four hundred years, but in 586 BCE, the Babylonians invaded the Land of Israel, destroyed the Temple, brought the Jews to Babylonia, and enslaved them once again. As slaveries go, however, the Jewish one in Babylonia wasn't all that bad. Soon, these "slaves" prospered. When Persia gained ascendancy over Babylonia fifty years later, the emperor Cyrus allowed the Jews to return to the Land of Israel, but only a small number did. Most Jews, with a polite—if Hebrew-accented— "Thanks, but no thanks," chose to stay in their new Babylonian homes.

The small number of Jews who returned rebuilt the Temple in Jerusalem. This Temple—the Second Temple—stood for about five hundred years, until 70 CE, when the Jews rebelled against their rulers *du jour*, the Romans, lost, and once again saw their sacred Temple reduced to rubble. The Jewish people scattered in every direction. A few remained in the Land of Israel, but most moved south, into Africa; north, to Europe; and east, to other places in the Middle East.

Diaspora Subcultures

Jewish life after the destruction of the Second Temple was a life of exile. No longer a ruling majority, these minority communities were deeply influenced by their surrounding cultures. In time, Diaspora Jewish communities arrayed themselves into a panoply of different subcultures. Though still united by Jewish religion and practice, they spoke different languages, ate different foods, and wore different clothes.

By the end of the tenth century, there were three broad groups of Jewish subcultures. The smallest was the Ashkenazim, or

Ashkenazic Jews. *Ashkenaz* is Hebrew for "Germany," and Ashkenazic Jews trace their roots to Jews who settled in northern and central Europe. The next biggest group was Sephardic Jews, who descend from Spain, Portugal, Greece, and other lands along the northern coast of the Mediterranean.

The Jews of Arab lands—northern Africa and the Middle East—were the largest group by far, and during the Middle Ages, many of them thrived and prospered in their exile. They were merchants and physicians, poets and philosophers; they spoke Arabic, Persian, Aramaic, Kurdish, Berber, and other languages; for the most part, they dressed and acted as any good Arab should.

And so it remained—for *centuries.* Ashkenazic Jews, Sephardic Jews, and the Jews of Arab lands knew about one another. They traded, read one another's books, and sometimes traveled great distances to visit one another. They felt proud of their own groups, and sometimes even superior to the others. But aside from occasional flare-ups, the different subcultures tended to interact as friendly rivals.

In 1492, everything changed. In that year—just three days before the voyage of Christopher Columbus—Spain's infamous Alhambra Decree took effect, expelling all one hundred thousand Jews from that country. Jews had been in Spain for many centuries—perhaps, some scholars believe, since biblical days. Suddenly, with the stroke of a royal pen, they were no longer permitted to live there.

Portugal expelled its Jews in 1497, and other Sephardic countries soon followed suit. Some Sephardim moved north, settling in Ashkenazic lands while proudly maintaining their Sephardic identity. Other Sephardic Jews fled to Arab lands. In fact, Spanish exiles fled to many of these communities in such great numbers that their culture soon overwhelmed that of the local Jews. As the Middle Ages waned, Ashkenazim lumped together all Jews in Arab lands—whether indigenous residents or descendants of Spanish exiles—as Sephardim. So, too, did many members of the communities themselves. As a result, the distinctive identity of Arabic Jews gradually melted away into the increasingly dominant Sephardic culture and practice.

Scholars estimate that at the end of the eleventh century, Ashkenazic Jews constituted only about 3 percent of the worldwide Jewish population. By modern times, however, with the political and economic ascent of Christian civilization over Islam, the balance had shifted, and Ashkenazic Jews greatly outnumbered their Sephardic counterparts.[1]

Until the nineteenth century, Ashkenazic Jews paid little attention to their Sephardic counterparts, and what attention they did pay often came out as a sneer. They prided themselves on the fact that under persecution, many Ashkenazim chose martyrdom rather than conversion, whereas Sephardim often converted to Islam rather than face death at the hands of their persecutors.

Sometimes, Ashkenazim went so far as to invoke Ashkenazic superiority to explain antisemitism and persecution. For example, after the pope ordered that the Talmud be burned in Rome in 1553, the chief rabbi of Poznan, Poland, suggested that the atrocity was the fault of the Sephardim. Was the Talmud burned because a tyrant bent on evil had ordered it? No. The burning of the Talmud, the rabbi reasoned, was a result of the fact that in 1551, Jews in Venice (some 250 miles from Rome) had published an edition of Maimonides's *Mishneh Torah*. And Maimonides was a Sephardic Jew! Evidently, according to this Ashkenazic rabbi, when the literature of great Sephardic sages is published, God responds by arranging the destruction of sacred Jewish texts.[2]

That view, however, changed dramatically during the nineteenth century, particularly in Western Europe. Under the light of modern science and historical scholarship, even Ashkenazim themselves came to see Ashkenazic Jewish life as insular and anachronistic, the "twisted" medieval logic of its scholars unworthy of an enlightened people. During the mid-1800s, Ashkenazic synagogues began incorporating the magnificent poetry of Sephardic Jewry into their worship. In Leipzig, Frankfurt, Cologne, Mainz,

Budapest, Vienna, Berlin, and elsewhere, Jewish communities built
their synagogues not as the tiny hovels or gabled wooden boxes
that had long characterized the synagogues of Ashkenaz, but as
majestic, ornately domed Moorish-style edifices, their intricate
designs evoking the exoticism and flavor of "the Orient." They
wrote contemporary fiction and poetry that focused on the lives of
Sephardic Jews, and their scholarship demonstrated a growing
awareness of the beauty and richness of Jewish life under Islam.[3]
Today, the fascination that European Jews showed for Middle
Eastern culture—their mythic (if somewhat myopic) conception of
the dark, mysterious, and exotic Arabian Jew—smacks of colonial-
ism. Lawrence of Arabia, Jewish style. The Jews of the time, however, would have argued that their view was not only deeply
respectful of their Eastern counterparts, but also a celebration of
enlightenment and modernity.

Moritz Steinschneider and Young Schechter

Among the individuals who effectuated this change was Moritz
Steinschneider, a quiet and unimposing giant of a scholar.
Steinschneider was born in Moravia in 1816 and received an intensive Jewish and secular education during his childhood. As a young
man, Steinschneider formed close relationships with many of the
most renowned Jewish scholars of the time, and in 1843, having
moved to Prague, he was ordained a rabbi. For years, he sustained
himself with rabbinic odd-job work—tutoring students, translating
textbooks, and officiating at weddings and worship services. Then,
in 1869, Steinschneider found two jobs that he would hold for
decades, one as an assistant at the Royal Berlin Library and the
other as director of a local Jewish girls school.[4]

By this time, Steinschneider had already gained a reputation
as a scholar. In 1845, the editors of the *General Encyclopedia of Arts
and Sciences* invited him to contribute a two-page article on "Jewish
Literature." With great diligence, Steinschneider worked on it for
three years, and when it was finally published in 1850, it was seven

times its intended length. Later, Oxford University's Bodleian Library hired him to catalogue their entire collection of printed Hebrew books. The massive project took him thirteen years to complete; when finished, it contained 15,000 entries—some 1,750 pages of text. His article on Maimonides alone was 82 pages long. The catalogue provided an index of printers, information on typography, geographical indices, and entries on every Hebrew work in the Bodleian that appeared before 1732. It became an indispensable tool for all serious studies of Jewish literature; Solomon Schechter would refer to it as "the Urim and Thummim of every Jewish student."[5]

Other libraries hired Steinschneider to catalogue their Judaica, and he published other bibliographic work, as well, for over a half century. His monumental 1893 work *The Hebrew Translations of the Middle Ages and the Jews as Interpreters: A Contribution to the Literary History of the Middle Ages, Mostly from Manuscript Sources* was published at his own expense, with a first printing of only three hundred copies.

Steinschneider focused much of his scholarship on a thorough examination of Arabic Jewish literature. He catalogued and described not only sacred texts, but also works of astronomy, mathematics, history, and more, revealing a world that other scholars hardly knew existed. They showed the influence of Islam over Jewish history and how extensively encounters between Jews and Arabs helped shape the Jewish people.

Moritz Steinschneider

Moritz Steinschneider also trained a generation of students eager to study manuscripts documenting the connection between Islam and Judaism. And in the late 1870s and early 1880s, one of Steinschneider's students in Berlin was a young rabbi by the name of Solomon Schechter.

Simon von Geldern, First on the Scene

One of the most puzzling aspects of the "discovery" of the Cairo Genizah is that it wasn't a discovery at all. By the time Western scholars became aware of its documents, the existence of Ben Ezra's Genizah was a widely known—if largely ignored—fact. Indeed, over the years, a few Western visitors had even glimpsed the Genizah and written of its massive heap of crumbling paper and parchment. But no one much cared.

However, during the eighteenth and nineteenth centuries, this began to change. Western European society in general had grown enamored of things Oriental, and—partly owing to Steinschneider's work—Western European Jews in particular had started turning to the East as a paradigm of refined Jewish culture. As a result, reports of a large genizah in Cairo raised some eyebrows, if only briefly. There was no rush of scholars or collectors to Cairo, but the small handful of Westerners who glimpsed the Genizah noticed a pile of documents that was quite large. Enticingly so.

The first known Westerner drawn to the Genizah was a German Jewish Bedouin sheikh named Simon von Geldern, great-uncle of the renowned author Heinrich Heine. Heine never met Von Geldern, but the luscious family lore about him sent young Heinrich's imagination soaring. Born in 1720, Simon von Geldern spent many years traveling throughout the Middle East and North Africa and later wrote of an ecstatic, mystical vision he had on Mount Moriah in Jerusalem. In his early thirties, he hooked up with a marauding tribe of Bedouins who, as Heine wrote, "did not profess Islamism but a kind of Mosaism, and had their resting place ... in one of the unknown oases of the north African desert."[6] Eventually, these quasi-Jewish nomadic thieves chose Von Geldern as their sheikh; he led them for the next several years as they pillaged valuable Middle Eastern booty wherever they could.

Periodically, Von Geldern returned to Europe, clad in Middle Eastern garb and telling stories of his desert adventures. Women melted in his presence. He was called Chevalier (Knight); he was called The Oriental; it was said that he could speak with the dead.

In 1753, Von Geldern and his merry mob of Bedouin bandits marauded its way to Cairo, and like any good German Jewish sheikh, Von Geldern visited the local synagogue. According to some accounts, he tipped the caretaker and took a peek into the Genizah; according to others, Von Geldern heeded warnings that disaster would befall anyone who entered the Genizah, and he stayed safely down below. Regardless, Simon von Geldern left bearing no Genizah material and later speculated in his memoirs about the "wealth of possibility" that might lay hidden in the Genizah's rubbish.[7]

And then, nothing. For over a century, there is no record of a Westerner visiting the Genizah. The pile grew, many older documents crumbled into dust, and except for those few moments when it received new papers, the attic remained dark.

Jacob Saphir, the Second Visitor

In the 1860s, the Genizah welcomed another Western visitor, albeit one who then lived in the East. Rabbi Jacob Saphir was born in

1822 in Oshmiany, Romania (now part of Belarus), and moved to Palestine when he was a young boy. Orphaned as a teenager, Jacob moved to Jerusalem and studied for the rabbinate. During the mid-nineteenth century, Jerusalem's impoverished Jewish community sent Saphir on several alms-seeking journeys to foreign lands. He traveled to India, Yemen, Egypt, and even as far as Australia.

In 1859, Saphir first visited the Ben Ezra Synagogue, where he glimpsed a Torah scroll said to have been written

Jacob Saphir

by Ezra the Scribe, namesake of the

biblical book. The caretakers told Saphir that they had a genizah, but, alas, they forbade him from entering it. The genizah, they explained, was guarded by a vicious serpent who refused to allow any visitors to enter. The caretakers may have been wary of foreigners or perhaps trying to coax some *baksheesh*—petty bribes—out of their visitor. Evidently, Saphir remained oblivious to their not-so-subtle hints.

When Saphir returned to the synagogue in 1864, he realized what the serpent-talk was really about. He discovered that a few Egyptian piasters discreetly passed to a synagogue caretaker somehow had the power to fend off an overly protective serpent. Later, he recalled his time in the Genizah:

> After I had labored for two days and was covered with dust and earth, I removed a few folios of some old books and manuscripts that I had chosen, but did not find any valuable information in them. Who knows what lies beneath? I was tired of searching, but I certainly came across no snake or similar reptile and, thank God, no harm came to me.[8]

Saphir was a manuscript salesman. Although he had visited the Genizah hoping to find manuscripts to sell to his customers, he found little salable material during his dusty two-day forage. Still, the manuscripts that he had seen in that stone chamber, not to mention the size of the Genizah pile, had certainly piqued his interest. "*Who knows what lies beneath?*"

Abraham Firkovitch, Karaite Historian

Another visitor to the Genizah at around this time was Abraham Firkovitch. Firkovitch, born in 1786 in the now Ukrainian city of Lutsk, spent much of his adult life in Crimea as leader of a community known as Karaites,[9] a group that rejects the authority of the Rabbis and whose history goes back to the ninth-century Middle East.

Abraham Firkovitch

By the Middle Ages, the Karaite community claimed tens of thousands of adherents, and Cairo was one of its main population centers. Despite occasional conflicts, the Karaites of Cairo and elsewhere usually got along with their Rabbanite counterparts. The two groups shared business ties, there were many cross-group friendships, and Karaite-Rabbanite marriages were far from uncommon.

But were the Karaites Jews, or were they something else? The question was important, especially when being Jewish could have life-or-death consequences. During the Middle Ages, when Jews under Islam enjoyed remarkable prosperity and prominent social status, the Karaites insisted that they were as Jewish as Moses or Rabbi Akiba. But in Czarist Russia, being Jewish had become dangerous, and Karaites often weren't so quick to proclaim their Jewish bona fides.

In 1836, a group of Rabbanite Jews in Crimea petitioned Czar Nicholas I to be released from military service. The czar asked them whether they believed in the Talmud, they said they did, and before they could say "St. Petersburg," they were wearing army fatigues.

Watching this scene unfold was the governor of Crimea, Prince Michail Woronzow, and his Karaite aide, Simchah Bobovitch. By 1839, Bobovitch had become head of the Crimean Karaite community and knew that if he wanted to avoid sending young Karaite boys off to years of brutal soldierdom under the czar, he'd best have proof that Karaites had long rejected Rabbinic teachings. So Bobovitch turned to his old tutor—the die-hard, anti-Rabbanite scholar Abraham Firkovitch. He provided Firkovitch with a salary, traveling expenses, and an authorization from the government to procure whatever evidence he could find to document the history of Karaite Jewry.

Firkovitch took on his assigned task with gusto, traveling throughout Crimea and the Caucasus gathering information about the history of his beloved Karaite community. For three years, Firkovitch visited every Jewish community he could, searching archives, poring through genizahs, and scanning headstones in search of familiar Karaite names. He gathered reams of information, and slowly a grand, epic Karaite saga emerged.

One attribute that helped Firkovitch create this saga was his willingness to play loose with the facts. If a date didn't fit, Firkovitch changed it. If he failed to find a certain biblical manuscript, Firkovitch penned it himself. If he needed a mold of a particular headstone to prove a point, he sometimes created one. It may have been bad scholarship, but it was great for community relations.[10]

In 1859, Firkovitch deposited his finds (and forgeries) into the Imperial Library of St. Petersburg. These documents gave birth to a new field of scholarly inquiry—Karaite studies. In later years, Firkovitch's ongoing searches took him to Cairo. From Egypt, he returned to Russia carrying approximately thirteen thousand Karaite manuscripts. Firkovitch never specified exactly where in Cairo he found these documents, saying only that he had collected material from the genizahs of several of the city's synagogues. In all likelihood, some of them may have come from Cairo's famous Genizah, but Firkovitch probably found most of them in the genizahs of other synagogues, especially in Cairo's remaining Karaite synagogues.[11] And of course, some of his "ancient manuscripts" may have been the creations of his own hand.

On his way back to Russia from Cairo in 1864, Firkovitch stopped in Jerusalem, where he met another manuscript collector who had also just returned from Cairo—Jacob Saphir. In his diaries, Saphir mentioned the meeting in passing and suggested that Firkovitch was a man of dubious character. It was the only time that the two men met.

Solomon Wertheimer, Jewish Manuscript Dealer

Slowly, the trickle of information about the Cairo Genizah wound its way westward, and eventually, some Genizah manuscripts themselves moved west. In 1890, Greville Chester, a noted British Egyptologist, visited the Ben Ezra Synagogue and discovered that the entire mass of Genizah documents had been moved outside while the synagogue was being rebuilt. Examining the sprawling piles of paper, he was able to secure several of the Genizah's liturgical tracts and Karaite documents and present them to Oxford University's Bodleian Library. Later, he sent some manuscripts to the Cambridge University Library as well. At around the same time, the famed Assyriologist Archibald Sayce also seems to have visited the Ben Ezra, and he too obtained several Genizah documents. Sayce sent his purchases to Oxford, helping the Bodleian assemble roughly twenty-six hundred Genizah fragments by decade's end. The prime minister of Austria, Archduke Rainier Ferdinand, got hold of some manuscripts as well, as did other lesser known Europeans who visited or worked in Cairo.

In 1893, Rabbi Solomon Wertheimer began corresponding with the Cambridge University Library. The twenty-seven-year-old

rabbi, who was born in Slovakia and had lived in Jerusalem since he was a child, had some medieval Jewish manuscripts to sell, cheap. And they were good ones, too. Some of his manuscripts were previously unknown passages of liturgy and poetry; others were important early fragments of the Jerusalem and Babylonian Talmuds. Whether Wertheimer had bought these fragments from dealers or had gone to Cairo to get them himself remains unclear. What was clear was that,

Rabbi Solomon Aaron Wertheimer

for only a few shillings each, Cambridge could have its pick of these priceless treasures.[12]

At the receiving end of Wertheimer's offers were the Cambridge University librarian Francis Jenkinson and its rising Jewish-academic star, Rabbi Solomon Schechter. Between 1894 and 1896, they arranged for the library to purchase some fifty documents from Wertheimer. Astoundingly, they decided to pass on many others, dismissing what would turn out to be significant manuscripts as "worthless" or "not wanted at all."[13] Jenkinson and Schechter seem to have been focused on other matters just then, and clearly they didn't yet realize where these Genizah finds could lead.

They probably didn't trust this Jerusalem manuscript hawker very much, either. Document sales, they learned, was only one of Wertheimer's gigs. As an aspiring scholar, he often published articles about the manuscripts he owned. Then, as now, the unwritten rule in academia is that the owner of a manuscript gets first dibs on the right to publish it in a critical edition. Wertheimer, however, did not play by that rule. Often, before selling a document, he would make a handwritten copy of it to use in his own scholarship. Many of his customers were later shocked to find Wertheimer's articles about the very same material for which they had paid so dearly.

One of Wertheimer's customers openly lamented this practice. In July 1896, the Bodleian's Adolf Neubauer—soon to be a Schechter rival in the race to obtain Genizah fragments—wrote about an old manuscript of the biblical book of Esther, which he had purchased from Wertheimer. Shortly after his article was released, Neubauer added this postscript:

April 14, 1896.

My essay was in type in February last, for insertion in the April number, but the infirmity of my eyes prevented me from reading the proofs, and I had to postpone the revision till the present date, when my learned friend, S. J. Halberstam, to whom I had sent a copy of this paper, informed me that the [manuscript had already] been published ... by

Rabbi Solomon Aaron Wertheimer of Jerusalem, from the
same MS, he believes, as mine. Yes, it is so, for the Jerusalem
Rabbi sold it to the Bodleian Library after having taken a
copy for publication, without stating the fact when he
offered it for sale…. I hope that Rabbi S. A. Wertheimer will
continue to bring to light interesting documents as he has
done up till now, but that he will remember the saying of
the early Rabbis, "*Tov Torah im derech eretz* [Scripture is good
when accompanied by proper etiquette]."[14]

Not only did Wertheimer play fast and loose with scholarly proto-
col, but he also had a reputation as an irresponsible caretaker of his
manuscripts. In a distinctly Solomonic moment of business acu-
men, he once published a Talmud commentary, and later, realizing that two halves of the commentary would sell for a better price
separately than together, he tore the commentary in half and sold
each piece to a different customer.[15] The move may have been bad
for scholarship, but it was very good for business.

Despite these shenanigans, however, Solomon Aaron Wertheimer
did play a pioneering role in bringing Genizah documents to the
Western world. He was responsible for some of the Genizah material
brought to Cambridge University and other European libraries,
and he published his own Genizah scholarship as well. Still, few
took notice, and most of the manuscripts he sold remained unexamined. Perhaps his reputation as a low-level scoundrel made his
scholarly buyers wary; perhaps they weren't yet ready for the find.
Wertheimer lived in poverty for most of his life, and during the
years before his death in 1935, he grew increasingly unhappy that
he never received proper credit for his role in revealing the importance of the Cairo Genizah:

I was the first to discover the dark, hidden, recessed treasures of ancient manuscripts in the confines of the old
Genizah in Egypt; and I was the first who published the revelations of those manuscripts from the midrashim of our

Rabbis of blessed memory and the responsa of the early Geonim, their poetry, etc. And it was me who published them throughout the world, so that the quality of that Genizah [became evident]. Then came different scholars who rescued the manuscripts of the Genizah from Egypt and brought their words to light and thus established permanent reputations for themselves. But nobody remembers the poor man who saved the city.[16]

Elkan Nathan Adler Amasses Largest Judaica Collection in the World

Meanwhile, Cairo locals began to take notice of an unusual new phenomenon. For some reason, people in Europe were becoming interested in the old papers that had long piled up in the attic of the Ben Ezra Synagogue and then sat out in the open and unguarded during the 1889–92 reconstruction. By the mid-1890s, Cairo's ancient Jewish manuscript market had become quite active. Visitors interested in purchasing antiquarian documents in the city could do so easily and affordably.

The growing market in these texts drew another visitor to the Ben Ezra Synagogue. This visitor, a prominent British attorney and Jewish activist named Elkan Nathan Adler, was quite unlike his predecessors. The son of the chief rabbi of Great Britain, Adler was born in 1861. He was an ardent Zionist and served on the boards of several Jewish organizations.

Adler was also a book and manuscript collector. Beginning in the 1880s, Adler's considerable fortune allowed him to make frequent trips to North Africa and the Middle East in search of new

Elkan Nathan Adler

ancient material for his collection. In time, his library grew to be one of the largest private collections of Judaica in the world, containing some thirty thousand books and over thirty thousand handwritten manuscripts.

Unlike most of his fellow collectors, Elkan Nathan Adler was far more than merely a patron of Jewish learning. As his collection grew, Adler's knowledge of Jewish manuscripts and booklore grew as well, and eventually he became a scholar in his own right. He published several books, including *About Hebrew Manuscripts, Jewish Travellers in the Middle Ages: 19 Firsthand Accounts,* and *A History of the Jews of London.*

In 1888, during one of his journeys to the Middle East, Adler traveled to Cairo to see what Jewish literary antiquities he might obtain there. With great pride, Adler's hosts gave him a tour of the Ben Ezra Synagogue and showed him the original, eight-hundred-year-old decree authorizing the construction of the building. Could he see the Genizah? He later recalled that "Cairene Jewish authorities told me that they occasionally buried torn or defaced Hebrew prints and Sifre Torah [Torah scrolls] in their Bet Chajim [cemetery] at Basatni [*sic,* Bassatin], but that nothing of importance"[17] remained in the synagogue. Apparently, Adler's hosts didn't like the idea of a wealthy European rummaging around in their genizah. It's possible that they did indeed view the Genizah documents as unworthy of investigation, but more likely they were dissembling, trying to put Adler off.

Adler took his hosts at their word. He didn't press to see the Genizah during that visit and at the time "expressed a confident opinion that nowadays no Hebrew MSS. of any importance are to be bought in Cairo!"[18] Later, he would eat those words.

Adler did, however, return to Cairo in 1896 and found that, since his previous visit, the Ben Ezra Synagogue had been thoroughly renovated and the contents of its genizah had sat outside in a pile for a time. He had also probably heard murmurings about the Genizah from Chester, Sayce, and other recent Western visitors to the Ben Ezra Synagogue.

On January 3, Adler met with Cairo's chief rabbi, Rabbi Aaron
Raphael Bensimon, and Youssef M. Cattaui, one of the city's most
prominent Jewish citizens. This time, perhaps aware that there was
a market for the documents, they handed their visitor an old Torah
cover and warmly invited him to examine the Genizah. Adler later
recalled:

> I ... was conducted by Rabbi Rafail [Bensimon] to the
> extreme end of the ladies' gallery, permitted to climb to the
> topmost rung of a ladder, to enter the sacred chamber of
> the Genizah through a hole in the wall, and to take away
> with me a sackful of paper and parchment writings—as
> much as I could gather up in the three or four hours I was
> permitted to linger there.[19]

When he returned home to London, Adler showed his sack of documents to Adolf Neubauer at the Bodleian. But Neubauer, like
Schechter and Jenkinson at Cambridge, was uninterested in
Genizah documents just then and later commented to an associate
that Adler's documents were "a lot of worthless rubbish for which
he paid high prices."[20]

Adler was quick to announce his discoveries, and within a few
years he published dozens of articles and two books on Genizah-
related subjects. The scholarly world gave Adler a polite "Jolly
good job, old boy" and a pat on the back for his discoveries, but his
announcements received nothing even remotely resembling the
wild enthusiasm that Solomon Schechter's announcement received
the following year.

In 1897, Adler supplemented his private collection with the
purchase of approximately six thousand "useless" Hebrew manuscripts from the Bodleian Library in Oxford.[21] Before he was
through, he would possess the largest personal collection of Genizah
documents in the world. Still, the size and significance of his cache
of manuscripts roused little attention. Neither did his scholarly
articles and books. Adler had neither the university affiliation of a

man like Schechter nor the red-haired rabbi's personal appeal and magnetism. Had he lived a century later and an ocean to the west, he would have appeared on C-SPAN rather than on *Oprah*, if he appeared on television at all.

During the early 1920s, one of Adler's business partners swindled him out of a large sum of money, and he was forced to sell his library. A small part of his manuscript collection went to the Hebrew Union College, in Cincinnati, but the vast majority of it went to New York's Jewish Theological Seminary, where it remains today. Despite this tremendous loss, Elkan Nathan Adler contin- ued his scholarly work until shortly before his death in 1946.

The Excitement Grows

As the nineteenth century moved through its final decade, news of a gigantic horde of Jewish manuscripts in the genizah of Cairo's Ben Ezra Synagogue made its way westward and entered the con- sciousness of European scholars. The news arrived just as Jews in the West were beginning to take note of the cultural riches of Middle Eastern Jewry, and during a time of growing fascination throughout Europe with all things Arab. Moreover, Victorian excitement for exploration and discovery was still running high— the century had seen Charles Darwin journey to the Galapagos, Dr. David Livingstone explore the African jungle, and Richard Francis Burton trek Arabia. Howard Carter, the British Egyptologist des- tined to discover King Tut's tomb in 1922, arrived in Egypt in 1891, spending the rest of the decade on excavations.

The stage was set for another discovery. The Genizah's moment was now. All that was needed was the right person to raise the curtain.

2
Solomon Schechter
The Rabbi of Christ's College

Solomon Schechter was born in Focsani, Romania, on December 7, 1850.[1] Nestled at the foot of the Carpathian Mountains, one hundred miles inland from the Black Sea, Focsani was a shtetl—a small, Jewish, *Fiddler-on-the-Roof*-type community of peddlers and farmers, pious sages and struggling shopkeepers. Like all shtetls, the rhythms of Focsani's daily life were governed in large part by Jewish law and Jewish custom. Men worshiped in the synagogue three times each day; women tended to the children and often ran the family business; Friday night and Saturday was the Sabbath—*Shabbes*—during which shops closed and families gathered in their homes to celebrate the sacred day together. Jewish law—the many regulations legislated in the Torah and interpreted by ancient and modern rabbis—governed life in the shtetl, and disputes of all kinds were brought to local rabbis for resolution.

Jews lived in such communities because Jews, like most ethnic groups, have always lived together in communities. But the shtetl world in which Solomon Schechter grew up was also a product of outside oppression. For centuries, the nations of Eastern Europe had required Jews to live in an area now comprising sections of Russia, Poland, Romania, and other countries, known as the Pale of Settlement. In the Pale, Jews were restricted to living only in certain areas, working only at certain professions, and, often, wearing certain clothing that marked them as Jews.

Despite these policies, however, Jewish life in the Pale flourished richly. There, Yiddish language reached is fullest expression as it provided text and context for the lives of its millions of Jewish residents. There, Jews established a unique mix of their own values and ideas with those of the surrounding non-Jewish culture. There, over time, Judaism thrived and developed even as it struggled against poverty and antisemitism.

Emancipation and Enlightenment

In the early nineteenth century, however, things began to change for shtetl Jews. And the changes originated not in Romania, or Poland, or anywhere else in Eastern Europe, but in France. In 1789, the French Revolution deposed the ruling monarchy under the banner of "*Liberté, Égalité, Fraternité*" and the new French society soon realized that if it was really serious about liberty, equality, and fraternity, then France would have to ensure that *all* citizens of the nation would be able to enjoy those rights—even Jews.

And so, after some melodious and highly voweled hemming and hawing, France tore down its ghetto walls and invited its Jews to become true-blue Frenchmen and Frenchwomen. Other countries in Western Europe soon followed suit—Germany, Austria, the Netherlands—and Emancipation spread country by country to Jews throughout Western Europe.

In the Eastern Europe of Schechter's childhood, however, the changes weren't as quick or dramatic. There, oppressive and isolating czarist laws remained in effect, and Jews still had to live under their restrictions in the Pale of Settlement. Eventually, however, some of the new modernist ideas did begin to spread to the Jews living in Eastern Europe. Gradually, the enlightened rationalism that was transforming life in Western Europe began making its way into the shtetl.

Jews—in secret at first, but then more openly—began studying Western literature, science, and history. Soon these new ways of thinking became a force to be dealt with, and students began to question many of the assumptions of traditional Jewish thought. These inquiries led nineteenth-century Eastern European Jewry to become a hotbed of political, religious, and economic thought, spawning ideological movements of all kinds. There were capitalists, socialists, and communists; religious modernists and religious traditionalists; Zionists and anti-Zionists. Life in the shtetl was a cacophony of different voices, each asserting its own version of the truth about the difficulties and complexities of the world and its Jews.

The Birth of Chasidism

One of the most significant of the Jewish religious movements of the day was Chasidic Judaism, which claimed among its many adherents the Focsani family of Isaac and Chayah Schechter. Chasidic Judaism was a populist movement founded by the followers of a late eighteenth-century charismatic rabbi by the name of Israel ben Eliezer, commonly known as the Baal Shem Tov (Master of the Good Name). What God wants most, it taught, is the devotion of the human heart. A song sung from deep within, a dance performed as a true expression of joy—these, and not legal or academic exactitude, are what God loves and desires most of all. At the same time, the Baal Shem Tov and his followers also promoted a new form of Jewish mysticism, teaching that passionate study and contemplation of Jewish sacred texts can allow the pious student to unite with the presence of God in the world.

When the Baal Shem Tov died in 1760, his followers fanned out through Eastern Europe. Each hung out his shingle as the Chasidic rabbi—"rebbe"—of that community, each developing his own following and brand of Chasidic Judaism.

One of the most popular groups was centered in the Russian town of Lubavitch—the Lubavitch Chasidim, who also call themselves Chabad. The movement was founded by a mystical scholar named Shneur Zalman of Lyadi (1745–1812), who emphasized "the mind ruling over the heart" and derived the name for his movement from an acronym of the names of the kabbalistic three "intellectual attributes of God": Wisdom (*Chochmah*), Understanding (*Binah*), and Knowledge (*Da'at*). Many of the other Chasidic denominations emphasized emotion, calling their members to ecstatic worship and rapturous religious practice. But early Chabad encouraged its followers to think before they sang, to contemplate before they danced.

And so it was that when a pair of twin boys was born to Isaac and Chayah Schechter in December 1850, one received the name Israel, after the biblical father of their nation, and the other Shneur Zalman, after the father of their Chasidic community.

Schechter's Early Years: Romania and Poland

From early in his childhood, Shneur Zalman (Solomon) Schechter came to be known in his community as an *iluy*—an "enlightened one," the boy-genius of the shtetl. Intellectual brilliance such as his was a highly prized commodity in shtetl life, for it allowed him to advance rapidly as a student of Torah, the greatest occupation to which a young Jewish man could aspire. "He had," as one observer noted, "the key to the treasury, and in the process of time, he could bring forth from the treasury things new and old."[2] Ironically, one fact that may have contributed to his intelligence was the poverty in which he was raised. Focsani was rather short on books as Schechter grew up, and this deficit redounded to Schechter's benefit, for it demanded that he commit as much as possible to memory, rather than relying on the printed word. When he was ten years old, Schechter made the first of what would be a lifelong series of moves west—this one to the nearby town of Piatra, to study in its yeshiva (rabbinic study academy). Legend has it that his parents originally refused to allow him to leave home at such a young age but relented only after their determined young yeshivah whiz-kid repeatedly snuck away on his own and walked through the snow to get there.[3] He later studied at a yeshiva in the town of Falticeni, and at sixteen, having reached the limit of what he could learn in the yeshivas of Romania, Schechter moved west again, to the far more prominent yeshiva in Lemberg (Lvov), Poland.

Immersed though he was in the study of ancient texts, Schechter was also exposed during these years to the secular learning of Haskalah, the Jewish Enlightenment. While his teachers and his elders spoke in Yiddish, saving Hebrew for prayer and Torah study, Schechter began reading Modern Hebrew literature and often wrote letters to his friends in Hebrew, too. Among his friends were scientists, anthropologists, and others whose teachings would have been somewhat less than welcome in the yeshiva.

Life in Vienna

Schechter had gotten the modernist "bug." In 1873, the twenty-six-year-old moved west yet again—this time to Vienna, where he could study in that city's famous "Beit Hamidrash" (house of study). Vienna of the 1870s was a highly cosmopolitan cultural center, especially in comparison to Focsani and the other far-smaller cities where Schechter had lived. It teemed with the finest of modern art, music, and scholarship; its citizens enjoyed the highest of the high culture of nineteenth-century Europe. And its Jewish life was just as sophisticated. Central European Vienna was the place where, for Jews, the scientific and technological advancements of the West converged with the deep Talmudic intricacies of the East—where Jewish learning could, in the eyes of its modernist scholars, embrace modern modes of thought and thus yield new truths and light for the world. During this era of dramatic cultural and scientific change, some Jews feared they might be swept away by the modernist, rationalist wave; undaunted and insatiably curious, Solomon Schechter learned early on to ride this new wave at its crest.

In Vienna, Schechter's teachers included some of the great minds of nineteenth-century Jewish studies. One of them was Meir "Ish Shalom" Friedmann (his nom de plume "Ish Shalom" means

"Peace Man"). Schechter studied rabbinics with Friedmann and later tutored Friedmann's two sons. Legend has it that Friedmann would often invite Schechter and other students to his home on Saturday afternoons; when the students' conversation became a bit too serious for his taste, Friedmann would say, "Come, my young friends, let us have a little gossip."[4]

In Vienna, Schechter also met the renowned scholar Adolf Jellinek, who took Schechter under his wing. When Schechter needed some extra income, Jellinek hired the young student to catalogue his library.[5] Another of Schechter's teachers was Isaac Hirsch Weiss, a pioneer in the historic study of the Talmud. It was under Weiss's tutelage that Schechter eventually received his rabbinic ordination.

Schechter's years in Vienna allowed him to realize as he never had before that modern scholarship wasn't necessarily the enemy of Jewish learning, as some of the teachers of his youth had taught. With the guidance of his new instructors, Schechter continued to study the ancient texts in which he had immersed himself during the years of his yeshiva learning, but now he did so with a historical and critical perspective that would have been seen as nothing less than heretical in the world of the yeshiva. He studied Jewish law, for example, not only as an eternal phenomenon, but also as one that existed in time—as a body of wisdom that had influenced and been influenced by the great forces of history over the ages. He began to study ancient manuscripts and saw in them the dynamic nature of the texts of Torah and Talmud, realizing that the scriptures we study today are often quite different than they were when first written. In Vienna, Schechter learned to love both Torah and modern learning with passion.

The Move to Berlin

But his studies weren't over. After his ordination as a rabbi in 1879, Schechter moved still further west, this time to Berlin. There he enrolled in the most modern of modern Jewish academies—the Hochschule für die Wissenschaft des Judentums, the Higher

Institute for the Scientific Study of Judaism. Founded in 1871, the Hochschule was created to be just what its name implied—a university of Jewish studies of the highest possible academic caliber. It attracted many of the greatest scholars of the late nineteenth century to its faculty, and many of its students would go on to become preeminent Jewish thinkers and leaders in the years to come. The Hochschule also welcomed non-Jewish students, as well—usually scientifically oriented and liberal-minded members of the Christian clergy. The diversity of the students sitting in the Hochschule classrooms allowed for an exchange of ideas and perspectives regarding Judaism and Jewish life, the breadth of which was simply unprecedented at the time. While studying at the Hochschule, Schechter met a younger student named Claude Montefiore. A scion of two British aristocratic dynasties,[6] Montefiore had come to the Hochschule from Oxford, where he had begun his Jewish studies. He soon came to love the scintillating atmosphere of Jewish learning that surrounded him in Berlin, and when it came time for Montefiore to return to England, he was reluctant to leave. Montefiore, never one to hurt for money, invited Schechter to accompany him on his return to London and to serve as his Talmud tutor.

The Riches of London

In London, Schechter found Jewish riches the likes of which he had never before encountered. Though few of London's Jews engaged in the kind of Jewish study to which he was accustomed, he did establish a close group of friends, mostly Jewish scholars and writers. The group, which included playwright Israel Zangwill, scholar Moses Gaster, historian Israel Abrahams, and several others, would meet regularly to discuss what was on their minds. Eventually, realizing that their meetings wandered from house to house and their conversations from idea to idea, they began calling themselves the "Wandering Jews" and, later, "the Wanderers."

In 1885, Schechter was introduced to a young Jewish woman from Breslau, Mathilde Roth. Orphaned as a young girl, Mathilde

Solomon Schechter, London, 1887

had been raised by her older brother and trained as a teacher of languages and literature. She had come to London the year she and Solomon met, working as a teacher and living in the house of Michael Friedlander, a prominent scholar who was head of Jews College. Motivating her move to London even more, perhaps, were the unparalleled study opportunities available there. In London, she hoped to study at Queens College and, as she wrote in her memoirs, "to read in the treasures of the British Museum, the National Gallery, and the endless private collections."

Given her passion for exploring the literary riches of London and her association with the city's Jewish scholars, it is no surprise that she and Solomon Schechter were soon drawn to one another. The couple fell in love and married in June 1887 at a ceremony attended by many of the great Jewish academicians of late nineteenth-century Western Europe.[7]

Mathilde was evidently included in many of the Wanderers' gatherings. Late in her life, she recalled those meetings clearly:

> We were all young and strong and keen, and every evening in our large and cozy study, around the huge log-fire, we read, and talked, and discussed every problem under the sun. There never were more jolly, sparkling, deeply earnest and spirited talks, and it is a pity that we were all so absorbed in living our lives that we failed to write down the best thought of those men of letters, who were at the time prodigal of their ideas. When Zangwill became too radical and Schechter stormy, and Lucien Wolf mysterious in diplomatic discussions, and Israel Abrahams, a born neutral, would say pacifically: "You are both right," and Asher Myers, the late editor of the *Jewish Chronicle*, and kindest of friends,

decided with his invariable pronunciamento: "I think Schechter is right," Joseph Jacobs, the most amiable of the group, would often clear the atmosphere with his original remarks and laughter.[8]

Schechter had an exuberant and charming personality, and many of his fellow Wanderers would later recall that he provided the group with much of its jovial energy. Indeed, Solomon Schechter would remain close with many of its members for the rest of his life.

London provided Schechter with another new opportunity, as well. When he wasn't tutoring Montefiore, he often spent time in London's British Museum and at the Bodleian Library at Oxford University. At the time, these institutions held two of the world's largest collections of antiquarian Jewish manuscripts, which included some of the oldest known copies of classical Jewish literature—Bible, Talmud, Midrash, and more. Away from the yeshiva world of his youth, Schechter felt deep loneliness in London. But the hours he spent beneath the arched ceilings of those book-lined halls surely brought him comfort. "As in Germany with the Bible," he wrote to a friend, "so here the holy literature of Judaism is tended only by Christians.... There is no spiritual life here, and I feel myself dead. The manuscripts in the British Museum are my only consolation."[9]

One can almost picture the lonely young Rabbi Schechter first stepping across the threshold into the literary wonderland of the Bodleian, his eyes ablaze as they scanned shelf after shelf of its Judaic treasures. His moves west had taken him far from his Focsani childhood. In Focsani, Schechter had many study partners, but few books. In London, it was just the opposite.

It was in London that Schechter began to establish a name for himself as a scholar, contributing to various rabbinic journals and editing in 1887 a version of *Avot d'Rabbi Natan*, a "minor tractate" of the Talmud. He also became a frequent contributor to the *Jewish Quarterly Review*, which Montefiore founded with Schechter's friend Israel Abrahams in 1888.

Schechter's reputation continued to grow, and his erudition in Jewish texts was soon known throughout Europe. With increasing frequency, scholars turned to him for assistance in understanding various passages of ancient Jewish law and lore, which he was happy to provide. He also came to be widely known among the largely non-Jewish British aristocracy as an embodiment of Jewish knowledge and a readily available scholarly resource.

Bridging Two Worlds in Cambridge

Among his associates at this time were some members of the faculty of Christ's College, at Cambridge University. Christ's College was an institution devoted in large part to the training of Christian clergy and whose Bible scholars studied the ancient texts in light of modern scientific knowledge. Long known as the most liberal of Cambridge's many colleges—John Milton and Charles Darwin had served on its faculty—Christ's College even welcomed the input of "heretics and Jews,"[10] particularly if the heretic or Jew in question had the scholarly bona fides of a Solomon Schechter. So, in 1890, when a lectureship in "Talmudics" opened at Christ's College, Schechter was the natural choice.

In June of that year, Christ's College invited Schechter to join its faculty. Mathilde had given birth to the couple's oldest child, Ruth, two years earlier, and their son Frank was born on the very same day Schechter received the offer from Cambridge. Their younger daughter, Amy, would be born a few years later.

Schechter was now the rabbi-professor of a college named Christ's. As his reputation there grew, so did his loneliness. He was the only Jewish "don" in the entire university, and although there were some pulpit rabbis in the area, he became increasingly isolated from his fellow Jewish scholars. At the same time, however, at Cambridge Schechter was surrounded by a veritable host of non-Jewish scholars of religion, many of whom would make enormous contributions to their fields of study. Some, such as Professor Frances C. Burkitt of Trinity College, Dr. Charles Taylor, master of

St. John's College, and Dr. James Rendel Harris of Clare College, became close friends of Schechter's and would, directly or indirectly, come to play important roles in the greatest of his scholarly achievements.

Solomon Schechter was forty years old when he moved to Cambridge. With his full beard, his curly red hair, and his thick Yiddish accent, he surely felt a bit out of place amid the denizens of Cambridge's refined ivory towers. But, in many ways, it was only because this shtetl Jew was willing to put himself in this foreign environment—and because Cambridge itself was open to welcoming a Jewish scholar such as Schechter—that he was able to bridge worlds and make the great contributions for which he is now remembered.

It would still be several years before Schechter would find an opportunity to truly make his mark at Cambridge, but when the moment arrived—thanks in part to a pair of feisty, scholarly Scottish sisters—Schechter seized it.

3

"The Giblews"

The Sisters, Their Adventures, and the Documents That Opened the Genizah

The manuscripts in the Cairo Genizah document the lives and literature of a community of medieval Jews whose members often interacted with their Muslim neighbors. However, two of the most prominent figures in the modern Genizah story are neither medieval, nor Jewish, nor Muslim, but nineteenth-century Presbyterian Scotswomen—wealthy, erudite twin sisters, world travelers and discoverers of great literary treasures. It was the contribution of these remarkable women that first sent Solomon Schechter along the trajectory that eventually led him to the Genizah.[1]

Margaret Dunlop Gibson and Agnes Smith Lewis, whom the students of Westminster College later referred to as "the Giblews," were twin sisters, born in Irvine, Scotland, twenty-five miles southwest of Glasgow, in 1843. Their mother died when they were only three weeks old, leaving their father, John Smith, to raise the two girls on his own. Smith was a "solicitor"—an attorney—and earned a comfortable income from his work. But the timely death of a wealthy cousin who was grateful for some legal work Smith had done for him led to a bequest that dropped the Irvine lawyer into the lap of luxury.

Smith doted on his daughters, but as a single parent, he had to relegate many day-to-day responsibilities of child raising to others, and Maggie and Agnes grew up under the care of nannies and governesses in their large Ayrshire home. The women who helped raise the girls were gentle but firm, providing the twins with far more guidance and instruction than affection or love.[2] Lacking a female role model, they never quite achieved the social refinement common for girls of their standing at the time; they didn't mix easily in groups, their clothing was rather unstylish, and from early on, many of the girls' schoolmates saw them as "frumps." Consequently, as they grew up, Margaret and Agnes turned to one another for emotional support, developing an intense twin-sister bond that they would share for their entire lives.

When they grew a bit older, their father sent the girls away to school in Birkenhead, near Liverpool, and later to a school near London, where the girls received the finest education then available to young British women. They both excelled in their studies, particularly in foreign languages such as French, German, and Latin.

John Smith died in 1866, leaving his twenty-three-year-old, recently matriculated, and still single twin daughters facing a curious question: What were they supposed to do with themselves? They were orphaned, jobless, curious, intelligent, and wealthy. What now?

They decided to travel. The girls had visited other places in Europe with their father when they were younger, but their learning and love of language left them eager to visit more distant places— sites described in the Bible and Greek mythology, places where they could use the languages they had studied in daily conversation, lands that most Europeans of their day could see only in their dreams and imaginations.

So, with a young former schoolteacher of theirs named Grace Blyth in tow as chaperone, Maggie and Agnes

Agnes Lewis and Margaret Dunlop Gibson

headed east, traveling to London, Nuremburg, Munich, Vienna, Pest, Varna, Constantinople, Cyprus, Alexandria, Cairo, Aswan, Jerusalem, Damascus, Greece, Venice, and Paris. Grace would become their lifelong companion, accompanying them on their travels and, with the help of Margaret and Agnes, maintaining a residence nearby that of her former charges.

When the trio returned, they settled in London, and the sisters joined the local Presbyterian church. They continued to study foreign languages and traveled regularly to the Mediterranean and the Middle East. Agnes published four mediocre romance novels: *Eastern Pilgrims, Effie Maxwell, Glenmavis,* and *The Brides of Ardmore.*

Marriage, All Too Brief

In 1883, the twins, now forty years old, were returning home from a trip to Greece and Italy, when, in the Black Forest spa town of Wildbad, they met up with one of Grace's cousins, a Presbyterian minister and man of letters named James Young Gibson. Gibson, a sickly man who suffered periodic bouts of depression, had distinguished himself as a Presbyterian clergyman and as a translator of *Don Quixote* and other works of Spanish literature. He and Maggie seem to have been engaged to be married a few years beforehand, when Gibson, suffering from malaise, repeatedly delayed the

wedding. But when the couple reconnected during the twins' return from Greece, there were no further delays. On September 8, he and Margaret Smith were married.

Sadly, however, the marriage would not last long. In 1886,

Castlebrae, home of Agnes Smith Lewis and Margaret Dunlop Gibson while the couple was on a short vacation, James Gibson suddenly became ill and died a few days later. Maggie was devastated. The couple had been married for only three years.

Six months later, in January 1887, Maggie and Agnes decided to take a two-week trip to Cambridge. During their visit, Agnes met the eccentric but charming librarian of Corpus Christi College, Samuel Lewis. The couple fell in love, and on December 12, 1888, Samuel Lewis and Agnes Smith were married. Maggie joined them on their honeymoon.

Agnes and Samuel had a happy, albeit unconventional, marriage. College rules demanded that Samuel live in his college rooms during the week, and he was only able to go home to join his wife and sister-in-law for meals and during the weekends. Nevertheless, in March 1890, the couple built a new house for themselves (and for Maggie, of course) just across the River Cam, on the lower slopes of Castle Hill, the ancient ruins of early Cambridge.

They called the house Castlebrae, Old Scottish for Castle Hill. It had more than twenty rooms, including a study, a drawing room, and a grand dining room with French windows looking out to the front drive. In later years, Maggie and Agnes shared a bedroom upstairs. At first they slept in the same bed, with a piece of tape down the middle demarcating each sister's turf. When they grew older, they replaced that larger bed with two smaller ones—twin beds, of course.

Alas, Samuel Lewis was not to enjoy his grand new manse for long. On March 31, 1891, on a train with Agnes as they returned home from a visit to Oxford, Samuel suddenly died, perhaps as the result of a massive stroke. He was fifty-five years old.

Antidote: Travel

Having mourned the deaths of her father and James, Maggie knew the pain of grief all too well. And she also knew one of the best antidotes to her sister's grief would be a good long trip abroad. Maggie suggested to Agnes that they embark upon another journey.

This time, they decided, they would go to Mount Sinai. There was a Greek Orthodox monastery called St. Catherine's at the foot of the mountain, and the sisters had dreamed of traveling there ever since they were young. In 1859, German biblical scholar Constantin von Tischendorf had visited St. Catherine's and discovered a manuscript of Christian scripture that was older and more complete than any other by almost six hundred years. James Rendel Harris—a friend of Schechter's as well as the sisters'—had recently visited the monastery and come back with rave reviews of the manuscript riches that its library contained.

Almost offhandedly, Rendel Harris added a tantalizing detail to his description of the monastery. Beneath the archbishop's rooms was a dark chamber, and off that dark chamber was a dark closet, and in that dark closet were chests filled with old Syriac manuscripts. Rendell Harris hadn't had time to explore the contents of those chests during his visit, but he suspected that they might contain some very ancient material—perhaps some of the most ancient Christian texts known to exist. If his suspicion was correct, then the language of the texts would be similar to that of Jesus himself, and their contents would be priceless.[3]

By this time, Margaret and Agnes had added several more languages to their repertoire—Hebrew, Arabic (Classical and Modern), Greek (Classical and Modern), and others. One language they didn't know, however, was Syriac, a dialect of Aramaic spoken in the Middle East from the second through the eighth centuries CE. Since many of the manuscripts they hoped to see at Mount Sinai were written in Syriac, Margaret and Agnes's ignorance of the language could prove to be a real deficit.

So Agnes learned Syriac. Picking up a language that hasn't been spoken for centuries would be a challenge for anyone at anytime. But for a woman in 1890s England, it was especially problematic. Even though she and Margaret were well-respected citizens of Cambridge, neither could enroll in the city's prestigious university. It had a "no girls allowed" policy, and there were no exceptions, not even for a very wealthy, deeply committed, aspiring student of

Maggie and Agnes in the Sinai, 1892–93

Syriac. Agnes began her studies on her own; with Hebrew and Arabic already in her lingual quiver, adding basic Syriac was relatively easy. Later, Agnes hired Rev. R. H. Kennett, a friend of her husband's and one of the university's top Semitic language scholars, to tutor her in Syriac over lunch every Monday at Castlebrae.

Having hired the best of the best as her private tutor, Agnes soon become proficient in Syriac. First they went to Cairo, where they hired a guide, gathered supplies, and finagled the letters of introduction they'd need to help ensure a welcome from the monks at St. Catherine's Monastery. Margaret and Agnes feared that the monks, like the dons at Cambridge, would have a no-girls-allowed policy, too. From Cairo, they traveled to the Gulf of Suez, at the northern end of the Red Sea, and crossed it by sailboat. The forty-nine-year-old Cambridge twins then began a ten-day camel ride to the mountain. It was a grueling trip.

St. Catherine's Monastery, Mount Sinai

When the group arrived at St. Catherine's on February 7, 1892, the resident monks greeted them warmly. The following day, the monks showed their visitors their library. It was scattered throughout the monastery—some volumes were prominently displayed in a "Show Library," others in the monks' private rooms, and some in a dark chamber halfway up a staircase. Margaret and Agnes, of course, were eager to get down into the closet behind the chamber beneath the archbishop's rooms, but they had to be patient. Finally, their guide asked whether there was anything in particular that they wanted to see, and Agnes saw her opportunity. "All your oldest Syriac manuscripts," she said, "particularly those which Dr. Harris had no time to examine."

The monks took the sisters downstairs. They entered the chamber beneath the archbishop's room and walked to the dark closet they had so dreamt of seeing. It was visible only by candle-light. Inside the closet were two small wooden chests, from which the monks removed several manuscripts. The party quickly moved upstairs, where they could examine the documents in the library, under better light.

Soon after they sat down, Agnes noticed an odd-looking clump of old parchment. Remembering the moment, Agnes later wrote, "It had a forbidding look, for it was very dirty, and its leaves were nearly all stuck together through their having remained unturned probably since the last Syrian monk had died, centuries ago, in the Convent."[4]

Agnes had come upon a palimpsest—a parchment that had been written on, erased, and re-inscribed with a new text. As with many palimpsests, the older writing wasn't completely erased, and enough remained to allow both texts—the undercoat and the newer overcoat—to be mostly legible. This particular palimpsest was 358 pages long. The newer of the two texts, a tract called "Lives of the Saints," was a collection of female saints' biographies and would eventually be dated to 778 CE. The older text was an early fourth-century version of the Christian Bible. It was the third-oldest copy of Christian scripture ever discovered—older than any other Syriac Bible known to exist—and it represents a version of the text closer to the original than any other. The only comparable document is the Cureton Manuscript, discovered in Lower Egypt in 1838 and dated to sometime between the second and fifth centuries. But the text of the Cureton Manuscript is fragmentary, and this remarkable manuscript—known today as either the Lewis Codex or the Sinaitic Palimpsest—fills in many of its gaps. The clump of old parchment that the twins discovered in the monastery library thus gives the world a glimpse of Christian scripture in one of its very earliest forms.[5]

Using cumbersome equipment they and their camels had lugged across the desert, the sisters now resolved to photograph each page of their find. The work, however, was difficult. They had never used a camera before, and everything they knew about photography came from a few brief instructions from the Kodak salesman in London, Rendel Harris, and their fellow ship-passengers earlier in their journey.

Photographing the manuscript took ten days. The equipment was temperamental and the work tedious; sometimes they accidentally cut off the top line of text when they took their pictures. But the images they brought back to England sufficed as evidence of their find.

For most scholars, this would have been the find of a lifetime. And although it was indeed a significant one for Margaret Dunlop Gibson and Agnes Lewis, the twin sisters from Irvine were just getting started.

Rabbi Schechter's Request

Margaret and Agnes planned to spend the spring of 1896 sitting quietly at home, reviewing finds from their earlier expeditions. But then they heard that there might be some valuable manuscripts available in Cairo, and they decided to go and have a look. And while they were there, the sisters reasoned, why not go to Jerusalem to see what they could find in that city, as well?

A few days before they left, the sisters hosted a small luncheon at Castlebrae. Among the invited guests were Rabbi and Mrs. Solomon Schechter, whom they had met through their friend William Robertson Smith, a Presbyterian Orientalist and Bible scholar who had helped recruit Schechter to Cambridge. Since the Schechters' arrival in 1890, Margaret and Agnes had grown close to the rabbi, and even closer to Mathilde. In largely Anglican Cambridge, the Jewish Schechters and the Presbyterian twins shared an outsider status, one that tightened their bond. Cementing the friendship even further was the fact that Solomon Schechter and the twins shared a passionate interest in antiquarian manuscripts. Schechter was eager to hear about the sisters' upcoming trip. As they chatted, Agnes and Margaret asked whether there was anything they could bring back to the Schechters as a gift. "If you could purchase some Hebrew manuscripts from one of the little antiquity shops," the rabbi responded, "please feel free to do so."[6]

Egypt and Palestine: In Search of Ancient Literary Treasure

The sisters' stay in Cairo went as planned, and Margaret and Agnes were able to purchase a small bundle of Hebrew manuscripts. Next, they boarded a boat for Palestine, hoping to disembark at Jaffa and travel to Jerusalem. But a cholera epidemic had broken out in Jaffa, and its port was quarantined and closed. Beirut's port was closed for the same reason, so they sailed back to Egypt and the sisters took an evening train to Suez. Just as on their Sinai expedition four years earlier, they mounted camels and set out in pursuit of ancient literary treasure, determined to reach Jerusalem by hook or by crook. The erudite, fifty-three-year-old ladies, with their wide-brimmed hats and poofy Victorian dresses, were becoming highly experienced camel riders.

The six-day trek from Suez to Gaza was, as Agnes later recalled, "much more difficult than we anticipated." The sand was deep and difficult to traverse—even for the camels. Water was hard to find and often brackish. The path was covered with sand. Were it not for the telegraph poles along the way, the group would have gotten hopelessly lost.[7]

When Margaret and Agnes traveled to Mount Sinai in 1892, they had followed the path of the ancient Israelites. Now, cameling their way across the northern edge of the Sinai desert, they walked in the footsteps of Christ. Despite having to brave miserable storms along the way, Margaret and Agnes pressed on from Gaza toward Jerusalem. Each day, their waiter and cook would walk ahead of the group to pitch the tents and prepare camp for the evening. One day, however, the travelers were dismayed to discover that their advance party was nowhere to be found. Clouds gathered overhead as they searched in vain for the men and the precious tents they carried. Eventually, it began to rain, and the group had to huddle underneath a flimsy luncheon tent that they had carried for daytime stops. The following morning, Agnes and Margaret threw in the towel. Reaching a village called Bittir, they boarded a train that took them the rest of the way to Jerusalem.

Arriving in Jerusalem in late March, the sisters visited the ancient city's holy sites, checked out some archaeological excavations, and observed the Greek Orthodox "Descent of the Holy Fire," an Eastern Orthodox ritual at the Church of the Holy Sepulchre. They photographed manuscripts at a Syrian monastery and purchased some more manuscripts to take home.

The sisters stayed in Jerusalem for about four weeks. Leaving on April 17, they traveled to the Plain of Sharon, along the Mediterranean coast. There, they met an antiquities dealer and purchased yet another bundle of manuscripts, bringing the total manuscript haul from this expedition to more than two thousand. The ladies packed their new purchases away with the others, unaware of the enormous transformation that the documents would soon bring to scholars and students around the world.

Ottoman customs officials took great bureaucratic glee in erecting hurdles to their departure. The twins had planned to travel to Beirut and had sent Maggie's trunk ahead. But then the weather turned bad, and the sisters decided to head straight home, instead. As they prepared to depart, the officials delayed Maggie's attempts to reclaim her luggage. Had she paid the required duties? Was she *really* the Margaret Dunlop Gibson who owned the trunk? And what *were* these old vellum texts packed with her lacy dresses and frilly undergarments? Their canny guide reminded the officials that the law forbade them from confiscating travelers' Bibles. "Do you not see that these [manuscripts] are in Hebrew? ... And the ladies say their prayers in Hebrew. Do you want to prevent them saying their prayers?"

The two Presbyterian Scotswomen only got out of Palestine by passing as Jews.[8]

With their box of "dirty scraps of vellum" safely packed into Maggie's portmanteau, Maggie and Agnes left Palestine via steamer on April 21 and arrived home on May 3. It wasn't until their return to Cambridge that they examined their purchases more closely. Most of the documents were easy for Margaret and Agnes to identify, but several of the scraps stumped them. To identify these mystery documents, the sisters would need to seek outside expertise.

Maybe Rabbi Schechter could help.

4
May 13, 1896

Rabbi Solomon Schechter walked briskly down St. John's Street, in Cambridge, England. It was a warm, sunny morning, and all around him the high gabled roofs and steeples of the city's great university towered imposingly against the blue sky.

But it is unlikely that Schechter thought much of weather or architecture just then, for he had just received some tantalizing information. A few minutes earlier, as he walked past the shops along King's Parade, Cambridge's main business district, he had encountered Mrs. Agnes Lewis. The two were delighted to see one another, and Schechter eagerly asked about her recent expedition to the Middle East. The trip had been wonderful, Agnes told him. Not only had she and her sister seen sites from the Bible and had several memorable adventures, but just as Rabbi Schechter had suggested, they also had purchased some antiquarian Hebrew documents. She and Mrs. Gibson had identified most of the manuscripts as biblical texts, Agnes told Schechter, but a few remained unidentified. How fortunate it was that she had run into Rabbi Schechter, for she and her sister had only recently resolved to ask him about the mysterious documents. Would he be interested in coming to their home to examine them sometime?

Indeed, he would be interested. And the results of his examination would open vast panoramas of knowledge few could have imagined at the time.

The Mystery Documents

Taking his leave of Mrs. Lewis, Schechter walked down King's Parade, past University Library, past the soaring steeples and green lawns of Trinity College. His curiosity had certainly been piqued. What could the Lewis-Gibson mystery documents be? Of course, they could be worthless souvenirs. But he and Mathilde had known the sisters for several years now, and Schechter knew that they had an eye—or rather two sets of eyes—for priceless manuscript finds. These were, after all, the very women who had found the Sinai Palimpsest a few years back. They were the very women whom Schechter's friends, Frances Burkitt and Rendel Harris, had seen fit to accompany on a difficult journey to Mount Sinai. At the very least, the haul from their recent trip was worth checking out.

He crossed the River Cam, turned right on Chesterton Lane, and a moment later, he turned left and walked up a wide driveway—Castlebrae. The large, red-brick home looked strong and solid—adorned, but with restraint. Just like the sisters. The finely trimmed landscaping shone bright in the late morning sun. Schechter knocked on the door.

A servant answered and presented Schechter to Mrs. Gibson. Maggie, surely knowing why he had come, welcomed Schechter warmly and invited him into the dining room. She fetched the Hebrew manuscripts and laid them out on the table in front of him. Schechter looked closely. As he began his examination, Agnes Lewis returned, having just completed her errands, and joined them in the dining room.

The manuscripts were faded and crumbling, but still quite legible. Holding up one vellum leaf, he said, "This is part of the Jerusalem Talmud, which is very rare. May I take it away [to examine it]?"[1]

"Certainly," replied Agnes.

Schechter then turned his attention to another manuscript. He scanned it briefly, and his pulse quickened. Restraining himself, he uttered one of the great understatements of nineteenth-century scholarship. "The other," he said, "may be important also."

Continuing, Schechter asked, "May I take it away and identify it?"

"Certainly."

"May I [...] publish it?"

"Mrs. Gibson and I will be only too happy if you find that it is worth publishing."

Schechter carefully placed the manuscripts in his bag and hurried off toward the University Library.

The Book of Ben Sirah

Schechter wasn't precisely certain what that second manuscript was, but he *thought* that it might have been a page of the original Hebrew version of the book of Ben Sirah. Also known as Ecclesiasticus, Ben Sirah is a book of wisdom literature, similar in many ways to the biblical book of Proverbs. Scholars believe that it was originally written in the second century BCE, around the time of the Hasmonean uprising, whose miracles Jews still celebrate each year at Chanukah. Its fifty-five chapters comprise a series of moral and ethical teachings, calling upon its readers to seek wisdom, care for the poor, and, truth be told, distrust women. "Be the first to stop eating, for the sake of good manners," it teaches, "and do not be insatiable, lest you give offense" (31:17). "Do not desire a multitude of useless children, nor rejoice in ungodly sons" (16:1). "Keep far from a man who has the power to kill, and you will not be worried by the fear of death. But if you approach him, make no misstep, lest he rob you of your life" (10:13).[2] Ben Sirah—Ecclesiasticus—did not "make the cut" for inclusion into the Jewish Bible. Nor is it in Protestant Bibles. Catholic scholars, however, saw in some of its passages allusions to the Trinity—the threefold nature of God—and included the book in their Bible, in the section known as the Apocrypha.

Primarily because it wasn't canonized into the Hebrew Bible, the original Hebrew version of the book slowly fell into disuse over the years. The ancient Rabbis cited the original Hebrew several times in the Talmud, but the latest section of the Talmud was codified around the year 500 CE. St. Jerome mentioned having seen a

Hebrew version of the text in the fourth century, and Rabbi Saadya Gaon, one of the great sages of medieval Jewry, claimed to have seen it as well, but he died in the year 942.[3] The Ben Sirah that appeared in Catholic Bibles typically got there by way of Greek and Syriac translations compiled centuries after the book was first written. The original Hebrew, however, had been lost to history.

Or so everyone thought.

Schechter's interest in the book was more than just academic. Just a few years earlier, he'd been involved in an academic dispute with another scholar about this very text. Schechter's opponent in this smackdown was a forty-eight-year-old professor of Arabic at Oxford named David Samuel Margoliouth. Margoliouth's family had, like Schechter, migrated to Great Britain from Eastern Europe. However, unlike, Schechter, the Margoliouths had converted from Judaism to Anglicanism along the way and had become active in that church's efforts to proselytize to Jews.[4] D. S. Margoliouth had worked for a time as an Anglican priest before going into academia. He was, as the ancient Rabbis might have delicately put it, an apostate to Judaism. Observers noted that he had "a deep voice, an 'exotic and vivid appearance,' and an outstanding linguistic ability."[5]

In true religious-convert fashion, Margoliouth's scholarly work often strove to minimize the historical and religious importance of his ancestral faith, Judaism, and to maximize that of Christianity. So, in 1889, in his first big lecture as an Oxford don, he argued that the Hebrew version of the book of Ben Sirah was of little consequence whatsoever. He suggested that the truly authoritative versions of the book were those in Syriac and Greek and that the Rabbis who quoted the book had translated its passages into Hebrew from earlier versions in those languages. The Hebrew, Margoliouth argued, was written not during the time of the "Old Testament," but rather at around the time of the Christian scriptures, and was thus more instructive about Christianity than about Judaism. By the time scholars definitively prove my point, Margoliouth insisted, "we shall have a dated document in a language nearer to the mother tongue of Christianity, the language of Christ and His Apostles, than any extant."[6] Schechter pounced. In a thoroughly researched article in an 1891 edition of the *Jewish Quarterly Review*, he assembled, translated, and annotated every Ben Sirah quotation he could find that appeared in classic Rabbinic literature and made a convincing case that the Hebrew version of Ben Sirah *was* an original and *was* written during biblical times— Old Testament biblical times. "The version of Ecclesiasticus available to the Rabbis," Schechter suggested, "was mostly written in pure [i.e., biblical] Hebrew."[7] Margoliouth's suggestion that the Hebrew was a later translation, he argued, was simply incorrect.

Still, absent a copy of the real thing, Schechter's argument on behalf of a full-fledged Hebrew book of Ben Sirah remained only a theory. How Schechter's eyes must have lit up, then, when he first glimpsed the manuscript on the Lewis-Gibson dining room table.

The Ben Sirah Fragment Revealed

With the documents tucked safely away in his case, Schechter left Castlebrae and crossed back over the River Cam in the direction he had come. It was about 12:30 p.m. Once again he passed the imposing entrance to Trinity College and headed toward King's Parade. But now, shopping and errands couldn't have been further from his mind. Before reaching King's Parade, he turned right and stepped into the dark confines of the University Library. There he consulted a copy of the Apocrypha and cross-checked it with the manuscript he had just taken from Castlebrae.

Schechter's pulse raced. Quickly, he fetched a sheet of library stationary and, with his hand shaking in excitement, dashed off a note to Agnes Lewis.

"Dear Mrs. Lewis,

I think we have reason to congratulate ~~ourself~~ ourselves. For the ~~piece~~ fragment I brought with me represents a piece *of the original Hebrew of Ecclesiasticus*. It is the first time such a thing has been discovered. Please *do not*

speak yet about the matter till tomorrow. I will come to you
tomorrow at 11 p.m. [*sic;* surely he meant 11 a.m.] and talk
over the matter with you how to make the matter known.

In haste and great excitement

Yours Sincerely,
S. Schechter."[8]

Despite his request to Mrs. Lewis that she and Mrs. Gibson keep
the matter under wraps, Schechter wasn't quite ready—or wasn't
quite able—to display such discretion himself. He mailed the letter, and on his way out of the library, he ran into several of his colleagues and spilled the beans immediately.[9]

Schechter rushed home. Bursting through the front door, he
called out to Mathilde, "As long as the Bible lives, my name shall
not die!" Evidently, Rabbi Schechter wasn't feeling very humble
just then. And having had some time to think about his discovery,
he wasn't feeling very patient either. "Now telegraph Mrs. Lewis
and Mrs. Gibson to come immediately."[10]

And one other thought may have flashed through his mind:
Margoliouth, this one is *mine*!

The British post of that time was remarkably efficient; intra-
city letters rarely took more than a couple of hours to arrive at their
destination. Still, it was the telegram that arrived at Castlebrae first,
delivered by a messenger at 1:33 p.m. The cable read: "Fragment is
very important; come to me this afternoon." Agnes and Maggie sat
down to lunch before heading over to the Schechter home. While
they were eating, the letter Schechter had sent from the library
arrived, filling them in on more details of the find.[11] We don't know
whether the sisters finished their lunch.

That evening, Agnes wrote to two scholarly journals, the
Athenaeum and the *Academy*, to announce the discovery of the Ben
Sirah fragment, and Schechter wrote in a similar vein to the
Expositor, which a few years previously had been a forum for discus-
sion of Margoliouth's theory about Ben Sirah. Some years later,
Agnes mused:

My sister and I may be excused for not having recognized the value of the leaf which we are now proud to possess. The Apocrypha is almost unknown to Scottish children, it is never put into their hands, and we were therefore not familiar with its text as we are with that of the Bible. Moreover, who even amongst scholars three years ago set any store whatever by Hebrew paper? Dr. Schechter, on the other hand, knows Hebrew as his native tongue, and had given special attention to Ecclesiasticus…. He was therefore eminently fitted to be the pioneer of discoveries of which we hope that we have seen only the beginning.[12]

The fragment Schechter had examined consisted of seventeen lines from chapters 39 and 40 of Ben Sirah. It matched the Greek and Syriac in some places, and in others it did not. There were places in which the translations had been inaccurate, incomplete, or just plain wrong. In short, the fragment he found represented a small piece of the

Schechter's letter to Agnes Lewis, May 13, 1896

Ben Sirah manuscript that Schechter examined at Castlebrae

original Hebrew of Ben Sirah—a book that had been in hiding for almost a millennium.[13]

After identifying the Ben Sirah fragment, Schechter sent a postcard describing the find to his friend, Adolf Neubauer, at Oxford's Bodleian Library. Neubauer, sixty-five years old and suffering from failing eyesight, had worked diligently to expand the Bodleian's collection of Jewish manuscripts since he began working there in 1873. He had been a valuable ally to Schechter in the Ben Sirah controversy with Margoliouth a few years earlier, and the two men had become friends. Two weeks later, Neubauer wrote back to Schechter saying that he couldn't read Schechter's postcard, but that he and his assistant, Arthur Cowley, had "coincidentally" discovered nine Ben Sirah pages in the Bodleian. Schechter was incensed at Neubauer's bogus account, realizing that what really happened was his postcard had sent Neubauer and Cowley digging through their own pile of Cairo manuscripts, hunting for additional Ben Sirah pages. Right then and there, the friendship between Solomon Schechter and Adolf Neubauer ended forever.[14]

Neubauer's Secret

What Schechter didn't know was that Neubauer had a secret—a secret involving a noted British Assyriologist, a shadowy German nobleman, and an enormous trove of manuscripts in Egypt.

The Assyriologist was the aforementioned Archibald Sayce, the Bodleian's primary source of Genizah documents. During the academic year, Sayce was a professor at Oxford University, but since 1890, for health reasons and professional interests, he had been wintering in Cairo. He first learned about the Cairo Genizah in 1892, just as workers completed the reconstruction of the Ben Ezra Synagogue. For some reason, however, Sayce didn't mention the Genizah to his associates in Oxford until 1895. "It is still filled with MSS & books," he wrote to Neubauer in March 1895, "the larger and more accessible of which have been torn to pieces in order to sell the papers which have come to Europe." Then, offhandedly, he continued, "The Jews in charge of the place have offered to sell the whole collection for £50 with £5 bakshish."[15] Sayce tried to negotiate the purchase of the entire body of Cairo Genizah documents for almost a year, but his efforts failed. "As soon as any money is paid to the old Rabbi and his colleagues," wrote Sayce, "they immediately get dead drunk upon it, & nothing can be done with them until their funds are exhausted."[16]

The nobleman was Count Riamo d'Hulst, a German officer during the Franco-Prussian war of 1870–71. The background of Count d'Hulst is unclear; he seems to have lived in Luxembourg for a time, and he was often referred to as an Austrian. What is clear is that the count had worked as an excavator and site supervisor for the Egypt Exploration Fund from 1886 to 1893. In 1889, when the Ben Ezra renovation began and Genizah documents were strewn about the synagogue grounds, the Fund sent d'Hulst to conduct excavations in Old Cairo. There he unearthed coins, tombstones, pottery, and "a number of fragments of some Hebrew manuscripts found at Fostat."[17] In the course of his work, d'Hulst evidently established good relationships with Cairo's Jewish community, and they periodically allowed him to examine the old manuscripts at the Ben Ezra Synagogue. In 1890, he sold some fragments to Oxford. The sale took place just before that of Greville Chester, thus making him one of the first—if not the very first—Westerner to visit and remove manuscripts from the Cairo Genizah in the late nineteenth century. D'Hulst later recalled that in 1889—six years before Sayce offered to buy the entire collection of Genizah documents—he could have purchased them all on Oxford's behalf for as little as twenty pounds. Such a purchase, Oxford's librarians later learned, would have been a pretty good deal.

In the early 1890s, d'Hulst began dealing in antiquarian manuscripts, and he met Archibald Sayce. It was d'Hulst who first told Sayce about the Genizah in 1892, and Sayce was eager to use d'Hulst's connections in the Jewish community to help him get access to the collection. Thus, while he was negotiating the purchase of the *entire* Genizah collection with local Jewish leaders, Sayce also turned to d'Hulst for help in getting *pieces* of the collection to send back to Oxford.

Evidently, Count d'Hulst succeeded in gaining entry to the reconstructed Genizah early in 1895, and that November Sayce wrote Neubauer that he was sending a box of manuscripts to Oxford, with three more boxes to follow in short order. Together, the boxes contained almost ten thousand pages; by early February 1896, they had all arrived at the Bodleian.

When Neubauer examined the massive shipment of documents, he was unimpressed. It contained letters, some business documents, a few Bible fragments, Rabbinic texts, and so on. Most of it, in Neubauer's view, was nothing more than rubbish. On May 9, 1896, the Bodleian Library "agreed to authorize the giving away, exchange or sale of unbound fragments of Hebrew writing recently purchased [which are reportedly] not worth adding to the collection of Hebrew MSS." Bodleian records do not include the name of the purchaser, but the person who bought them was Elkan Nathan Adler.[18]

A few days later, Neubauer received Schechter's postcard informing him of the Ben Sirah discovery. Neubauer knew that the documents Mrs. Lewis and Mrs. Gibson had brought from the Middle East most likely came from the Cairo Genizah—the very same Cairo Genizah that had been the source of the shipment he had just received from Sayce. Could there be additional pages of

Ben Sirah in the Bodleian Genizah collection? Fortunately, Neubauer realized, the documents had not yet been sold; there was still time for a closer look. Maybe those old papers weren't so worthless after all.

Sure enough, he and Cowley soon discovered nine more leaves of the very same Ben Sirah manuscript as the one the ladies had shared with Solomon Schechter. Now, Neubauer realized that there were indeed treasures to be had in the Genizah, and since Schechter would surely want them, too, there was no time to waste in getting them. Neubauer got to work planning a trip to Cairo.

Meanwhile, Schechter realized that several of the documents Mrs. Lewis and Mrs. Gibson brought back from their travels were clearly labeled as having come from Fustat—Old Cairo. Schechter knew of the Genizah in Cairo, of course, but until now he hadn't given it much thought. With his discovery of the Ben Sirah pages, however, the Cairo Genizah had captured his attention. Maybe there were more Ben Sirah pages still in the Genizah; maybe the Genizah held other precious treasures, as well. Schechter had no idea what the old attic held but decided that it offered sufficient promise to merit a trip to Cairo.

He would have to be discreet, of course. Others, like Neubauer, would certainly be hot on the Genizah trail, too, and Schechter wanted to get there first.

The race was on.

5

A Battlefield of Books

"The whole synagogue is a gem of antiquity."
ELKAN NATHAN ADLER, DESCRIBING CAIRO'S BEN EZRA SYNAGOGUE, 1888[1]

"[The Genizah is] a heterogeneous mass of confusion."
AGNES LEWIS, 1898[2]

In December 1896, Solomon Schechter embarked on his journey toward the Genizah. The trip was difficult to plan. Schechter had to wait to travel until after the fall term—Michaelmas term, as it was called in Cambridge. Most of his funding had come from Dr. Charles Taylor, of St. John's College at Cambridge. Taylor, a devoted Anglican, was not only a highly accomplished Hebraist and supporter of Jewish scholarship, but he also came from an affluent family and was able to provide generous support to Schechter's research. With Taylor's funding, Schechter was able to avoid having the university pay for his trip, which would have demanded going public with word of his expedition. Schechter was determined not to allow Neubauer to get to the Genizah first, so secrecy was of the utmost importance.

Schechter's other friends in England had done what they could to help as well, providing letters of introduction, funds, and some coaching on the ways of Arab life. Prior to that time, Schechter had never been farther south than Italy. He had heard and read about Egypt since he was a child, of course. It was the place where Jacob and his sons went to escape famine in their homeland. It was the land that brutally enslaved the ancient Israelites and from which they fled under Moses's leadership—a miraculous and awesome event that Schechter relived every spring at his Passover Seder. Lest the Jewish people ever consider a return to their old slave stomping grounds, God had been quite clear in the book of Deuteronomy: "You shall not return this way ever again" (17:16). From the Exodus on, the land of Egypt was under an eternal "no-travel" order for Jews.

And yet, there Schechter was—in Egypt. Amid the noisy tumult, spicy aromas, and brightly colored souks of nineteenth-century Egypt, he realized that it wasn't only the country's history that made him feel like an outsider; so too did its modern Arab culture and mores.

Schechter's boat had landed in Alexandria, just over one hundred miles north of Cairo, and his first visit was to that city's chief rabbi, Elijah Hazzan. The fifty-seven-year-old, Turkish-born sage was a staunch defender of religious Orthodoxy in its struggle against modernity. Schechter explained that he had come to examine the papers of the Cairo Genizah. He hoped that examining its manuscripts in the light of modern advances in paleogra-phy and historical criticism might lead to some significant discoveries.

Paleography? Historical criticism? Hazzan had heard of such things, but he couldn't fathom what they had to do with the junk up in the Cairo Genizah. With a dismissive shake of his head, he tried to warn his British visitor off such a foolish pursuit. "You will find very little there but loose sheets."[3]

Documents being placed in the Cairo Genizah, as illustrated in a diorama at Beit Hatfutzot: The Museum of Jewish People, Tel Aviv

Schechter kept his tone cool and measured. He reminded the rabbi that Cairo was home to one of the world's oldest Jewish communities and that some of the documents in its Genizah could be over a thousand years old. Cairo's prominent Jews often corresponded with other Jewish leaders in Palestine, Mesopotamia, and elsewhere, and many of their letters were likely to have made their way to the Genizah. Some of the most renowned Jewish scholars in history lived in Cairo, including the great rabbi-physician-philosopher Moses Maimonides (1138–1204). Certainly some significant manuscripts relating to their lives and work were up there, as well. And with luck, Schechter added, Cairo's dry climate had helped preserve the documents from the ravages of time. "Loose sheets," indeed.[4]

Cairo: Two Cities in One

From Alexandria, Schechter took a 3½-hour train ride to Cairo.[5] On the carriage from the train station to his hotel, Schechter saw that Cairo was a meeting place of vastly different cultures and eras, unlike any other in the world. Here was an imposing colonnaded museum

Cairene Sight

resembling the Parthenon; there, worshipers entered a Muslim shrine. Here, merchants rode donkeys to purchase wares for their shops; there was a café straight from the Champs-Elysées.

Cairo, Schechter realized, was actually two cities—one Egyptian, the other European. Together, they formed a teeming metropolis with one foot firmly planted in antiquity and the other in modernity. Egyptian Cairo was an ancient city. Its streets were narrow zigzag-ging alleyways; donkeys provided the primary mode of transportation; goats, cows, and even camels wandered among the hordes of human pedestrians. Above it all towered a forest of minarets, from which muezzins called worshipers to prayer five times each

Mohammed Ali Square, Cairo, mid-1890s

day. "*Allahu akbar*, God is great," the cry began. To Cairo's many pious Muslims, it was a timeless credo that gave rhythm and structure to their lives.

Modern Cairo, on the other hand, was far more European in flavor. Built during the 1860s and 1870s, it was originally designed to impress the many dignitaries who flocked to Egypt for the 1869 dedication of the Suez Canal. This Cairo consisted of wide boulevards, elegant hotels, and a grand opera house. At its heart was the Azbakiyyah Garden, Cairo's version of a Parisian park, featuring shops, cafés, restaurants, pedal boats, and even a shooting gallery.[6]

In short, Schechter arrived at a time when old Egyptian Cairo and its modern European counterpart dwelt alongside and intermeshed with one another as fraternal twin cities. Almost 600,000 people lived in Cairo, which put it right between Warsaw and Brussels on the list of the world's largest cities, and far above Africa's next largest metropolis, Alexandria, which was home to only about 320,000. Its streets teemed with finely dressed Western tourists, local shopkeepers hawking their wares to passersby, clusters of old men smoking ornate water pipes, fez-wearing Egyptian soldiers perched high atop their camels, British colonial officials, and nine-year-old donkey drivers lined up outside the hotels shouting out what little English they knew: "Lady, you want ride? This donkey named George Washington—best in all Cairo!"

And one bearded rabbi from Cambridge in search of old Jewish documents.

Schechter checked into the Hotel Metropole, a forty-room pension just south of the Azbakiyyah Garden, and right around the corner from the Opera House. The hotel was neither as grand nor as costly as the more elegant Shepheard's or Savoy hotels nearby, but the *Baedeker's Guide* described it as "well spoken of." Despite its second-tier status, the Metropole attracted many dignitaries and provided Schechter with several good social opportunities.

Among Schechter's first tasks in Cairo was to meet—and woo—Rabbi Aaron Raphael Bensimon, whose support he needed to ensure access to the Genizah. Bensimon was born in Jerusalem in 1848 and had served as Cairo's chief rabbi since 1891. Surely, Bensimon was initially uncomfortable with his British visitor. Bensimon had been working to defend Judaism against the threat of Western values and mores, while Schechter, with his European accent and Cambridge letters of introduction, had clearly embraced those values. Bensimon spent most of his professional energy dealing with matters of *halakhah*—Jewish law. Schechter,

though an ordained rabbi, spent most of his time studying *history*, for some reason. And most puzzling of all, Schechter seemed particularly interested in the junk up in the Genizah.

But Schechter was dignified, charming, and witty. Plus, he was from Cambridge, and those letters of introduction did have some impressive-looking seals. Bensimon saw that an alliance with Schechter could be of benefit to his community. It took many cigarettes and gallons of coffee over several days, but

Rabbi Aaron Raphael Bensimon

eventually Schechter suc-
ceeded in winning the
prelate over. Within days,
the rabbi from Cambridge
and the rabbi from Cairo
had become fast friends.

Schechter also met
with Youssef M. Cattaui, a
lay leader of the Cairo
Jewish community. Cattaui

The home of Youssef M. Cattaui

was a scion of a large and very prominent Cairo Jewish family.
Having made a fortune in banking and real estate, the Cattauis
lived in palaces in Cairo's most elegant neighborhoods; eventually,
three streets in the city would bear their family name. Cattaui's
support, too, was important for Schechter to secure access to whatever might be in the Genizah.

Schechter rode to Cattaui's home, and Cattaui welcomed him
cordially. Unlike Rabbi Bensimon, Cattaui was eager to extend
himself to Schechter. Cattaui was, after all, an aristocrat—a
European-style aristocrat. His wealth had allowed him to enjoy the
riches of Western culture even in an outpost as distant as Cairo,
and he yearned for more. Prominent visitors from places such as
Cambridge were always welcome in his home.

Schechter's schmoozing paid off. He earned the respect and
the affection of the leaders of the Cairo Jewish community, and
within a few short days, Rabbi Bensimon offered to show him to
the Genizah.[7]

The Ruins of Fustat

Together, Schechter and Bensimon rode to southern Cairo, to its
oldest neighborhood, Fustat. It was a journey of just over three miles
in distance, but many centuries in time. Founded as Egypt's capital
in 642 CE, Fustat was built around a walled Nile-side citadel called
the Fortress of Babylon, or Qasr al Sham; it was also called the

Fortress of Candles, perhaps for the candles that illumined its towers to mark the beginning of every month. By the eleventh century, the city was an international center of trade and the arts, featuring churches, markets, twelve-meter-high fortifications, and a populace of 120,000 citizens—far more than Venice's 100,000 residents, and certainly more than in Cairo, Fustat's small suburb to the north.

Arriving in Fustat, Schechter was saddened to see that the neighborhood lay in ruins. Reduced in status ever since the conquering tenth-century Fatimids moved Egypt's capital to neighboring Cairo, Fustat had declined further during the Middle Ages when the course of the Nile shifted roughly four hundred meters to the west, leaving Fustat high, dry, and strategically irrelevant. People continued to live there, but without the governmental spiffing-up that it received when it was the riverside capital, the area had long fallen into decrepitude. From the thirteenth to sixteenth centuries, large sections of Fustat were used as a garbage dump.

The men descended from their carriage and continued over the ruins on foot. Along the way, Schechter reflected on the building he was about to visit. Although later archaeological evidence would reveal that the synagogue had been built during the mid-eleventh century, legend in Schechter's time had it that the structure had been converted from a Coptic church to a synagogue shortly after the Muslim conquest of Egypt in 639 CE, making it a site of profound antiquity.

Over the years, other legends developed about the place, suggesting that it had been visited by biblical noteworthies such as the prophet Jeremiah; Ezra the Scribe, who supposedly penned a Torah scroll for the congregation; Elijah; and even Moses. Each of these men bestowed a bit of their sanctity on the synagogue; visiting the room where Jeremiah prayed reportedly could heal people suffering from eye diseases, for example. Moses is even said to have worshiped there. By the time of Schechter's visit, many local Egyptians had come to think of the Ben Ezra Synagogue as a magical place, indeed.[8]

Schechter had good reason to hope that there might be valuable manuscripts in the Genizah. Jews had lived in Fustat ever since it was first founded, often in great numbers. A visitor to the community in 1170 estimated its Jewish population at about seven thousand people.[9] Unlike their European counterparts to the north, the Jews of Egypt, and of Fustat in particular, often thrived during the Middle Ages. Many Fustat Jews were accomplished businessmen, government officials, poets, and artists. Its merchants traded with their counterparts in lands as distant as Morocco, Italy, and China.

The community may not have been as large as that of Cordoba or Baghdad or as sacred as that of Jerusalem, but it was significant. Fustat's position on the medieval Jewish landscape gave it a standing similar to that of Chicago in contemporary America.

Like Chicago, Fustat Jewry teemed with diversity. Not only did its residents span the economic spectrum, but there were also religious and cultural differences among the community's three Jewish subgroups: the Palestinian Jews, with allegiance to the authorities of the Land of Israel; Iraqi Jews, who cast their lot with the sages of Babylonia; and Karaite Jews, who rejected Rabbinic authority and cast their lot with no rabbis at all. Divided though they were, the three populations lived in relative harmony in Fustat.

Since the early 1890s, medieval manuscripts from the Fustat Jewish community had been surfacing on the European antiquities market, and Schechter himself of course had just identified one as a page of a long-lost book of the Bible. While he couldn't be certain, he had good reason to believe that this trip would prove to be worth the effort.

The Jewel among the Rubbish

Together, the men walked through the ruins of the ancient fortress and approached the synagogue. The building, small by the standards of the grand synagogues Schechter had visited in Europe, was of fair size by Egyptian standards—about twenty meters long and ten meters across. Reconstructed a few years earlier, the handsome structure stood in stark contrast to the dilapidated buildings around it. Schechter undoubtedly noticed the piles of rubbish still heaped outside the synagogue and would have wondered whether the heaps contained any valuable old papers.

In deference to his guest, Rabbi Bensimon let Schechter enter first.

Schechter walked through the arched entryway and immediately scanned the room. The sanctuary was plainly decorated—the community had not yet raised funds to restore the interior—but still the space retained a grandeur of design and construction. Five pillars lined each side of the synagogue, supporting the women's gallery balcony overlooking the nave. The pillars continued upward into an arched wall supporting the ceiling above the women's gallery. From beneath the arches, sunlight shone in through windows along each side of the building. Brass chandeliers hung from the ceiling, and behind a raised platform in the front of the room stood the *aron hakodesh*, the sacred ark, holding the Torah scrolls.

Rabbi Bensimon introduced Schechter to the synagogue's caretakers and explained that their visitor had come to examine the Genizah. They nodded and escorted Schechter back out the doorway through which he had just entered. Schechter was probably puzzled as to why they were having him leave, but as soon as he was outside he realized what was going on. The women's gallery was accessible only by way of a bridge connecting it to a small building next door. The caretakers explained that the outbuilding was that of the *waqf*—the Jewish community's charitable foundation—and design changes implemented during the 1892 reconstruction made it necessary to erect the bridge for access to the women's gallery.

Once inside, the caretakers pointed over the rail and across the room. The entrance to the Genizah was on the opposite side of the sanctuary to their right, high up on the front wall. The group turned left, walked along the balcony, made two right turns, and in a few moments they stood beneath a shapeless hole high on the eastern wall of the synagogue. The caretakers leaned a crudely built ladder against the wall, handed Schechter a lantern, and invited him to proceed.

Climbing to the Chamber Above

Schechter climbed the ladder, his eyes focused on the darkened Genizah entrance above him. Pausing on his way up, he glanced around to orient himself. Through the arched window over his left shoulder, sunlight shone into the basilica-style sanctuary, illuminating its stately pillars and brass chandeliers. Below, Schechter could see a large wooden reading table and chairs for several dozen worshipers arranged around it. From where he stood near the thirty-foot-high ceiling, the room and its furnishings looked tiny.[10]

Reaching the top of the ladder, Schechter carefully stepped through the small opening into the chamber, and as his eyes adjusted to the darkness, the Genizah and its contents slowly came into view. It was a rectangular room measuring about twelve by fourteen feet, its walls exposed gray brick reaching more than twenty feet from floor to ceiling. Thick clouds of dust floated in the air, billowing more heavily with each step he took. Schechter's eyes continued to adjust to the darkness and the dust. Then, gradually, the clouds parted.

It was a mountain of texts.

The moderately sized room was packed tightly from wall to wall. There were no boxes or baskets, just papers and words—more words than could ever be counted. Some documents lay flat; others were crinkled and clumped together like monstrous, dried-up spitballs; still others seemed to crumble before his eyes. Many of the old documents had turned to dust; they floated in the air all around him, and he couldn't help but inhale some of them. The quantity and the chaos were staggering.

Later, Schechter recalled his impressions:

One can hardly realise the confusion in a genuine, old Genizah until one has seen it. It is a battlefield of books, and the literary production of many centuries had their share in the battle, and their *disjecta membra* are now strewn over its area. Some of the belligerents have perished outright, and are literally ground to dust in the terrible struggle for space, whilst others, as if overtaken by a general crush, are squeezed into big, unshapely lumps, which even with the aid of chemical appliances can no longer be separated from their contents. In their present condition, these lumps sometimes afford curiously suggestive combinations; as, for instance, when you find a piece of some rationalistic work, in which the very existence of either angels or devils is denied, clinging for its very life to an amulet in which these same beings (mostly the latter) are bound over to be on their good behaviour and not interfere with Miss Jair's love for somebody. The development of the romance is obscured by the fact that the last lines of the amulet are mounted on some I.O.U., or lease, and this in turn is squeezed between the sheets of an old moralist, who treats all attention to money affairs with scorn and indignation. Again, all these contradictory matters cleave tightly to some sheets from a very old Bible. This, indeed, ought to be the last umpire between them, but it is hardly legible without peeling off from its surface the fragments of some printed work, which clings to old nobility with all of the obstinacy and obtrusiveness of the parvenu.[11]

Schechter realized that he was looking at the literary ruins of a lost civilization. Where was he to start? How was he even to begin examining the chaos of treasures before him? Schechter was an expert on Jewish manuscripts, and before him sat a quantity of texts far greater than *all* of the manuscripts he had ever before studied. In fact, he was looking at a collection that turned out to be larger and far more important—in terms of mass, depth, and range—than all other collections of antiquarian Jewish manuscripts in the world combined. Cambridge had approximately eight hundred Hebrew manuscripts in its collection at the time, and Oxford's Bodleian Library held about three thousand more—but this dwarfed them all, hundreds of times over.[12]

The Genizah was an awesome sight. Seeing it must have stilled and satisfied Solomon Schechter as never before. It was a moment few scholars could ever hope to experience.

We can imagine Schechter grabbing documents left and right, giving each a quick glance before laying it aside and going on to the next. Here—part of a Bible written in an ancient Hebrew script; it might date back as far as the ninth century. And here—another Bible with some of its letters inked-in with gold leaf. Gilt lettering had long been forbidden in Jewish Bibles, so this text probably dated at least as far back as the early Middle Ages. And here's a page from a prayer book that looks to be from the twelfth century or so ... but wait ... beneath the text there appears to be the faint outline of *another* text, this one even older. A psalm? The document is a palimpsest—a text written atop an older, poorly erased text to save the cost and trouble of obtaining scarce writing supplies.[13] And over here is a pile of correspondence—the Hebrew letters look familiar, but the words are gibberish ... no, not gibberish, *Arabic*! Judeo-Arabic, to be precise. This Jewish dialect of the local vernacular, written in Hebrew characters, was the language of many documents in the Genizah, and it was a language in which Schechter was not very proficient. He'd have to save those for later. But here's another Judeo-Arabic piece—a court document? And this one looks like a lease of some sort. Here's a *ketubah*—a Jewish marriage certificate. And just below it is a *get*—a divorce decree—for the same couple. Whoops.

Each move he made stirred up clouds of ancient dust. Each scrap he examined was a new and priceless treasure. Taking this trip to Cairo, it turns out, had been a good idea after all.

A Mountain of Texts

Schechter had to tear himself away from his piece-by-piece Genizah examination to look at the big picture. He offered three hundred pounds for the entire pile of manuscripts,[14] and Cairo's Jewish leaders, all of whom probably shared Rabbi Bensimon's bewilderment at the interest this rabbi was taking in the tattered papers heaped in their synagogue attic, accepted the offer and told Schechter that he could take as much of the stuff up there as he liked. But Schechter had a problem: "As a matter of fact, I liked it all."[15]

Without delay, he hired local laborers to assist him in his work and dove into the colossal task of sorting through the Genizah. Schechter was unable to focus on individual sheets for long, for the Genizah held literally hundreds of thousands of documents. Back at Cambridge, he would often spend many weeks examining a single manuscript and preparing it for publication. Now, facing a mountain of such manuscripts, he realized that at his usual pace, the work would take a lifetime—no, *many* lifetimes—to complete.

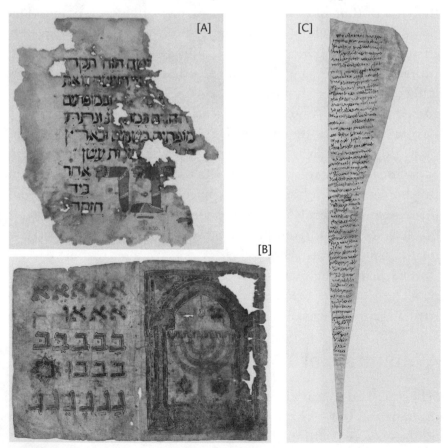

Genizah fragments: a Haggadah [A], a schoohouse primer [B], a legal document [C]

Over the next two weeks, Schechter found scriptural passages dating back to the tenth century, some adorned with previously unknown commentaries in the margins. He found fragments of the Talmud, many of which varied from what later became standard versions of the work, and some representing tractates lost for centuries. The Genizah also contained "autograph documents"— handwritten letters, notes, lists, and scribbles inscribed not to be works of literature, but simply as part of the day-to-day lives of the members of a literate society. There were business records, court documents, poems, amulets, and medical instructions.[16]

He came across a leaf from a child's reading primer that appeared to date back to the eleventh century. The page was decorated with a six-pointed star, but that symbol had never been seen on Jewish documents anywhere near that old. He saw a page of a Passover Haggadah decorated with pictures of animals forming Hebrew letters. There was even a narrow strip of paper that looked to be a document transferring the ownership of a house, which began, "The following sale was effected with one handshake."

Schechter had told Elijah Hazzan in Alexandria that he suspected the Genizah might hold some material relating to Moses Maimonides, the great twelfth-century sage and court physician. But in the Genizah, Schechter came across documents that appeared to have been written in Maimonides's own hand.

It is likely that Schechter had heard, at least in passing, of a sixth-century poet from Palestine named Yannai, one of the earliest composers of a form of Hebrew verse called *piyyut*. The brief article about Yannai in the 1903 *Jewish Encyclopedia* notes that he "was apparently a very prolific poet ... [but] most of his poems are lost." Later encyclopedia articles about Yannai would be more informative, however, because mixed into the pile of documents Schechter found in the Genizah were no fewer than eight hundred of Yannai's poems.[17]

The Genizah, Schechter could see, held schoolbooks, travel records, and some of the oldest known versions of sacred Jewish texts. He found Torah scrolls, magical incantations, and letters from Jewish travelers. Some of the Genizah documents, Schechter observed, were quite large—sixty to seventy centimeters from top to bottom—and others were tiny scraps bearing only a few words or letters of text. Many of the texts were written in Judeo-Arabic, others in Hebrew, still others in Judeo-Persian and Indian languages, and at least one in a language that, still today, over a century later, scholars have not yet identified. There were alms requests, sermons, love letters, and doodles; there were calendars, liturgical texts, mathematics, and astrology.

Schechter soon realized that the Genizah held a great deal of printed matter stored there during recent centuries. But he was partial to handwritten manuscripts and didn't want to bother with these post-Gutenberg additions. Schechter probably suspected that some of the printed documents were significant, but the printed material was more recent and therefore less likely to have scholarly value than the older, handwritten manuscripts. Moreover, there were probably identical copies of the printed material elsewhere— it was *printed*, after all. In contrast, each individual manuscript is a unique creation of the scribe who penned it and often differs significantly from other manuscripts of the very same texts. Schechter focused on the manuscripts and left the printed matter behind.[18]

Years later, scholars realized that Schechter's exclusive focus on the manuscripts meant that he ignored printed material of great significance. For example, the Genizah contained dozens of printed amulets—long pieces of paper bearing Arabic prayers for good fortune that people would roll up and put in small pouches hanging from their necks. The fact that these prayers were printed in quantity rather than written out by hand indicates not their worthlessness, but only that the wearing of Arabic amulets was a common practice for medieval Jews.

But despite knowing that some of the printed documents in the Genizah might be valuable, Schechter was overwhelmed; he faced an astounding number of documents, and his manuscripts-only decision seemed a sensible first step in his culling.

The decision was far easier to make than carry out. The paper and parchment scraps had been dumped into the Genizah over the centuries with no mind to order or tidiness. And when Ben Ezra's renovation was completed in 1892, the old roof having collapsed four years earlier, most of the Genizah's contents were taken up from the synagogue grounds and simply dumped en masse back into the newly reconstructed Genizah. The caretakers hadn't even bothered to remove the remains of the old roof. Many documents, as Schechter noted, had been ground to dust over the centuries, and those that survived were often on the verge of crumbling into oblivion, as well. Handling them was very delicate work.

A letter of reference from Moses Maimonides

Working at the Cairo Genizah was not at all like working in the hushed, hallowed halls of Cambridge. For starters, the laborers he hired were different from Cambridge research assistants. Schechter later recalled:

> [The local workers] declined to be paid for their services in so many piastres *per diem*. This was a vulgar way of doing business to which no self-respecting keeper of a real Genizah would degrade himself. The keepers insisted the more on *bakhshish* [small bribes], which, besides being a more dignified kind of remuneration, has the advantage of being expected also for services not rendered.[19]

When word got out that a British, *baksheesh*-wielding rabbi was working at the Ben Ezra Synagogue, an endless parade of visitors made its way to Schechter at the Genizah.

In fact, the whole population within the precincts of the synagogue were constantly coming forward with claims on my liberality—the men as worthy colleagues employed in the same work (of selection) as myself, or, at least, in watching us at our work; the women for greeting me respectfully when I entered the place, or for showing me their deep sympathy in my fits of coughing caused by the dust.[20]

Miserable working conditions in the Genizah added to the difficulty of his labor. Although Schechter described the Genizah as having been "of fair dimensions," he was being generous. The modest stone chamber was stuffed with an enormous volume of papers. Accessible only by ladder, it was dark and cramped. Insects swarmed out of the festering pile of texts, and the dust was oppressive—at times almost suffocating.

Cairo Is Not Cambridge

During the previous several years, Schechter had grown accustomed to the pristine ivory towers of Cambridge scholarship. But in Cairo, what he saw and felt at every turn reminded him that he wasn't in Cambridge anymore. Not even close.

Even Cairo's Jewish community was different. Schechter was a thoroughly European Jew with thoroughly European sensibilities. Never before had he known Jews who spoke Modern Arabic. Fortunately, he could speak Hebrew with Rabbi Bensimon, and he could use his smattering of French with Cattaui and many of the others. Never before had he been surrounded by Jews with such Middle Eastern features. They were Jews, of course, but their dark skin made them look like Arabs—which, of course, they also were. And never before had Schechter seen a Jewish community so imbued with Arab customs and mores. For wealthy men in the city, flowing robes, fezzes, and sometimes even turbans were de rigueur. Cairo opened Schechter's eyes to a Jewish culture he had heard about, but whose richness he had never appreciated.

And the Genizah he found in Cairo would do the very same thing for others. It would reveal a rich culture long ignored by most of the Jewish world and would expand Western notions of what it means to be a Jew. The Genizah, for example, held thousands of poems—some religious, others secular—and revealed the enormous literary accomplishments of medieval Egyptian Jewry. Its court documents showed the civility with which Jews and Egyptians interacted for many centuries. Its business records put Jews at the very heart of Middle Eastern mercantile life as they interacted with associates and customers locally and in faraway lands. The thousands of letters in the Genizah spoke of the passion of a woman for her beloved, the despair of a man swindled out of his lifetime savings, the hard work of tradesmen arranging their deals, and countless other details of life in medieval Jewish culture. One of the first documents Schechter found, for example, was a letter written in about the year 1000 from Rabbi Chushiel ben Elhanan of Kairowan, Tunisia, to Rabbi Shemariah ben Elhanan of Egypt. The two men were preeminent scholars in medieval North Africa, and their correspondence detailed the active nature of daily life at their academies as students and sages studied Torah together. This and other documents revealed a Jewish world that until then had existed only in the barest of outlines.

Between the long shifts he put in at the Genizah, Schechter found time to schmooze with other local residents. For example, at the Metropole, he met Charles Henry Butcher, chaplain of All Saints Parish, whom he invited along with Butcher's wife and a few other acquaintances to an enjoyable afternoon tea with Rabbi Bensimon. Schechter described Butcher as "a delightful fellow."[21]

He also met and mixed with British diplomats, including Lord Cromer, the British agent in Cairo, who was, in the words of one historian, "the virtual ruler of Egypt." Cromer, whose given name was Evelyn Baring, was fifty-six years old and had held diplomatic posts in Egypt for fourteen years. An imperialist par excellence, Cromer filled most key government positions with British officials and had little respect for the abilities of the people he governed. "We need not always inquire too closely what these people … themselves think is in their own best interests," he wrote. "It is essential that each special issue should be decided mainly with reference to what, by the light of Western knowledge and experience … we conscientiously think is best for the subject race."[22] At the time, Cromer was working to stanch the flow of illegal antiquities out of the country, but he took a keen interest in Schechter's work—Schechter was from *Cambridge*, after all—and the two men began what would be a lifelong friendship. When it came time to ship the Genizah documents home, Schechter's personal relationship with Cromer proved enormously helpful in cutting through the red tape. And the fact that Cromer had filled government posts with Cambridge-respecting Brits didn't hurt, either.[23]

Schechter also befriended Sabbatai Manjubi,[24] the local leader of the Karaites, who still thrived in Cairo, though in numbers far smaller than during the Middle Ages. On a walk with Manjubi one day, the two men were having a friendly chat in Hebrew when Schechter tripped on a cobblestone, almost fell, and lapsed into English. "Damn!" When Manjubi asked him what that strange word meant, Schechter explained, "We have in our language a little word of one syllable which is full of theological meaning and is used as a sort of charm against people who annoy us."[25]

When Schechter learned that Rabbi Bensimon had never visited the Pyramids, Schechter took him there. "It cost me about ten shillings," he wrote Mathilde, "but that is the only way to make yourself popular." Evidently Schechter's efforts to endear himself to the local rabbi continued to succeed. In another letter, he noted, that "the Rabbi is very kind to me and kisses me on the mouth, which is not very pleasant…. I am just back from the Genizah and brought two big sacks with fragments. I must have a bath at once. You have no idea of the dirt."[26] His letter leaves modern readers wondering whether it was the dirt or the kiss that made him crave a bath.

Schechter befriended other local leaders, as well, and he managed to find time to enjoy the pleasures of Cairo. "Cairo is a glorious place," he wrote his wife, "enjoying an Italian opera, French dancing masters, English administration, and Mohammedan houris [voluptuous young women]. The last are very ugly," he made sure to add, "and I do not wonder that they are so careful as to cover their faces."[27]

The Genizah work continued. Each day, Schechter would have an early breakfast at the Hotel Metropole, then exit to the street and hire one of the open-air two-horse victoria cabs waiting at the curb to take him on the 3½-mile trip to the Ben Ezra Synagogue. Walking the final several hundred feet through the ruins of old Fustat, he would arrive at the synagogue, climb the stairs in the *waqf*, cross the bridge to the women's gallery balcony, make a left and two rights, and ascend the ladder to the Genizah. For the next several hours, workers would hurry to and from the Genizah entrance, carefully holding piles of delicate old manuscripts amid the swirl of activity around them. There were frequent interruptions from British diplomats, Cairo's Jewish leaders, and those aforementioned local residents with claims on Schechter's "liberality." Still, dust covered, stooped, and squinting in the darkness, Schechter pressed on. The Genizah was a "battlefield of books," and the rabbi had come to tend its wounded and its dead.

The Sisters Arrive

As he prepared for his trip, Schechter had invited Mrs. Lewis and Mrs. Gibson to accompany him. But Mrs. Lewis came down with a bout of fever and rheumatism, which, among other factors, delayed the ladies' departure for several weeks.

Finally, on January 9, the sisters departed by steamer for Egypt, arriving in Cairo on January 21. They checked into the Hotel d'Angleterre, an upscale alternative to Schechter's nearby Metropole, freshened up, and at 5 p.m., went to visit Schechter.[28] Schechter, exhausted from his work, was delighted to see them and immediately invited them in for tea. Instead, they adjourned to the more elegant Hotel d'Angleterre for their tea, and Schechter filled them in on the progress of his work. "He has found a few good

things amongst heaps of, well, I won't say rubbish, but quite unim-
portant stuff," Mrs. Lewis wrote to Mathilde that evening. "That is
the way in all Eastern libraries, but in this case he has been choked
with dust and bad air and has worked like a horse."[29] Fortunately,
the ladies had brought the rabbi a care package from his wife,
which included a "respirator"[30]—a device similar to a gas mask—to
help him breathe in the dusty confines of the Genizah.

Agnes and Margaret found Schechter so engrossed in his work
that he was becoming something of an absentminded professor-
rabbi. For example, he complained over tea that having "no idea that
Cairo was such a gay place," he had neglected to bring his black dress-
suit. But then, two weeks later, they reported that he showed up to
dinner wearing the suit "and looked very well indeed." Mrs. Lewis
reported, "Occasionally, he does leave a thing about, and forgets it.
But it turns up." At tea with Butcher and Bensimon, Schechter
agreed to serve as the Hebrew-English interpreter. But when Rabbi
Bensimon spoke in Hebrew, Schechter turned to Butcher and
repeated verbatim what the rabbi had said. He repeated it so verbatim in fact, that he did so in the original Hebrew.[31]

Shortly after their arrival, Schechter escorted the ladies to the
Ben Ezra Synagogue. "It is a very plain synagogue in one of the
most densely populated quarters of old Cairo," Agnes Lewis would
later recall. "A very broad gallery runs round three sides of it, and
above one of these there is a door high up in the whitewashed wall,
to which the roughest of rude ladders gave access. As its rungs were
very wide apart, I dared not attempt to mount it."[32]

Agnes and her sister would turn fifty-four years old that year.
They were almost certainly clothed in the long dresses and white
gloves proper for Victorian ladies of the time, and Agnes herself
was still suffering from rheumatism. None of these factors, however, was what made Agnes reluctant to climb up to the Genizah
that day. It was the widely spaced rungs on the ladder.

But the synagogue beadle who was there that day did climb
the ladder, "and as he jumped down on the other side," Agnes
wrote, "we could hear the crinkling of vellum leaves under his

feet."[33] Her description of ancient manuscripts crinkling beneath trampling feet is enough to make any bibliophile wince. Margaret was evidently the more adventurous twin that day. Having seen the ease with which the beadle mounted the ladder, she too climbed up and had a look inside the Genizah.

Sadly, there are no known photographs of the Genizah from this time. Schechter was too focused on its contents to worry about taking any pictures, the locals never bothered to preserve any images of the room where they dumped their "junk," and Mrs. Lewis, an inveterate and highly organized photographer, made an uncharacteristic goof that day. "One of the many regrets of my life," she recalled, "is that on the occasion of our visit to [the Genizah] we left the little Frena [camera] in the hotel, and I am therefore unable to present my readers with a picture of its exterior."[34] Although photographs of the Genizah entryway would become available soon after the sisters' visit, the first properly executed range of photos of the Genizah's interior would not be taken for another 113 years; the photographer would be my fifteen-year-old son Jacob, who accompanied me on my trip to Cairo in February 2010 (see p. 220).

In the thrum of activity at the Ben Ezra Synagogue—as friends, workers, and hangers-on continually streamed in and out of the building—a certain volume of Genizah material seeped out of Schechter's control and into Cairo's black market. Some of it may have left earlier, of course, for even before Schechter's arrival local salesmen had learned that Genizah manuscripts could fetch a good price. But Schechter's visit raised local awareness even further. The old papers were valuable, and several clever entrepreneurs figured out how to get hold of some of them and resell them to the growing, manuscript-hungry herd of Western collectors coming to Cairo.

At one point, "a certain dealer in antiquities who shall be nameless" approached Schechter himself with some Genizah texts for sale, and Schechter became furious. The synagogue caretakers had told him that the Genizah fragments were his for the taking, and now he was being forced to pay for them. To Schechter, it was nothing short of extortion. "My complaints to the authorities of

the Jewish community brought this plundering to a speedy end,"
he later recounted, "but not before I had parted with certain
guineas by way of payment to this worthy for a number of selected
fragments, which were mine by right and on which he put exorbi-
tant prices."[35] Under his breath, Schechter may also have muttered
a "sort of charm" at the huckster. "Damn!"

Mrs. Lewis and Mrs. Gibson were able to help, too. Using
their own funds and their longtime contacts in Cairo's antiquities
market, they were able to reclaim many of the "pilfered" manuscripts so that the texts could rejoin the Genizah collection.[36]
Agnes later recalled how she and Maggie processed the fragments:

> We bought a leather portmanteau to pack them into, and
> as there is no particular satisfaction in importing dirt, I sat
> down to the work of cleaning them in the bedroom of our
> hotel. This I did with great eagerness, for every scrap that I
> detached from its neighbours might possibly have been
> concealing another leaf of the [original document that
> spurred Rabbi Schechter to investigate the Genizah], but in
> this I was disappointed. They were so wet that I had to
> spread them out on trunks and tables in the sunlight to dry,
> removing a quantity of sticky treacle-like stuff with bits of
> paper which I afterwards destroyed.[37]

Seeking to build upon his success, Schechter visited other genizahs
and several small synagogues in the city. He also went to the local
Jewish cemetery in the Bassatin neighborhood, where Cairo's
Jewish leaders had told him he might find more scraps. Most com-
munities empty out their genizahs every few years and bury the
contents in their local cemetery. For some reason, however, the
Jews of Cairo never did this, so Schechter found only a few frag-
ments in the cemetery, and none of them excited him very much.
"The people here understand so little," Schechter wrote to
Mathilde. "They believe that where there is any rubbish the mad
English will be interested."[38]

While Agnes Lewis was busy drying her documents and removing their molasses-like goop, Schechter was packing his for shipment. By late January 1897, he had amassed over a dozen sacks of manuscripts and carefully packed them into eight large "tea chests" for shipment back to Cambridge.[39] As he began preparing for his departure, Schechter became increasingly concerned about the fate of these precious quarries. He had promised to visit his brother in Palestine after finishing his work in Cairo, so he wouldn't be able to personally accompany his finds back home.

Schechter was concerned, of course, about how the documents would fare during shipment, but even more about what could happen to them after they arrived. He had not yet publicized his discovery, but before he left there had been so much buzz about his work among the scholars in Cambridge that he feared somebody might tamper with or even steal them before his return.

Schechter felt a keen sense of ownership over these manuscripts. Although he had taken this trip under the aegis of the university, the expedition was privately financed, primarily by Dr. Taylor. Cambridge University had no official claim on the Genizah documents. Schechter and Taylor did.

Schechter wrote to his wife and to Francis Jenkinson, the Cambridge University librarian, demanding that the crates he sent be kept sealed until he could open them himself. "I want the MSS to be considered as my private property," he said, "so that the boxes must not be opened before I have returned. For I am very anxious to be the first to examine them properly."[40]

In Cairo, Schechter had estimated that he was sending back an astonishing 100,000 manuscripts. The real number was closer to 190,000.[41]

Count d'Hulst's Excavations

Having made the transfer arrangements, Schechter left his treasures in the care of Reginald Henriques, a British Jewish businessman he had befriended in Cairo, and went to visit his brother. As he departed for Palestine, Schechter was unaware that Neubauer, Sayce, and Count d'Hulst were still conniving to get some Genizah manuscripts of their own. Unlike Schechter, Count d'Hulst had been in Cairo during the 1889–92 rebuild of the Ben Ezra Synagogue. He had seen the Genizah documents shortly after they had all been removed from the Genizah and brought to the synagogue courtyard, and he had done some excavations in the area himself. He knew that although many of the manuscripts had since been redeposited into the Genizah, others had been moved to the cemetery and other burial places near the synagogue. Schechter had removed many of the Genizah documents, but not all of them. And Count d'Hulst had a very good idea where the remaining ones might be found.

Neubauer, who had originally planned to travel to Cairo himself, had decided not to make the arduous trip. Instead, he published the Bodleian Ben Sirah finds in partnership with Cowley and then met with Sayce and d'Hulst in Oxford. There, the three men hatched a plan for d'Hulst to excavate the area around the synagogue and other local rubbish heaps in search of more Genizah manuscripts.

The excavations began in late 1897 or early 1898. In April, Henriques wrote to Schechter in Palestine:

> I am having an exciting time about your Geniza. And but for my intervention everything now left would have been carried off to the Bodleian.... I was out there last Saturday, and I found a gentleman who introduced himself as "Comte de Hulst" with some twenty Arabs digging outside the enclosed space of the Synagogue.... He claimed to have a permit from the Public Works Department and to be working for the Bodleian.... He seems an interesting sort of man. I saw Cattaui and got his permit limited to the area outside the precinct where there is probably nothing of value.[42]

There was, d'Hulst discovered, an amazing amount of material still moldering on the synagogue grounds. In April, he reported:

> I have already recovered more than two big grain sacks full & an unusual large quantity of these papers are manuscripts; there is also a larger amount of parchment amongst them.... A large part of the courtyard of the synagogue has been covered about one meter high with the same papers.[43]

Evidently, the printed documents weren't the only ones that Schechter chose to ignore. From d'Hulst's report we learn that, at the time of his visit, there were still massive heaps of manuscripts outside the synagogue from the 1889–92 renovation, some of which had come from the Genizah. The community had buried some of the material, but much of it remained out in the open. Because Schechter needed to limit his search, he chose to ignore everything outside and focus only on what the synagogue caretakers had returned to the Genizah chamber itself.

In recounting his experience at the Genizah, Schechter never mentioned the treasures that he may have left behind on the synagogue grounds. Perhaps he worried that such information would attract manuscript seekers; perhaps he hoped to return to examine those documents himself someday. There is even some indication that the primary reason Schechter had solicited the help of Reginald Henriques was to have Henriques sift through the Genizah material in the piles outside the synagogue and send whatever valuable material he found to Schechter at Cambridge.[44]

Schechter's friend Israel Abrahams visited the Ben Ezra Synagogue just over a year later and wrote home to his wife, saying, "There is *a great deal* left. I should not wonder that there is as much again as Schechter took.... It is a real sell Schechter pretending that he had brought away everything."[45]

D'Hulst's excavations lasted for fifty-five days, and in May 1898, he wrote that he was sending the Bodleian sixteen large sacks of documents in four large wooden boxes. By then, Neubauer was in failing health, and the Oxford's funding of d'Hulst's work had dried up.

The Bodleian received d'Hulst's shipment, sent him a note of thanks, and then proceeded to dispense with the vast majority of the documents. They retained only about two hundred folios and sold the rest, presumably to Elkan Nathan Adler.[46]

Count Riamo d'Hulst would no longer play a role of any consequence in the Genizah story. Like Solomon Wertheimer, he would eventually lament the fact that the role he did play had receded into the shadows. In 1914, some of d'Hulst's friends began pressing Oxford University to provide the now financially strapped count some monetary support for his earlier Genizah work, and the following year a committee looking into the matter agreed that d'Hulst deserved a "handsome vote of thanks," recommending that he be paid twenty-five pounds for his past services, even though he had agreed to work for free at the time.

In 1921, d'Hulst's wife wrote several letters to the British High Command in Egypt, explaining that her husband was interned during World War I as an enemy alien—or perhaps as a spy—and had died in destitution of malaria shortly after his release.[47] Though Oxford University never adequately recognized d'Hulst's contributions, in 1923 seventy-seven-year-old Archibald Sayce sent d'Hulst's widow a letter acknowledging that "it was in fact, to the Count's knowledge of the language and manners of Egypt that the discovery of the MSS was originally due."[48]

Return to Cambridge

In late spring 1897, Solomon Schechter returned from the Middle East to Cambridge and began to unpack his priceless finds. He later wrote:

> Looking over this enormous mass of fragments, I cannot overcome a sad feeling stealing over me, that I shall hardly be worthy to see all the results which the Genizah will add

to our knowledge of Jews and Judaism. The work is not for one man and not for one generation. It will occupy many a specialist, and much longer than a lifetime. However, to use an old adage, "It is not thy duty to complete the work, but neither art thou free to desist from it."[49]

Schechter was correct, of course. The task of unpacking the texts of the Cairo Genizah—of cataloguing them, studying them, and recording the stories they told—remains unfinished even today. But however daunting it was, Schechter refused to desist from the work. Instead, immediately after his return, he drafted several other scholars to assist him and, with their help, began sorting through his finds, page by page, scrap by scrap, faded letter by faded letter. And with each new passage they read or manuscript they studied, Schechter and his colleagues opened wider the window on forgotten lives and lost civilizations.

6

Unpacking the Boxes

"I shall begin the examination work after the [Passover holiday. It] will take many weeks."

SCHECHTER TO JUDGE MAYER SULZBERGER, APRIL 16, 1897[1]

One day shortly after his return to Cambridge, Solomon Schechter walked to the University Library to look at the manuscripts he had sent from Cairo. In the Genizah, he had given the pile only a cursory look. Darkness, dust, and the chaotic hubbub of the Ben Ezra Synagogue made it impossible for him to give the documents the close, careful examination that characterized his other scholarly work. Now, however, amid the ivory towers of this bastion of British academia, Schechter would have the time and the quiet he needed to give these treasures the attention they deserved.

Walking into the library that day, Schechter surely felt some trepidation. Did all of the boxes arrive? Did a high-handed customs official hold some of them back? Did the documents stay dry and safe on the ship? Did any curious nosey-bodies manage to sneak in and get a look at them before Schechter himself returned? He had done all he could to ensure the documents' safe delivery before he left Cairo, but he couldn't be sure that his arrangements had worked.

They did. Waiting for him in the library, Schechter found the eight massive wooden crates he had shipped from Cairo awaiting his arrival just as he had hoped. No red tape had hampered their shipment; nobody had tampered with them; everything he had sent looked present and accounted for.

Schechter got right to work. Prying off the lid of the first crate, he peered into the box. It looked like the inside of a dustbin. There were thousands of tiny scraps inside—some lay flat, others were crumpled and wadded; most were torn and deteriorating. Lining the bottom of the box was a layer of ancient confetti—the crumbled remains of the lives and literature of generations long past. Schechter looked up. Stacked neatly along the walls were seven other boxes just like this one. This was going to be a tremendous amount of work, and he was eager to get started.

A Scholarly Dream Team

After a quick glance at a few documents, Schechter wrote to some of the world's most prominent scholars of Judaica, inviting them to participate in what would surely be a once-in-a lifetime opportunity. Together, he and the others would "unpack" these boxes of Genizah treasures and share their riches with the world.

To work on the palimpsests and the postbiblical Hebrew documents, Schechter turned to his Cambridge friend and benefactor Dr. Charles Taylor, already known for his translations of Ecclesiastes and the Ethics of the Fathers (*Pirke Avot*). For Greek texts, it was Frances Burkitt, also of Cambridge and a former Mount Sinai traveling companion of Mrs. Lewis and Mrs. Gibson. Arabic texts in the Genizah would go to Hartwig Hirschfeld, a Prussian-born scholar who, at forty-three, had already established a name for himself as an expert in Judeo-Arabic literature. Herbert Leonard Pass would handle the biblical manuscripts. Pass, born Jewish, had converted to Christianity while a student at Cambridge and was ordained an Anglican priest in 1916. The Syriac material in the Genizah, of course, would go to Mrs. Lewis and Mrs. Gibson. Others would help, too—Elkan Nathan Adler and Schechter's friend Israel Abrahams among them.

Together, they comprised Solomon Schechter's Genizah dream team, an elite cadre of Judaic scholars poised to take on an unprecedented challenge of enormous promise.

One of Schechter's greatest supporters in his Genizah work at Cambridge was the university librarian, Francis Jenkinson. It was Jenkinson who had interceded with Professor Charles Taylor and arranged for Taylor's financial support of Schechter's trip to Egypt. Jenkinson had helped Schechter get letters of introduction for entrée into Cairo's academic circles, and he even arranged for Schechter to do some of his dictation at home rather than at the library, where he could feed his cigarette addiction while he did his work.

Now Jenkinson assigned Schechter a room in the library where he could conduct his research. It was a long, narrow space on the second floor, with high, arched windows along both of the long walls, providing good lighting throughout the day. The expansive space would allow Schechter and his assistants ample room to conduct their research, and in pre-electrified and often cloudy Cambridge, the light streaming in from both sides of the room was particularly helpful.

Searching for Ben Sirah

Schechter's first priority for his own research was Ben Sirah, and there was no time to waste. Other scholars, spurred by Schechter's discovery at Castlebrae, were eagerly pursuing additional Ben Sirah material, and for Schechter to maintain his position as the world's leading Ben Sirah expert, he needed to publish—quickly.

When Schechter originally announced his Ben Sirah find the previous May, he was circumspect about the origin of his source. He did say that the Ben Sirah page belonged to Mrs. Lewis and Mrs. Gibson and that they had obtained it on a recent trip to the Middle East. But he omitted any mention of Cairo or the Genizah. Yes, Schechter did suspect that the fragments may have come from the Genizah he had been hearing about, for many of the Lewis-Gibson manuscripts bore markings indicating they had come from Fustat.

But he couldn't be absolutely certain. For all he knew, the Genizah might have held great riches, but he needed to check it out for himself, as it could have proved to be empty, unremarkable, or a dud for some other reason. To have

Solomon Schechter with Genizah manuscripts, Cambridge University Library, summer 1897

made any major proclamations before his visit would have been imprudent and potentially embarrassing. Furthermore, if the Genizah *was* the gold mine he suspected it might be, then he definitely wanted to wait until he could go to Cairo before going public. Why share a treasure map before going to collect the riches for yourself? Even his broader write-up of the other Hebrew manuscripts in the Lewis-Gibson collection said only that the ladies had acquired them "on their travels during the last three or four years."[2]

The newly discovered ancient Hebrew version of Ben Sirah would be published in stages, almost like a serial novel. Watching it emerge in this piecemeal way, Schechter wanted to do all he could to get his byline on as many installments as possible.

The first installment, of course, had been Schechter's excited announcement in 1896 that he had found a single leaf of the book in the Lewis-Gibson collection. Scholars and librarians throughout Europe began sniffing around their own collections for similar treasures. In January 1897, while Schechter was in Cairo, Oxford's Cowley and Neubauer published the second installment in the Ben Sirah series—a paper announcing that they had found nine pages of the same Ben Sirah manuscript in the Bodleian's collection. In the preface, they acknowledged Schechter's identification of one of the Lewis-Gibson leaves as having come from the original Hebrew of the ancient book. They thanked Mrs. Lewis for the courtesy of allowing them to inspect the document themselves and mentioned that they had some quibbles with a few details of Schechter's reading of the text. They also threw in a subtle attempt to claim credit for the Ben Sirah discovery:

> Almost simultaneously the Bodleian Library acquired, through [noted Egyptologist] Professor [Archibald] Sayce, a box of Hebrew and Arabic fragments, among which we recognized another portion of the same text of Sirach, consisting of nine leaves, and forming the continuation of Mrs. Lewis' leaf.[3]

Their chronology, while technically correct, was misleading. Cowley and Neubauer had indeed discovered their Ben Sirah leaves "almost simultaneously" with the time that Schechter identified his—in the same way that a second-place horse crosses the finish line "almost simultaneously" behind the winner. As we have seen, it was only because of Schechter's find that Cowley and Neubauer thought to search the Bodleian for more pages of Ben Sirah.[4]

Racing to establish his priority as the discoverer of Ben Sirah, Schechter dove into his boxes of manuscripts, feverishly searching for whatever material from the ancient book he could find. Scholars and students who knew him at the time remember him working frantically and for long hours in his Genizah room at the library, even damaging his health in an attempt to find more leaves of Ben Sirah. Ordinarily pleasant and gregarious, Schechter became grumpy and ill-tempered during these days, often bickering with Jenkinson over minor mishaps. Jenkinson wrote that Schechter "nearly went out of his head" during those early months of Genizah research.[5]

His search filled his every daylight hour that spring and summer, revealing new treasures with each page he examined. There were Syriac manuscripts to send to Mrs. Lewis and Mrs. Gibson, biblical texts to send to Dr. Pass, and palimpsests for Taylor to see. Many of the manuscripts were in Arabic; Schechter, unable to read them, set those documents aside for later.

But what about Ben Sirah? Even with the Oxford finds, the manuscript was far from complete. Could it really be that only a small section of that Ben Sirah manuscript made its way to the Genizah? Could the missing pages have been destroyed in the crush of the Genizah pile? Might they have become the dust he inhaled while sifting through the documents in Cairo? Or the confetti lining the bottom of the boxes in Cambridge?

And then, one afternoon in midsummer—when the days are long and the Genizah hours plentiful—Schechter noticed one particular crumbling piece of paper in the piles of Genizah documents around him. The page was square, similar in size to the Ben Sirah leaf he had seen at Castlebrae—about 7½ inches on each side. Like the Lewis-Gibson manuscript, it was written in two vertical columns. The handwriting was similar to the other document, and it looked to be about the same age. Examining it more closely, Schechter realized that the page matched the Ben Sirah manuscript he had seen at Castlebrae. It was another leaf of the very same book!

It was only one page, of course. Perhaps there were more.

Sure enough, soon another page of Ben Sirah surfaced; then, another. At the end of August, Schechter wrote to an American friend, "My first glorious Genizah day was last Friday [August 27], when I discovered in one afternoon a piece of Greek, a Syriac palimpsest, and the most important portion of Sirach, *hodu ladonai* [thanks be to God]."[6]

Soon, in what must have seemed exasperatingly similar to what he encountered in Egypt, visitors began showing up at the door of Schechter's Genizah garret—only a few at first, but as word of what was going on up there got out, the trickle of curious seekers swelled into a mighty stream. It was gratifying for Schechter to be at the center of such attention, of course, but the unexamined piles of manuscripts still screamed for attention, and all of these visitors were very distracting.

There were other frustrations, as well. The documents strained his eyes, and he sometimes had to take breaks to bathe them in lotion. During the short, gloomy days of the British winter, his

Genizah work was especially challenging. "It is a very dark day," he wrote to a friend in January 1898. "Two miles I walked from my house to the Library and was unable to read a single fragment on account of the fog. It was never as bad as this minute."[7]

Still, Schechter pushed ahead, and each day he continued to discover exciting treasures in the Genizah boxes—palimpsests, early Syriac literature, autograph documents of Maimonides, and other Rabbinic literature. "The contents of the Genizah," he noted soon after his return from Cairo, "turn out to be of much greater importance than I could have ever dared to hope for."[8]

But despite the excitement of these discoveries, Schechter still couldn't rest on his laurels. For one thing, he still had Margoliouth to deal with. Back in 1890, when the discussion was still a theoretical exchange regarding a "lost" book of ancient literature, Margoliouth had pooh-poohed the significance of the original Hebrew of Ben Sirah. Now, despite the announcements of the newly discovered Hebrew Ben Sirah pages, Margoliouth was not going to be easily put off. In 1899, he published an article entitled "The Origin of the 'Original Hebrew' of Ecclesiasticus." The snide quotation marks around "Original Hebrew" in his title say it all. Schechter's discovery, he argued, represents not the original version of the Ben Sirah text but a later retranslation of an earlier Greek version of the text. The original version, Margoliouth argued, was in Greek; the Hebrew only came later. He suggested a scenario by which sometime after the year 1000, an Arabic-speaking Jew hears of this lost book of the Bible and sets out to translate it into Hebrew from the Greek, Syriac, and Persian versions of the text then available to him. Sadly, Margoliouth suggested, the translator doesn't do a great job. When the manuscript is finished, it

> falls into the hand of a pedant, who knows Hebrew better than the master did, but knows nothing else. And he scores a few poor and worthless emendations on the margin ... and has fair copies made, and sells some, but not

many; *for the Jews like to get good value for their coin* [emphasis added].

This is the only account that I can excogitate of this extraordinary book. And having read it over many times, I regard it as the true one.[9]

Schechter, still searching through his manuscripts, hadn't yet published his own findings about Ben Sirah.

To the scholarly world, the third installment in the Ben Sirah series came from a cousin of D. S. Margoliouth. On April 4, 1899, George Margoliouth announced in the *Times of London* that he had discovered two more leaves of Ben Sirah in the British Museum's manuscript collection.[10] Soon afterward, George distanced himself from his cousin with regard to whether the book was first written in Hebrew. "The textual evidence in favour of the Hebrew being the original," he argued, "must be regarded as very strong."[11]

Finally, by late 1899, it was time to publish. Scholars had identified a total of twenty-three leaves of Ben Sirah by that time, eleven of which Schechter had discovered himself. To produce *The Wisdom of Ben Sirah*, Schechter collaborated with Charles Taylor. Schechter transcribed the text, provided notes, lengthy commentary, and an introduction; Taylor translated the manuscripts into English, compiled the footnotes, and wrote an appendix. The book includes Schechter's rejoinder to Margoliouth's argument that Ben Sirah was originally written in Greek, then translated into Persian, and later into Hebrew. Schechter argued, "The argument of M[argoliouth] in this case is too artificial to be convincing; but with its steps reversed it would be simple and natural, and it would go to prove that the Greek came from the Hebrew through the Persian."[12]

Schechter supported this assertion with a detailed and systematic destruction of Margoliouth's argument, citing Greek, Syriac, and Hebrew sources to show that the book was originally written in Hebrew, and not translated into the language from an earlier version.

Along the way, Schechter throws in some salty jabs. Margoliouth "was not a good enough scholar to know" how to translate a certain Syriac term. Margoliouth tried to "explain away" obvious inconsistencies in his interpretation of the book. His commentary includes statements that are "questionable or incomplete."[13]

Ben Sirah pages continued to appear. In 1901, Cambridge and Oxford jointly released a facsimile edition of all known Ben Sirah manuscripts in Hebrew. By that time, sixty pages had been found, comprising four separate editions of the ancient book. The pages, which had sat for centuries gathering dust in the Genizah, were now scattered about in no fewer than six libraries throughout Europe: the Taylor-Schechter collection at Cambridge, the British Museum, the private library of Mrs. Lewis and Mrs. Gibson, Oxford's Bodleian Library, the library of the Consistoire Israelite in Paris, and the private library of Rabbi Moses Gaster, leader of the British Sephardic community.

During the following decades, scholars identified several more Ben Sirah pages. In 1949, Joseph Marcus of The Jewish Theological Seminary in New York identified a manuscript in the JTS Genizah collection as containing forty-six verses of yet a fifth manuscript. In 1957, Israeli scholar Jefim Schirmann found a folio of one of the earlier manuscripts, and two more in 1959. In 2008, scholars announced that a manuscript owned by a collector named Gifford Combs of Los Angeles had also been identified as having come from the Book of Ben Sirah.[14]

Until his death in 1940, D. S. Margoliouth remained unconvinced of the antiquity of the Hebrew Ben Sirah, believing instead that it was a medieval translation of earlier Greek and Persian versions of the text. The argument was finally put to rest in 1964, when Yigal Yadin discovered Hebrew Ben Sirah manuscripts among the first-century Dead Sea Scrolls in his excavations at Qumran. Schechter and Margoliouth were long gone by then. Neither would live to see the definitive resolution of their disagreement. Of the long, epic drama of the original Hebrew of Ben Sirah, this was the final episode. For now.

Palestinian Haggadot: A Reminder of Ritual Renewed

Solomon Schechter was far from the only scholar interested in Genizah texts during the late 1890s. In fact, during the months following Schechter's return from Cairo, a wide variety of Genizah-related articles suddenly began appearing in the *Jewish Quarterly Review* and other academic journals. Schechter's massive haul from Cairo, and the renewed interest in looking at Genizah documents that it inspired, had transformed the landscape of Jewish scholarship. If the "lost book" of Ben Sirah turned out not to have been a lost book after all, then who knew what other precious finds were waiting to be discovered in Schechter's garret and in the Genizah collections of other European libraries? Pre-Genizah scholars, breathing the air of nineteenth-century optimism and self-satisfaction, had a sense that as a group they were doing a pretty good job of keeping up in their studies of the manuscripts then available to them. Now, suddenly, reams of unexamined texts demanded their attention. Now, suddenly, they had a lot of catching up to do.

Most of the early Genizah research focused on its literary documents—Talmudic texts, biblical passages, poetry, and other documents created to be read over and over again. This was the material that Schechter's "dream team" studied. Scholars knew that there was other material in the Genizah, as well—letters, business records, court documents—but these they put aside. To them, an ancient Rabbinic text or an early variant of a biblical passage was far more interesting than, say, a deed on some property or a children's schoolbook.

Israel Abrahams, Schechter's longtime friend from London who would later succeed him at Cambridge, published some of the first texts.[15] "Among the many interesting MSS which Mr. S. Schechter has obtained from the Cairo Geniza," his article in the *Jewish Quarterly Review* began, "are some curious fragments of the Passover Hagada."[16] Abrahams, perhaps while helping Schechter sort through the manuscripts, had come across several passages from the Passover Haggadah (plural, Haggadot), the prayer book that Jews have used for centuries during their Passover Seder meals. The Haggadah is a guidebook, filled with biblical and Rabbinic passages to guide Seder participants in recalling and reliving the journey of their ancestors from slavery in Egypt to redemption in the Promised Land.

Abrahams's fragments were the tattered remains of thirteen different Genizah Haggadot. Some were written on paper, others on parchment. Most measured three to six inches on each side, and they ranged in length between two and sixteen pages. Some of the Haggadot could be read quite clearly; others were mutilated and faded and could only be read with difficulty.

Abrahams examined them closely. He had no doubt that they were Passover Haggadot, yet there was something odd about them. Some of the verbiage didn't look quite right. All ancient manuscripts—even those of the same texts—vary slightly from one another, usually due to scribal error. A biblical verse will contain a misspelled word; a scribe will mistakenly omit a short phrase; a rabbi will be quoted in one manuscript in a slightly different way than he is in another. But the Haggadot that Abrahams examined deviated enormously from the standard versions of the text. Some were far shorter than the Haggadot Abrahams knew; others carried different instructions as to how to conduct the Seder ritual. One of the most beloved parts of the ritual for many families is a passage called "The Four Questions," customarily read by the youngest child at the Seder who can read them. Some of Abrahams's texts had only three questions. Another traditional passage reads, "In every generation, each Jew must feel as if he himself went out of Egypt." In one of Abrahams's Haggadot, that line read similarly, but with a significant change in tense: "In every generation, each Jew must feel as if he himself is going out of Egypt," contemporizing the ritual in a way that the other versions did not. One of Abrahams's versions tried to provide a standard quotation from the Bible, "And [the Egyptians] set taskmasters over [the Israelites] to afflict them with their burdens" (Exodus 1:11). However, this particular version of the Haggadah mistakenly replaced the final Hebrew word in the verse, *b'sivlotam*, with the similar-sounding *b'simlotam*, thus rendering the passage, "And the Egyptians set taskmasters over the Israelites to afflict them with their dresses."

Abrahams was right to take note of these unusual Haggadot. Thanks in part to his work, later scholars would realize that several of them were unusual because they were Palestinian Haggadot, not Babylonian. For the most part, by the twelfth century, the Babylonian, or Iraqi, take on Jewish culture and religion had come to predominate. Palestinian forms played a more minor role, and Karaism almost none. During the Middle Ages, however, it was far from clear that the Babylonians would win in the end. Each had its own synagogues, and the Ben Ezra, as we've learned, belonged to the Palestinians.

It shouldn't surprise us, then, that the Genizah held many liturgical documents representing Palestinian religious practice as opposed to the Babylonian rite reflected in Jewish prayer books of today. However, until the Genizah was discovered, modern Jews didn't even know the extent to which there ever was a distinct Palestinian rite to begin with. Certain Palestinian customs had seeped into the Babylonian and survived, but their distinctive Palestinian characteristics had long ago melted away into the Babylonian custom. It was only due to documents such as the Abrahams's Haggadot that scholars and students of the Jewish past were able to reclaim knowledge otherwise lost of Palestinian forms of Jewish religious practice.

The documents taught other important lessons, as well. Customs such as those that constitute the Passover Seder are so old that it sometimes seems as if they've been around forever. As Jews renew the ancient rituals of the Passover Haggadah each year—as they sing its songs, read its words, and eat its foods— many find it particularly meaningful to know that they are echoing the music, words, and menus of countless generations of Jews who preceded them. In many ways, they are. However, the liturgical texts of the Cairo Genizah remind us that these words and practices are often far more dynamic than we realize. Jews once read *three* questions rather than four? The foods of the Seder once differed from the ones we eat today? Haggadot contained typos?

We are mistaken in thinking that Jewish liturgy has been around for millennia in precisely its current form. The documents of the Cairo Genizah remind us that ancient words never stagnate. Often imperceptibly, sometimes violently, ancient Jewish rituals move and shift and create new realities in each generation. They are the liturgical tectonic plates of the Jewish world.

Palimpsests: What Lies Beneath

Among the most enticing manuscripts of the Genizah were its palimpsests. Palimpsests, so named from the Greek term for "re-scraped," usually appeared at times when writing supplies were scarce. Paper and parchment were often hard to come by during the Middle Ages, so it was common for scribes to take a used piece of parchment or paper, scrape it clean, and write their own text on its surface.

But even after the scribe completed his work, the document continued to change. Often, over the course of time, as the manuscript aged, the remnants of the old ink would interact with the ambient air in such a way as to cause a chemical reaction that re-darkened it. Slowly, invisible and long destroyed old words would reappear on the pages where they were originally written.

The resulting document would have two layers of text. The newer layer is often quite legible; behind it, in faint yet readable letters, floats an older text that refuses to disappear. Like the Genizah itself, palimpsests testify to the power of the written word to convey meaning for centuries, long after its first owner discards it.

The Genizah held dozens of palimpsests, and Schechter set them aside during his first scan of the texts. The upper, newer, of these manuscripts were usually Hebrew Rabbinic texts, such as Talmud or Midrash. The texts that hovered beneath the Hebrew, however, were usually Christian passages in Greek or Syriac, often from the New Testament.

Surely, the scribes who penned the older texts would have been horrified to know that their holy books would one day fade into the shadowy background behind later Jewish literature. The

Old Testament, or Hebrew Bible, was supposed to have given way to the New Testament, not hover behind it.

And just as surely, the scribes of the newer texts would have found it unsettling to know that the older texts they erased would one day reappear to mess up their creations on what they thought had been blank sheets of parchment or paper.

Schechter sorted the palimpsests according to the languages of their under-texts. He sent the Hebrew-Greek ones to Charles Taylor, and the Hebrew-Syriac ones to his old friends Mrs. Lewis and Mrs. Gibson. In 1900, both books were published.

The Lewis-Gibson volume, *Palestinian Syriac Texts from Palimpsest Fragments in the Taylor-Schechter Collection*, focused on thirty-four individual Genizah manuscripts, thirty of which they had received from Schechter, and four of which came from their private collection, purchased when they went to see Schechter in Cairo in early 1897. In her introduction to the book, Mrs. Lewis describes the Genizah and the enormous, densely packed heap of crumbling documents she and Mrs. Gibson saw there. "Over the centuries … they have squeezed and hurt each other, whilst all the time some of them were keeping for us very precious secrets." She described the arduous work it took to separate the individual pages of the manuscript clumps:

> I found each little bundle of heterogeneous leaves glued together…. Sometimes a handful which I supposed to consist of three leaves would be found to conceal a dozen, each differing in character from its neighbours, and amongst the dust which covered them I discovered not a few very tiny insects. Thus the numerous holes with which our palimpsest leaves are studded have certainly been produced by long adhesion to a slowly mouldering mass of parchment and paper.[17]

She added that in a few instances, and only with the permission of the Cambridge University librarian, the sisters had applied an ammonia-based chemical reagent to help render the texts more legible. Describing the way she and Margaret had studied two of their own Genizah palimpsests, Agnes wrote:

> Fragments I and II of our collection would have been perfectly illegible without it; the under script in these was mistaken by me for a faint brown streak of dirt; and it was thus left to Dr Schechter, who knew the appearance of the Hebrew script in the fragments of his own collection, to recognize that this streak was really an ancient text.[18]

But despite the watery decay and nibbling insects, and despite the difficulty of reading them, the palimpsests in the Lewis-Gibson collection were quite legible. They featured Talmud, Midrash, or some liturgical Hebrew poetry on top, and various Jewish and Christian scriptural passages in Syriac floating faintly beneath.

Moreover, the finds were historically significant. "We feel justified in saying," wrote Agnes, "that no earlier specimen of the language is

A Genizah palimpsest, showing an eleventh-century page of Talmud over a seventh-century translation of Psalm 102

known than these texts of Jeremiah, Joel, Hosea, Corinthians, Thessalonians, Timothy and Titus. We are certain, also, that these are not parts of a Lectionary, but are the remains of an early Syriac version, translated from the Septuagint."[19]

In other words, the faded Syriac that lingered beneath the Hebrew on the palimpsests represented some of the earliest known biblical manuscripts in the world.

> We can hardly venture to hope that these somewhat scrappy texts will do much to dissipate the cloud of mystery which enshrouds the early history of the Palestinian Syriac dialect, but we shall be disappointed if they do not lead competent scholars, ... after due examination of the fragments themselves, to assign a possibly earlier date than they have hitherto done to the Palestinian Syriac version of the Scriptures.[20]

Taylor's work was snappily entitled *Hebrew-Greek Cairo Genizah Palimpsests from the Taylor-Schechter Collection, Including a Fragment of the Twenty-Second Psalm According to Origen's Hexapla, Edited for the Syndics of the University Press.*[21] It was a write-up of three separate documents. One was a curious version of Jewish scripture called the Hexapla—a six-column translation of the Jewish Bible into a variety of ancient languages and scripts.

Another palimpsest had a fifth-century copy of Aquila's translation of portions of Psalms 100–102 behind an eleventh-century edition of a part of Tractate *Ta'anit* from the Babylonian Talmud. A third consisted of five small scraps of the Gospels of Matthew and John behind various early Rabbinic texts.

In his work on these palimpsests, Taylor's emphasis is decidedly on the Greek under-texts rather than on the Hebrew overtexts. He publishes photographic plates of the documents oriented so that the Greek is right side up, which often involved flipping the Hebrew under-text 90 or 180 degrees. Although he does acknowledge in the preface that "the upper writing of the fragments is not without interest,"[22] this Christian Hebraist approached his texts as a pious Christian, eager to discover early versions of Christian scripture in them … and the Hebrew was interesting, too.

The Damascus Document

Genizah studies during these years included work on many other kinds of texts, as well. Between 1897 and 1907, hundreds of books and articles were published describing various documents in the newly discovered Genizah collections at Cambridge and elsewhere. Hartwig Hirschfeld published a series of fourteen articles in the *Jewish Quarterly Review* about Arabic documents from the Genizah, describing, among other treasures, some early copies of the renowned Babylonian thinker Rabbi Saadya Gaon, as well as a number of original leaves of Maimonides's work, handwritten by the sage himself. Cowley and Neubauer published several Genizah texts from the collection at Oxford's Bodleian Library. There were even some articles about legal documents from the Genizah that appeared in an American magazine called *The Green Bag: An Entertaining Magazine for Lawyers.*[23]

In early 1900, Solomon Schechter came across two apparently related and overlapping texts,[24] one far more complete than the other. The more complete document—which in his write-up he called Text A—consisted of sixteen pages of text, some of which were quite mutilated. Looking at the style of its handwriting and other factors, Schechter estimated that it dated back to the tenth century. Text B was just a single leaf with writing on both sides. It was a pretty close copy of a chunk of Text A, and this one, Schechter suggested, came from the eleventh or twelfth century. Though Text A was far more complete than Text B, both constituted different versions of the same document.

This curious text, it turns out, was part of a prominent collection of manuscripts whose fame would one day far exceed that of the Genizah. But in turn-of-the-century Cambridge, Solomon Schechter was unaware of this larger collection, because the document before him was the only one that had come to light. The remainder of the collection wouldn't be discovered for almost half a century.

The document was difficult to study. For starters, whoever penned Text A—the older of the two versions—did a lousy job. "We have here to deal," Schechter explained, "with a very careless scribe, who not only may have had a very poor copy before him, but also disfigured his text in several places by his inability to read his MS. correctly."[25] The scribe misspelled words, misquoted the Bible, wrote of "an assembly of treacherous men in a later generation" when he really meant to refer to those men in a "former generation." And that was just on the first page!

Text B, which was evidently based on Text A, wasn't much better, and its scribe added some mistakes of his own.

The section of the text that survived its stay in the Genizah jumped within a span of eight pages from a discussion of laws concerning vows, to material about the organization of the group for whom it was written, to a few lines about the laws of the Levites working in the ancient Temple, to material about the Sabbath, back to Levitical law, back again to Sabbath law, to material about how the group was to relate to non-Jews, to dietary laws, back yet again to the Levites, to laws about the organization of the group, and so on.

The document was in Hebrew—Biblical Hebrew in some places, Rabbinic Hebrew in others. Rarely were its biblical citations accurate, and sometimes they were so far off as to be almost unrecognizable.

Looking at the document as a whole, Schechter concluded that it contained the history and laws of a long extinct Jewish sect. It told of the group's charismatic leader, "the Teacher of Righteousness," also referred to as "the Only One," "the Only Teacher," "the Lawgiver Who Interprets the Law." The text intimated that at some future day, the Teacher would die and then reappear with a brand-new name—Messiah.

Other Jewish texts suggest that the Messiah will descend from King David. This one didn't have much use for David, describing instead the Messiah as a descendant of Zadok, the first High Priest of the ancient Temple, who lived during the tenth century BCE. Under the leadership of the Teacher, the text taught, the group broke away from the Jewish people and moved to Damascus, where the Teacher eventually died. His death was only temporary, of course, for the Teacher would one day rise again during the time of redemption.

Even after the death of the Teacher, the sect lived on. Those whose views drifted from the group's norms were expelled, and eventually the group developed an elaborate and formal set of rules for itself. The community consisted of four different estates (priests, Levites, Israelites, and converts); a ten-member governing council; a High Priest; and a censor, who served as a judge, tax collector, and membership director.

Who were these people? Clearly, they were Jews, Schechter said. They adhered strictly to the Torah and other parts of the Jewish Bible. But unlike most Jews of the second century BCE, they also embraced the teachings of many additional books that weren't in the Jewish Bible. Their literature discussed the teachings of several biblical-era books, some of which are of unknown origin. Even the most infamous breakaway sect from Judaism, the Samaritans, weren't so eclectic and inclusive in their canonical tastes. The group lived by an unusual festival calendar, unknown in other Jewish circles, and seemed to have a special "thing" against the Pharisees, the group that eventually became the Rabbis. The Pharisees, this sect argued, twist the teachings of the Torah, they support divorce and polygamy just as King David did, and perhaps worst of all, some of them are friendly with the Greeks!

The text would come to be known as the Damascus Document, and Jewish history knew of no sect identical to the one it described. However, Schechter noted, one ancient Jewish author did make passing reference to a group that might just fit the bill. In his *The Book of Lights and High Beacons,* Jacob Kirkisani, a tenth-century Karaite sage, described the High Priest Zadok as one of his heroes. "Zadok was the first who exposed the Rabbanites and contradicted them publicly." Kirkisani described the followers of Zadok—Zadokites—

in ways similar to the sect Schechter was studying in his mysterious document. The Zadokites prohibited divorce, had a weird calendar, and couldn't stand the Rabbis. To Schechter, these perspectives indicated just who the producers of the Damascus Document really were. They were Zadokites. They weren't the priestly Sadducees, who are also known as Zadokites in Hebrew, but rather a different anti-Rabbinic group

The Damascus Document

known by the same name. Later, Schechter argued, this group somehow merged with a Samaritan sect known as Dositheans, remnants of which are found today in the Falasha Jews of Ethiopia. How they connected with *that* group, Schechter admitted, remained a mystery.

Subsequent scholarship would show that Schechter was absolutely correct to identify this group as an unusual and noteworthy breakaway sect. On many of the other details, however, he didn't do quite as well.

In 1947—fifty years after Solomon Schechter's visit to Cairo, and 275 miles to the northeast—a sixteen-year-old Bedouin shepherd named Muhammad Adh-Dhib was tending his flock near the northern tip of the Dead Sea. At one point, he noticed that one of his goats had strayed into a cave high on a cliff overlooking the brackish Dead Sea water below. Muhammad tossed a stone into the cave to roust out the goat and was startled to hear the sound of breaking pottery when it landed. Muhammad climbed up to the cave to investigate, and there he found several earthenware jars—some intact, others broken. Inside the unbroken jars and scattered among the shards of the broken ones were four strips of old parchment texts. Really old.

Young Muhammad Adh-Dhib had discovered the Dead Sea Scrolls—the literary remnants of an ascetic sect known as the Essenes, who had moved to their remote desert outpost, Qumran, during the second century BCE.

Archaeologists unearthed a total of about nine hundred scrolls in and around the caves of Qumran. As scholars studied them, they came across a group of fragments that looked familiar. The Damascus Document! Not only did it show up on a total of ten fragments discovered in two separate caves, but one of the original four scrolls that Muhammad Adh-Dhib discovered was also closely related to it. The curious manuscripts of the Damascus Document that Schechter found in the Genizah turn out to have been early copies of these Essene texts. The Damascus mentioned wasn't the literal Damascus in Syria, it was a metaphorical "Damascus"—the Boonies, Sticksville. In this case, Jericho.

Later scholars found accounts from around the year 800 of Karaites, drawn to Essenes and their writings because of their opposition to the Rabbis, who traveled to Jericho and copied some of their texts. The Karaite network was strong, and soon those documents made their way to Cairo.[26]

Sitting in his Cambridge Genizah garret, then, Solomon Schechter became the first modern scholar to study one of the Dead Sea Scrolls. Of course, he didn't realize it at the time, for the Dead Sea Scrolls wouldn't be discovered for another fifty years.

Ownership of the Texts

As Schechter and others dove into their Genizah research, an administrative question remained unanswered: who owned the texts at Cambridge?[27] Technically, Schechter and Taylor did. Schechter was the one who had traveled to Cairo to get them, Taylor was the one who had funded his trip, and Schechter had made it perfectly clear in his correspondence from Cairo that, while he eventually planned to donate them to the university, he saw the texts as belonging to himself and his benefactor. And yet, it was clear to everyone that ownership of the collection would soon need to pass to the university. An archive of this size and value far exceeded the curatorial abilities of any individual or small group. Only a major library could give it the necessary care; only an institution experienced in housing such manuscripts could adequately catalogue and preserve them. Furthermore, the treasures of the Cairo Genizah rightly belonged to the Jewish people, or even to humanity at large. For Schechter and Taylor to have held onto them as their own private collection would have been unseemly and boorish; it would have flouted the enlightened values of nineteenth-century scholarship.

However, Schechter and Taylor weren't about to fork over their Genizah manuscripts without a few stipulations. They worried that the Arabic-focused Orientalists at Cambridge might not give these Jewish documents their due. They also felt that Schechter deserved some sort of compensation for the collection, but they wanted to avoid coming across as crass and greedy. Taylor and Schechter both wanted to ensure their own continued access to the collection even though they were transferring ownership of it to the university.

Finally, Schechter wanted to limit other scholars' access to certain parts of the collection. He had no problem with the university letting scholars use most of the texts. But he did want the library to hold some of the manuscripts, such as the Ben Sirah texts, as his own private stash—the university would own them, but Schechter wanted to be the only one permitted to use them. Taylor disagreed with Schechter on this point and advocated open access for the entire collection.

In the end, Schechter and Taylor reached a negotiated agreement with the library. Ownership of the Genizah texts would be transferred to Cambridge University; they would be kept as a separate collection, to be called something along the lines of "The Taylor-Schechter Collection from the Genizah of Old Cairo"; the university would officially thank the Jewish community of Cairo; nobody would be allowed to use the collection for three years without the donors' consent; Schechter could borrow whatever he wanted; the university would sort, catalogue, and preserve the collection "by binding, mounting or otherwise," within ten years; and Schechter and Taylor would keep the Greek fragments and the Ecclesiasticus fragments "until they have brought out complete editions of them." Additionally, Schechter would be appointed curator in Oriental literature at the University Library, allowing him to earn some extra cash without making the whole deal feel like a commercial transaction. Schechter and Taylor assured the university in writing that they planned to publish the Greek and Ecclesiasticus material within two or three years. The university estimated that cataloguing and preserving the documents would cost approximately five hundred pounds, and set aside that amount accordingly. Their estimate was, to say the least, a bit low.

These treasures of the Cairo Genizah, entombed for so many centuries in a small attic in Egypt, were now ensconced in the safe, clean confines of one of the world's great libraries. No longer would they crumble into dust; no longer would they fight with one another for space; no longer would they molder unseen in the darkness. Now, they would be preserved and shared with all who sought to see them. Now, they would see the light of day once again. Since his trip to Cairo, Solomon Schechter had brought the Cairo Genizah and its treasures to widespread scholarly attention. But by the time he left Cambridge in 1902, only a small number of the manuscripts had been identified and catalogued. Hundreds of thousands lay piled in boxes, waiting to be examined. Earlier, Schechter had lamented that the work would take "many a specialist, and much longer than a lifetime" to complete. He was correct, of course, but what he left out was that it was his erudition, insight, and passion that had first sparked this magnificent burst of learning in the first place.

7

More Treasures Come to Light

The Genizah after Schechter, 1902–50

Shortly after Solomon Schechter returned to Cambridge from Cairo in the spring of 1897, he wrote to his friend Judge Mayer Sulzberger, a Philadelphia philanthropist and bibliophile. Sulzberger was one of Schechter's confidants, and Schechter had written to the judge during his trip to Cairo with information about his discoveries. In this letter, however, Schechter focused not on medieval manuscripts, but instead on his career:

> I was approached from New York with the question whether I should care to come to New York to take charge of the chancellorship of The Jewish Theological Seminary.... I have not answered [the person who invited me] yet; but ... I hardly need tell you that America has certain attractions for me.[1]

The Jewish Theological Seminary Association had been founded in 1886 as an institution to train rabbis to serve America's growing Conservative movement. However, when Schechter was first invited to take its helm over a decade later, it was still struggling. Plus, Schechter had just gotten back from Cairo and was only beginning to sink his teeth into his Genizah work. It was not a good time for an overseas move.

Undaunted, his fans in America continued to push for him to come to the Seminary. Finally, in 1901, the directors reorganized the school and renamed it The Jewish Theological Seminary of America (JTS), and Schechter agreed to become its president. Taking about one hundred Genizah documents he was then researching along with him, Schechter moved with his family to New York and officially assumed his position in March 1902.

On November 20 of that year, at the Young Men's Hebrew Association on New York's Upper East Side, Rabbi Schechter rose to deliver his inaugural address. Before him sat a crowd of more than one thousand people—merchants, scholars, bankers, and other notables—celebrating what promised to be the beginning of a new era of Jewish history. These leaders of American Conservative Judaism hoped that their rabbinical training academy as it was now organized would help build a religious movement in this country that was deeply committed to Jewish norms and practices while also embracing the values of modernity. It was to be more deeply committed to Jewish law than Reform, more modern than Orthodoxy, and thus a uniquely American convergence of traditional religion and modern thinking. To lead its charge into the twentieth century, the reorganized Seminary had chosen as its first president Rabbi Solomon Schechter, a rising star from Cambridge University who had recently achieved notoriety as the discoverer of the Cairo Genizah.

Early in his address, Schechter cited his Genizah work as an example of the value of modern Jewish scholarship:

> This passionate devotion to the study of ancient MSS., which you may possibly have observed in some students, has not its source in mere antiquarianism or love of curios…. Every discovery of an ancient document giving evidence of a bygone world is, if undertaken in the right spirit—that is, for the honor of God and the truth and not for the glory of self—

an act of resurrection in miniature. How the past suddenly rushes in upon you with all its joys and woes! And there is a spark of a human soul like yours come to light again after a disappearance of centuries, crying for sympathy and mercy.... You dare not neglect the appeal and slay this soul again. Unless you choose to become another Cain you must be the keeper of your brother and give him a fair hearing. You pray with him if he happens to be a liturgist; you grieve with him if the impress left by him in your mind is that of suffering; you fight for him if his voice is that of ardent partisanship, and you even doubt with him if the garb in which he makes his appearance is that of an honest skeptic. "Souls can only be kissed through the medium of sympathy."[2]

Invoking Abraham Lincoln on the one hand, and Maimonides along with other great Jewish sages on the other, Schechter called for the Seminary to foster an expression of American Judaism that was both truly American and truly Jewish. After he finished, there was an outburst of applause, and hundreds of audience members swarmed the stage to shake Schechter's hand.[3] A new chapter had begun in the life of Rabbi Solomon Schechter. And with it also began a new century of modern Jewish scholarship.

Schechter's Vision

Schechter's new duties at the Seminary severely limited his ability to engage in Genizah research. He was able to publish several volumes and articles about Genizah documents, but as soon as he took up his new duties in New York, it became clear that the days of leisurely, uninterrupted manuscript study in his Genizah garret that he had enjoyed in Cambridge would be no more.

As his administrative duties grew, Solomon Schechter realized that the few documents he and his dream team had published amounted to only a tiny fraction of the total number of Genizah fragments available. Schechter and his team were getting on in years, and despite all of their hard labor, they had barely made a dent in the pile of unexamined material sitting in the "Genizah in-box."

Indeed, by the early twentieth century, it had become evident that the scholars' method of selecting the documents to publish—if, that is, one could really call their decision-making process a "method"—was inadequate to the task. Overwhelmed and excited by their newfound riches, Schechter and his colleagues had tacitly adapted a "browse and grab" manner of selecting the material they would study. "Oh, look," a scholar would say while perusing the texts, "an interesting biblical manuscript. I think I'll publish it." "Oh my," one of his colleagues would interject, "a very old fragment of Talmud. That's what I'm going to work on." Margaret Gibson and Agnes Lewis would come up with some Syriac, Taylor with a palimpsest, Schechter himself with another page of Ben Sirah, and off they all would go, each excitedly pursuing his or her own piece of the great Genizah project.

Clearly, their haphazard way of researching the documents would need to change. Schechter envisioned a systematic effort to produce one massive, comprehensive edition of the documents of the Cairo Genizah—a wall (or more) of books that would organize all available Genizah material into a single, usable library. When he first found the Genizah, of course, the documents were a chaotic "battlefield of books"—a literary junk heap utterly inaccessible to anyone interested in systematic study. The Genizah, in the words of scholar S. D. Goitein, was "the very opposite of an archive."[4] Now, for the most part, the manuscripts were safely stored on library shelves, but the vast majority of them had yet to be closely examined, not to mention transcribed, catalogued, organized, and studied. What's more, the Genizah documents, crammed together for centuries in a single small room, were now scattered across many countries. Over half of them were in Cambridge, but more than one hundred thousand manuscripts were housed elsewhere, in libraries throughout Europe and the Middle East.

What Schechter envisioned was a well-published Genizah mega-library—one that would organize the documents by chronology, geography, language, and so on, rendering them usable for modern scholars as never before. It would form, Schechter imagined, "the Greatest Historical Work on Jewish lore—published in the century."[5] To accomplish such a thing would take another generation of scholars, and perhaps another generation after that, teams of dedicated experts into the future, poring over the endless parchments, papers, and fragments.

It would take years, Schechter knew. But how, one wonders, would he have responded had he learned that it would actually take more than a century?

Jacob Mann, a "Colossal Scholar"

Jacob Mann was not a popular professor. He was a short, pudgy man, and when he sat in his professor's chair in the front of his classroom at the Hebrew Union College in Cincinnati, his feet barely reached the floor. He spoke English with a heavy Eastern European accent, tinged with long, snooty, British vowels, reminding his students with each word of their teacher's Galician upbringing and his twelve years of study in London. He was an exacting scholar, focused always on the particulars of the material at hand, describing in detail the texts before him and their connections with other material. He would enter each class promptly at the assigned time, sit down in his chair, take out his notes, and read them verbatim to the class. Word for guttural word. The young men who sat before him were preparing to become rabbis, and in many of their classes they were eager and attentive. But here, as their professor's monotone, European-accented lectures droned on, many of them wrote letters or did work for other classes. Rarely did he take questions; he studiously refrained from grandiose generalizations; he never threw in personal perspectives or cute anecdotes about the material he taught.

And yet, Jacob Mann was, as one of his former students later acknowledged, a "colossal scholar."[6] Born in Przemysl, Galicia, in 1888 and educated at Jews' College in London, Mann was a professor at Cincinnati's Hebrew Union College from 1921 until his untimely death in 1940. As a child, Mann received an Orthodox religious education, but as a young adult, just like Schechter before him, he drifted steadily westward from the shtetl of his childhood, moving intellectually and physically away from his Eastern European yeshiva training into the world of *Wissenschaft des Judentums*—the scientific study of Judaism. Ordained a rabbi in 1914, Mann immediately began publishing scholarly historical papers, most of which examined ancient and medieval manuscripts as sources of Jewish history.

Unlike previous generations of Jewish historians, Mann had a magnificent and largely unstudied trove of source material available to him—the documents of the Cairo Genizah. During his years in London, he had easy access to the collections of Genizah documents at the British Library, the Bodleian Library, and Cambridge. Additionally, Elkan Nathan Adler generously gave Mann access to his massive collection of Genizah manuscripts. As a young scholar eager to make his mark, it was only natural that Mann should devote his energies to studying these treasures. He was, after all, at the forefront of the second generation of Genizah scholars. In his generation were the men—at that time it *was* mostly men—who would take the helm of Genizah research from the aging Schechters, Abrahams, and the Giblews. Schechter's dream of a comprehensive Genizah mega-library would only come true if Mann and the other men of his generation could make it come true.

And so, in 1915, Jacob Mann began his Genizah work. Tirelessly, he worked his way through as many manuscripts as he could. As a historian, he was particularly drawn to the letters in the Genizah collection; reading them, Mann found invaluable information about medieval Jewish life. As a rabbi, he took special interest in the rabbinic correspondence and found reams of letters penned by some of the great sages of medieval Jewry. As a product of the shtetl, Mann's Arabic wasn't very strong, and he therefore laid aside the many Genizah documents in that language and focused on the Hebrew material.

Slowly, the bare outlines of a picture of medieval Jewry began to emerge and grow clearer. It was a picture of a Jewish society that had lay buried in the dust of history for centuries. The picture was far from complete, but the pieces of it that emerged opened the eyes of scholars and students throughout the Western world.

Early on, he looked with special interest at the writings of the Geonim (singular, Gaon), the leaders of the Middle Eastern rabbinic academies from the sixth to eleventh century, particularly those in Babylonia. During this period, Jewish individuals or groups would send questions of Jewish law that they couldn't figure out on their own to the Gaon: "Rabbi, a Jew in our community has converted to Islam, and now he's trying to get the Jewish courts to protect him in an inheritance claim. How should we respond?" "Rabbi, a member of our local Jewish community is accused of assaulting a non-Jew, and the non-Jewish courts have asked that we hand him over for trial. What would Jewish law have us do in this situation?" "Rabbi, is it permissible to display a bust of the king in our synagogue?"

It was to the responsa of the Geonim that Jacob Mann devoted his early scholarly efforts in Genizah research. Mann studied every Geonic responsum he could find. These responsa tended to be to questions asked by Jews who lived far away from Babylonia. After all, the Geonim frequently visited nearby communities in person, and there they could often get away with verbal responses rather than written ones. But questions from faraway places such as Persia, Yemen, Italy, or Egypt demanded written answers. Often the Geonim, their students, and the people who made the inquiries shared the correspondence with others, and often the mail went to—or through—Cairo. Consequently, the Cairo Genizah held many Geonic responsa that nobody had seen for centuries.

Nobody, that is, until Jacob Mann.

This work, like most Genizah research, was difficult. The manuscripts were old and tattered. Many of the original collectors of these responsa cared primarily about the legal bottom line and often omitted dates, addresses, and even the name of the Gaon who penned the response.

But Mann was able to overcome these obstacles and decipher much of what the crumbling papers said, and he realized that these old responsa contained a wealth of information. They painted a vivid picture, for example of Babylonian Jewry, the largest Jewish community in the world at the time. Many Babylonian Jews—also called Iraqi Jews—were the descendants of exiles brought there in captivity after Babylonia destroyed the First Temple in 586 BCE. Others had moved there more recently from Persia, Egypt, and elsewhere. The responsa portrayed a Jewish community that, while suffering persecution during the late Middle Ages, also thrived during much of its history, enjoying close relationships with its non-Jewish neighbors. The study of these precious Genizah documents deepened our understanding of Babylonian trials, taxes, terrors, and much, much more.

The responsa also provided information about other communities, as well. They shed light, for example, on medieval Palestinian Jewry—the persecutions it suffered at the hands of local Arabs, the activities of its rabbinic academies. There was also, of course, a great deal of information in the responsa about the Jews of Egypt, especially since in the early days of Fustat, its members often turned to the sages of Babylonia for rabbinic guidance. In fact, Jewish communities throughout North Africa appeared often in the Genizah responsa literature. There were responsa addressed to Jews in Fez, Kairowan, and other communities throughout the Maghreb. Those places were home to many great sages of their own, and the fact that there was such an active correspondence with Babylonia over Jewish legal issues was further proof of the preeminent status of the Babylonian academies. European Jewish communities—those in places such as France, Spain, and elsewhere—also benefited from these responsa. In fact, the Jews of Babylonia sent copies of the entire Talmud, as well as their newly standardized prayer books, to several of these communities. And when a community in, say, Greece wanted to know if it was allowed to feed its silkworms on the Sabbath, its members wrote to the Babylonian authorities, and a copy of the correspondence ended up in the Genizah.

Between 1917 and 1921, Jacob Mann published a series of articles in the *Jewish Quarterly Review* entitled "The Responsa of Babylonian Geonim as a Source of Jewish History," in which he shared some of this rich body of material.

Mann's Genizah work, however, was far from limited to Geonic responsa. He was also engaged in a far more comprehensive project, the chief aim of which was "to produce a skeleton of the contemporary history of the Egyptian and the Palestinian Jewries."[7] He studied hundreds of manuscripts and, in 1920, published the first volume of *The Jews in Egypt and in Palestine under the Fatimid Caliphs: A Contribution to Their Political and Communal History Based Chiefly on Genizah Material Hitherto Unpublished.* A second volume followed in 1922.

It is a massive work. Drawing on the manuscripts he studied, Mann traces the developments of the Jewish communities of Egypt and Palestine from 969 to 1204 CE, describing their politics, religion, the daily lives of its members, and much more. He goes into detail about the Jewish scholarship of the time, providing, for example, a seven-page account of a debate over how a particular Hebrew vowel was to be pronounced. Two dots, one over the other, placed beneath a Hebrew letter, is called a *sh'va.* Sometimes it is silent; sometimes it is pronounced as a little grunt, like the apostrophe in the Australian "G'day." Mann describes in great detail the debates as to which words call for which pronunciation of the vowel.

From the outset, Mann was aware that his work would draw a very small readership. In the introduction to the first volume of *The Jews in Egypt and Palestine,* he thanks his publisher, acknowledging that "a work of this kind, with no special appeal to the reading public at large, is not eagerly sought after by publishers."[8] And yet, as is common in scholarship, he engaged in this multiyear project anyway, confident that his contribution would somehow prove to be of lasting value despite the small reading audience it would attract.

I purchased my own copy of *The Jews in Egypt and Palestine under the Fatimid Caliphs* from a used book dealer over the Internet in early 2009. When I opened the package, I noticed that each of its two volumes bore a bookplate indicating that the set had previously been part of the library at a major American university. Carefully opening each of the two volumes, I noticed that they were in factory condition. Like many new books from the 1920s, their pages—originally printed on large sheets and folded into multipage "signatures"—had not been sliced apart and instead remained like pressed sleeves, making it impossible to open many of them for reading. Pasted inside the back cover of each volume were "Due Date" slips, both of which were blank.

It had been eighty-nine years since that book was published and shelved at the university library. And in all of that time, nobody had ever read it.

A Transcontinental Shift

As obscure as Jacob Mann was to popular reading audiences, his growing volume of Genizah research allowed him to achieve great prominence in scholarly circles. In fact, one of his successors, S. D. Goitein, credits Mann with nothing less than "creat[ing] the historical framework for all future study of the documentary Genizah."[9]

The ascent of Jacob Mann's academic star reflected an important transcontinental shift taking place in Genizah studies during the early twentieth century. When the documents of the Cairo Genizah first came to the attention of the Western world, most of the scholarship surrounding them took place in Europe, particularly in England. But then Schechter moved to America. And then World War I happened. And then, during the years leading to World War II, the antisemitism that had been simmering for centuries in many European countries broke out anew with unprecedented violence.

During the late nineteenth and early twentieth centuries, millions of Jews left Europe. Most headed west, toward America; a few headed east to help rebuild their ancestral national home in the Land of Israel. As European Jewry struggled and headed toward unimaginable cataclysm, Jewish communities in America and Palestine grew and flourished.

Genizah studies followed a similar path. As the twentieth century progressed, the number of Genizah scholars who lived in Europe steadily waned, while the number living in the United States and Palestine (later, Israel) increased dramatically.

Jacob Mann was only one member of this new generation of American Genizah scholars. Richard James Horatio Gottheil (1862–1936), an ardently Zionist professor at Columbia University who was also famous for having founded the Zeta Beta Tau (ZBT) fraternity in 1898, published *Fragments from the Cairo Genizah in the Freer Collection* with W. H. Worrell in 1927. Schechter's friend from England, Louis Ginzberg (1873–1953), whom Schechter hired as a faculty member at The Jewish Theological Seminary as soon as he became its president, published extensively on Geonic literature, the Palestinian Talmud, and other Genizah-related topics. Alexander Marx, one of Schechter's other early hires at the Seminary, published several historical and philosophical texts.

Marx was also head librarian at the Seminary, and in that capacity, he presided over what was arguably the greatest acquisition it ever made: the purchase of the lion's share of Elkan Nathan Adler's book and manuscript holdings in the 1920s, including more than thirty thousand manuscripts from the Cairo Genizah, sold by Adler to regain his financial footing after being victimized by a business associate.

Most of the documents Solomon Schechter had sent from Cairo to Cambridge in 1897 stayed in Cambridge when Schechter moved to New York in 1902. But with the JTS acquisition of the Adler collection, the institution Schechter came to America to serve became the owner of the world's second-largest collection of Genizah documents.

No longer, it seems, was it just Schechter who was following the Genizah documents. Now, having moved from Egypt to England to New York, many of the Genizah documents were following him!

The growing Jewish community in Palestine also began studying Genizah texts. Since the late nineteenth century, a small trickle
of immigrants had made its way to Palestine from Europe. Many who
came were young, idealistic dreamers, deeply committed to building
a Jewish nation in their ancient homeland. As fervent Zionists, they
were committed to creating a Jewish state to serve not only as a safe
haven for oppressed Jews, but also as a spiritual, cultural, and intellectual capital of the Jewish people. Such a state, of course, would
need to educate it citizens, and as early as 1884, members of the
fledgling Zionist movement proposed the creation of "a university of
the Jewish people." On April 1, 1925, the dream came true at the fes-
tive opening ceremony of the Hebrew University in Jerusalem.

When it first opened, Hebrew University had only 33 faculty
members and 141 students. But despite its small size it became an
important academic center, with its faculty making important contributions in the sciences, humanities, education, and other fields.
The Jewish history faculty was particularly strong, and it should be
no surprise that one area of focus for the department was in
Genizah studies.

Simha Assaf did significant work publishing Geonic texts and
other Genizah materials. Unlike Jacob Mann, Assaf was an Arabist
and was able to work with the innumerable Arabic texts he found
in the Genizah. Also unlike Mann, Assaf was interested in social
and cultural—as well as religious—history, and his work gave some
of the first glimpses through the window that opened to the day-
to-day lives of the Genizah people.[10] D. H. Baneth (1893–1973)
worked with Assaf, publishing additional Arabic Genizah texts, particularly those by Maimonides, Yehudah Halevi, and other philosophers. Yitzhak Baer, professor of medieval history, made invaluable
contributions, as well.

The Schocken Institute

In 1929, a German department store magnate and book collector
named Salman Schocken opened an institute for the study of Hebrew

poetry in Berlin. Schocken's overarching goal was to uncover the poetic spirit of the Jewish people—a Jewish version of the *Nibelungenlied*, the twelfth-century epic poem of knights and dragon slaying upon which Richard Wagner later based his four-opera series *The Ring of the Nibelung*. More generally, Schocken wanted to assemble and study the entire corpus of medieval Hebrew poetry—all of it. He hired Heinrich Brody, accomplished medievalist and chief rabbi of Prague, to direct the Schocken Institute, as well as several younger scholars—Abraham Meir Habermann, Jefim Schirmann, Menahem Zulay, and others.

Schocken's timing couldn't have been better. By 1930, the scholarly world become well aware of the documents of the Cairo Genizah, and by the end of the decade, a new technology called photocopying would make those manuscripts widely accessible. The Schocken Institute moved to Jerusalem in 1934, and by 1940, it had amassed copies of more than twenty-five thousand Genizah manuscripts. Schocken's scholars published articles about their research, and the institute itself released seven volumes of its studies.

Among the most significant discoveries of the Schocken Institute was the work of a seventh-century Palestinian poet named Yannai. The 1906 *Jewish Encyclopedia* article about Yannai is a four-inch blurb, describing Yannai as "apparently a very prolific poet," whose work survives in only three brief and very fragmentary manuscripts. The work of the Schocken Institute, however, unleashed a Yannai blizzard from the Cairo Genizah. Today, we have more than eight hundred of the poet's works.

The Thrill of Discovery, and Yet ...

The first half of the twentieth century, then, was a time rife with Genizah discoveries of all kinds. And each new discovery—each crumbling responsum, letter, or page of Talmud studied—brought new clarity and focus to the emerging picture of medieval Jewry in the Middle East, a picture showing that its Judaism was far more dynamic than most Jews ever realized. The familiar Jewish practices of today, the documents showed, weren't always just like they are now—and often, they were far different. Today, most Jewish communities read a portion of the Torah every week and get through the entire scroll over the course of a year. During Genizah days, many communities took three years to get through the scroll. Today, most Jewish communities read pretty much the same versions of prayers, printed in their prayer books. During Genizah days, many prayers differed wildly from community to community, and sometimes even from individual to individual. Today, only a small handful of *piyyutim*—medieval religious poems—are included in the Jewish worship services. Back in the days of the Genizah, there were many more.

In fact, back in Genizah days, there were two major forms of Jewish worship and practice—one dictated by the sages in the Land of Israel (or Palestine), the other by the sages in Babylonia. As a result of these differences, each camp wrote its own Talmud, which described the Judaism it felt was most fitting and proper. To speak, as many people do, of "the Talmud," is therefore inappropriate, for there are actually two Talmuds—the Babylonian Talmud and the Palestinian (or Jerusalem) Talmud. The sages concurred on most of the basics, but there were many details on which the two camps vehemently disagreed. For the most part, however, it was the Babylonian rite that held sway and stood the test of time.

Since the Ben Ezra Synagogue served Cairo's Palestinian Jewish community, it naturally practiced the Palestinian rite in its form of worship. The Genizah documents provide a window into a prominent and distinct form of Judaism that faded into obscurity many centuries ago.

What a vivid picture emerged as these documents came into view! The material recovered a nearly lost Jewish culture, thrilling scholars in the field, and yet ... hardly anyone else paid attention. Part of the reason for the relative silence that greeted these Genizah discoveries, even in the Jewish world, was the unique moment in history during which they occurred.[11] Simply put, when the Genizah discoveries were made, none of the major groups of Jews who might have taken interest in them needed or wanted the discoveries very much at all.

One might think, for example, that the liberal-minded Jews of the Reform and Conservative movements would have welcomed the new picture that the Genizah revealed with great enthusiasm. These were the movements whose scholars argued that Judaism was never the static, frozen, unchanging rock that Orthodox Jews said it was. Instead, they asserted, Judaism was always dynamic; from its very inception, Judaism changed and adapted to the ever-new and varying historical circumstances it encountered. The Genizah demonstrated that ongoing change in countless ways. The evidence it contained of so many different kinds of Jewish life and practice and of Judaism responding to various challenges by changing and adapting long-held practices accorded precisely with what these progressive denominations had been arguing for decades. For this reason, Reform and Conservative Jews should have rejoiced when they learned about the Genizah; they should have trumpeted its every revelation as yet more proof of their argument with Jewish Orthodoxy. Right?

Wrong. It's true that a handful of *researchers* operating within the Reform and Conservative movements did, indeed, thrill at these discoveries. Schechter was the first, of course, as well as many of his friends and colleagues at JTS. But the Genizah discoveries had little if any practical impact on the lives and practice of the rank-and-file of the Conservative movement.

Schechter's counterpart in the Reform movement was Rabbi Kaufmann Kohler (1843–1926). Four years Schechter's senior, Kohler became president of Hebrew Union College in February 1903, less than three months after Schechter was inaugurated at JTS. The two men had met in 1901, when Kohler visited Schechter at Cambridge. "It was one of the most delightful [days] I have ever experienced in that place," Schechter would later recall.

> The day was spent roaming over the contents of the Genizah
> and in conversation. Our thoughts turned to Judaism and

the subjects which occupied our minds were all of a theological or historical nature. We probably differed in a good many points, and please God we shall differ in many more—but this did not prevent our short acquaintance from ripening at once in to what might approach friendship.[12]

Despite his interest in matters-Genizah, the rank-and-file members of the movement that Kohler led didn't seem to take much notice of these issues; dusty old documents had little to do with the grand, decorous, and lofty American religion that the Reform Jews of early twentieth-century America were working to advance. For the most part, most scholars and leaders of the Reform movement didn't take much notice of the Genizah, either. They'd already shown that Judaism changes with the times, and they didn't need a heap of medieval Egyptian documents to prove it any further.

Just as Reform and Conservative Jews didn't give much attention to the Genizah, neither did Orthodox Jews. The Judaism that they practiced, after all, was the Judaism of the Babylonian rite. To the Orthodox, the Palestinian Judaism of the Genizah was mostly a relic of the past, and its documents therefore didn't excite them very much at all.

Genizah Prayers Given New Voice

Eventually, as the decades passed, a few Genizah texts quietly made their way into Reform Jewish liturgy. On November 2, 1972, two graduate students at the Hebrew Union College–Jewish Institute of Religion (HUC-JIR) in Cincinnati led a worship service celebrating Balfour Day, the fiftieth anniversary of the famous Balfour Declaration, in which the British government expressed sympathy with Zionist aims. The students, Lawrence Hoffman and Richard Sarason, compiled a service based largely on Genizah documents, reflecting the Palestinian rite of the Ben Ezra Synagogue rather than the Babylonian rite that later prevailed. In the introduction to their mimeographed prayer packet, they noted:

> We hope through this service, to illustrate the vast reservoir
> of creativity in our multi-faceted tradition; to give expression
> to the longings of our forefathers; and finally, to identify
> with our people through time, from the earliest expression
> of their hopes to the present rebirth of the land where
> those hopes were born.[13]

Both Hoffman and Sarason would later become faculty members
at HUC-JIR, not to mention two of the Reform movement's lead-
ing scholars of rabbinics and Jewish liturgy. In 1978, the Central
Conference of American Rabbis (CCAR) published *Gates of Repentance:
The New Union Prayerbook for the Days of Awe*. Hoffman was on the
CCAR Liturgy Committee at the time that this Rosh Hashanah and
Yom Kippur liturgy was compiled, and he managed to persuade
the editors to include a prayer from a Genizah manuscript.
Attesting to the deep roots of the Jewish people in the land where
the Genizah was amassed, the passage begins, "You raised up a vine
out of Egypt, O God, You scattered our foes and planted us."[14] When
the CCAR published its newest prayer book, *Mishkan T'filah*, Hoffman
succeeded in getting yet another Genizah prayer included—an
optional reading before the recitation of the *Sh'ma* that he and
Sarason had included in their Balfour Day service in 1972:

> Praised are You, Adonai our God, Ruler of the Universe,
> who hallows us with *mitzvot*,
> commanding us how to recite the *Sh'ma*:
> to declare wholeheartedly God's rule,
> to declare earnestly God is One,
> and to willingly worship God.[15]

These two passages—one recited annually in many Reform congre-
gations, the other on a weekly basis by only a few—give voice to the
long-silent Palestinian-affiliated community that amassed the
Genizah. To my knowledge, they are the only two prayers solely of
Genizah origin currently recited in Jewish worship.

Schechter's Legacy

Jacob Mann's work on the responsa of the Geonim; the discovery of so many previously unknown Yannai poems; Simha Assaf's Genizah scholarship at the newly opened Hebrew University in Jerusalem; the reappearance in Reform prayer books of some of the Genizah's long-lost liturgical passages—unfortunately, Solomon Schechter did not live to witness these exciting discoveries and scholarly achievements in the growing academic field he initiated. In early 1915, involved in a heated controversy over how best to prepare for the Jewish relief efforts that would be needed after the conclusion of World War I, Schechter underwent an operation from which he never fully recovered. On Friday, November 20, 1915, he was attending to some administrative matters at the Seminary and preparing for a lecture scheduled for later that day when he fell ill and was sent home. Reading a book later that afternoon, Rabbi Schechter suffered a seizure and died.

Today, Solomon Schechter is widely remembered in the United States as a founding father of American Conservative Judaism. But even more than his great accomplishments as a denominational leader, it was his discovery of the Cairo Genizah and the rebirth that this discovery gave to a forgotten Jewish world that may rank as his greatest legacy. His erudition, keen eye, and passion for learning helped bring from darkness into light a trove of precious Jewish papers, parchments, and texts ignored for centuries and nearly lost, making possible countless acts of "resurrection in miniature" for generations of scholars to come. Through the medium of his sympathy and shining intelligence, Solomon Schechter had kissed many souls indeed.

8

Professor Genizah

Shelomo Dov Goitein and the Mediterranean Society He Uncovered

One morning in early January 1954, an attendant hoisted a large wooden crate onto a table in the manuscripts reading room at the Cambridge University Library. *Thunk!* "Here are the manuscripts you requested, Professor."

Brushing the dust off his hands and clothing, the attendant heard a chair slide back from the other side of the table. Then, slowly, from behind the box, rose a five-foot-four bespectacled Jewish monolith, with a bald head, horn-rimmed glasses, and the smiling face of Dr. Shelomo Dov Goitein. "Thank you," he nodded. "Thank you very much."

"Is there anything else I can help you with, sir?"

"No, not right now. Thank you," said Goitein in his formal, German-accented English. Goitein was already removing the lid of the box and craning his neck to see inside.

As eager as Goitein was to see the manuscripts, he was also very tired. He had just arrived from New York. The previous week, at The Jewish Theological Seminary, Goitein had delivered an address at the annual meeting of the American Academy of Jewish Research. Before an audience of several dozen leading scholars of Judaic studies, he renewed Schechter's call for a complete collection of, if not

all of the manuscripts of the Cairo
Genizah, at least the Arabic material.
His lecture, entitled "What Would
Jewish and General History Benefit
by a Systematic Publication of the
Documentary Geniza Papers?" argued
that a volume such as this would
be invaluable to the study of the
medieval world, both Jewish and
non-Jewish.

Dr. Shelomo Dov Goitein

To illustrate his point, Goitein
told the audience that he had collected more than 130 Genizah documents related to trade between
India and the Mediterranean. Much
of this trade flowed through Cairo,
so Jewish merchants were heavily involved in it, and their papers
often landed in the Genizah. In the course of his research, Goitein
had found lists of trade goods that flowed to and from India, business contracts, correspondence between merchants and shipown-
ers, and much more. Several of Maimonides's rulings detailed how
these financial arrangements should work, and the other Genizah
documents showed how medieval Jews applied those rulings to the
real-life commerce in which they engaged. The Genizah, in short,
was a rich and exceedingly vast source of primary information about
the economics, technology, and politics of the medieval world.
However, as an Islamic historian had recently pointed out to him,
"so far not a single Muslim Arab document relating to that trade
has been found." The Jewish documents in the Genizah, therefore,
provided the only available view into this largely unexplored
medieval world. "It is my considered opinion," Goitein concluded,
"that only after the whole documentary Geniza is—not published,
this constitutes a separate problem—but transcribed, translated and
properly commented on, shall we know what it contains and shall
we have fulfilled our duty to Jewish and general historiography."[1]

One member of the audience that day was Professor Saul Lieberman, dean of the JTS rabbinical school. As Goitein spoke, Lieberman took special note of his comments about Maimonides. He remembered that Moses Maimonides had a younger brother, David Maimonides, a successful businessman, who made his fortune largely from the India trade. David's life was cut tragically short when, at the age of thirty-three, he was lost at sea on a business trip to India.

During the Q&A following Goitein's talk, Lieberman raised his hand. "Professor Goitein," he said, "it would be a fine thing—would it not?—if the Genizah could produce a letter from David Maimonides to his brother, Moses. Have you come across any such correspondence?"

Goitein had surely thought about the Maimonides brothers while researching the India documents, and he could imagine what such correspondence would look like. Moses and David Maimonides were very close. In fact, although Moses Maimonides wrote extensively to and about his brother David, he hardly ever mentioned his wife—we don't even know her name. It was his relationship with his brother that Moses Maimonides treasured most of all, and David's death cast him into a deep depression, from which it took him years to recover.

But Goitein was an exacting scholar. Sure, it would be wonderful to find letters between Moses and David Maimonides, but so far none had turned up.

"I could write a story about David Maimonides," he replied, "but I would not dare invent a letter."[2]

That was just the previous week in New York. Now Goitein was at Cambridge and eager to proceed with his research for what he referred to as his "India Book." He remembered that the Cambridge Genizah collection included more than one thousand manuscripts acquired from dealers just prior to and immediately after Schechter's 1897 trip to Cairo.[3] Nobody had ever catalogued these documents, much less given them even a cursory sort-through. For almost sixty years, they had sat in boxes at Cambridge, waiting for someone to read their words.

A letter from 'Aydhab, 1169 CE

It was almost as if they had been put into a second Genizah, though this one was far tidier and had much better lighting than the first.

Goitein reached into the box, carefully removed a document, and laid it onto the reading table. Most Genizah manuscripts were damaged in some way, but this one was in particularly bad shape. There were large holes on the top and bottom, and an even larger one eaten out of the middle. It was written on paper, relatively small—six by nine inches or so— and it was in Judeo-Arabic. It looked to be a letter of some sort. Goitein gave the page a quick scan, and one of the tattered words caught his attention.

"'Aydhab."

'Aydhab, a long-abandoned city in what is now a disputed area near the Egyptian-Sudanese border, was a major seaport for ships carrying goods between India and the Mediterranean during the Middle Ages. David Maimonides and countless other businessmen who traveled between Egypt and India back then passed through the sandy seaside oasis on their journeys. If this was a letter from 'Aydhab, it might hold some valuable information. Goitein put it aside, continued to look through the box, and selected several other manuscripts to study further.

After his initial scan, Goitein turned his attention back to the first letter he had removed. As he read it, Goitein's pulse quickened. There were smaller holes in the paper, adding to the difficulty in deciphering it that the larger ones presented, and the text was written in the terse, abbreviated style of medieval Jewish writers. Still, he was able to piece together much of its content:

To my beloved brother Rabbi Moses, son of Rabbi Maimon, may the memory of the righteous be blessed.

David, your brother who is longing for you—may God unite me with you under the most happy circumstances in His grace.[4]

Could it be? If this letter was actually one that David Maimonides wrote to his brother Moses from 'Aydhab, then it would represent a major contribution to the known biography of a man who was arguably the greatest Jewish thinker in history. "From Moses [of the Bible] to Moses [Maimonides]," an old Jewish adage said, "there was never another like Moses." Goitein read further:

I am writing this letter from 'Aydhab. I am well, but my mind is very much troubled, so that I walk around the bazaar and do not know—by our religion—where I am, nor how come that I did not imagine how much you must worry about me.[5]

The more he read, the more Goitein became convinced that this letter was what he had suspected from the beginning. After all, how many Moses ben Maimons with merchant-brothers named David could Cairo have had?

Goitein read further. In the letter, David told his brother of his adventures on the way to 'Aydhab. Shortly after the previous Passover, David had reached Qus, a city along the Nile that served as the launching point for caravans heading toward 'Aydhab. Knowing the potential hazards of desert travel, David booked passage on a Qus-to-'Aydhab caravan and began heading east. Early in the trip, however, David broke away from the caravan because ... because ... *ahhh!*—that hole in the letter! The words "Luxor" and "the desert" appeared twice, but the reason for David's departure from the caravan had crumbled into Genizah dust.

Then the text resumed:

So we traveled alone out of fear of him. No one has ever dared to embark on such disastrous undertaking. I did it only because of my complete ignorance. But God saved us after many frightful encounters, to describe which would lead me too far afield. We arrived in 'Aydhab safely with our entire baggage. We were unloading our things at the city gate, when the caravans arrived. Their passengers had been robbed and wounded and some had died of thirst.... We were saved only because we had taken upon ourselves those frightful experiences.[6]

Evidently, David had become afraid of something or someone on his caravan and had broken away with one or more of his traveling companions to make the journey on their own. The ensuing trip was arduous, but he arrived in 'Aydhab safely, only to find that many travelers in the original caravan weren't so lucky.

David had traveled to 'Aydhab to shop in its bustling markets and purchase goods from India. However, upon his arrival, he discovered that no such imports were available. "I found nothing to buy but indigo," David said. Rather than return home empty-handed, David decided to sail from 'Aydhab to India to purchase his goods directly. And after all he had just endured, David probably reasoned, how difficult could a sea journey of a few days really be?

David acknowledged, however, that he had heard of other travelers in the area who had encountered trouble when their boats foundered. But, he assured his brother, "do not worry. He who saved me from the desert with its ..." another small hole "... will save me at sea."

Another large hole in the letter—this one obscured five lines. Around its periphery Goitein could make out the words "desert" and "sea," each written twice. David continued:

And please, calm the heart of the little one [his wife] and her sister [Moses Maimonides's own wife]; do not frighten them and let them not despair, for 'crying out to God for what has passed is a vain prayer' [*Mishnah Berakhot* 9:3].[7]

After a couple more obscured lines, the text became legible once again:

I am doing all this out of my continuous efforts for your [plural] material well-being, although you [singular] have never imposed on me anything of the kind. So be steadfast; God will replace your losses and bring me back to you. Anyhow, what has passed is past, and I am sure that this letter will reach you at a time when I, God willing, have already made [it] most of the way. [Bracketed inserts from Goitein's translation.][8]

Shortly after writing this letter, David Maimonides boarded his boat for India. Although we have no record of the fate of this particular ship, the Genizah carries accounts of several boats going down around that time along the same route.[9]

Moses Maimonides never heard from or saw his brother again. It is likely that David's ship sank in the Red Sea on its way to India.

Eight years later, Moses was still grieving his brother's loss. In a letter he wrote during the late 1170s, he described the death of his brother as the worst misfortune that had ever befallen him:

On the day I received that terrible news I fell ill and remained in bed for about a year, suffering from a sore boil, fever, and depression, and was almost given up. About eight years have since passed, but I am still mourning and unable to accept consolation. And how should I console myself? He grew up on my knees, he was my brother, he was my student; he traded on the markets, and earned, and I could sit safely at home.... Whenever I see his handwriting or one of his letters, my heart turns upside down and my grief awakens again. In short, 'I shall go down to the nether world to my son in mourning' (Genesis 37:35).[10]

Goitein realized that the letter he had drawn out of the crate—the first one he examined among the hundreds of others around it—was not only a letter from David Maimonides to Moses Maimonides, but probably the *very last* such letter that David ever sent. Evidently, Maimonides or one of his descendants put it into the Genizah with his other papers, and it remained there until the late 1890s when a dealer sold it to Cambridge University as part of a larger batch of manuscripts. How often must the great sage have returned to it during the years of his grief. How deeply must it have wrenched his soul every time he reread its words. How steadfastly must he have treasured the letter during the years he held on to it before it made its way up into the Genizah.

And those holes in the paper? Perhaps they were the results of the ravages of time. Or maybe they are what happens when a man's tears fall upon his most treasured keepsake of all—the final words of his beloved younger brother.

Born into Two Worlds

Shelomo Dov Goitein was born on April 4, 1900, in the small, northern Bavarian town of Burgkunstadt, nestled about 140 miles from the nearest big cities—Munich to the south, Frankfurt to the west, and Prague to the east. Burgkunstadt was, in many ways, far to the west of Focsani, the shtetl of Solomon Schechter's childhood. Located in the heart of central Europe, Burgkunstadt was at the confluence of the two great forces of modern Jewish culture: the ancient customs and traditions of the East, and the science and Enlightenment of the West.

Like Schechter, Goitein was raised in a religiously observant home. Unlike Schechter, however, he didn't need to leave home to pursue modern, scientific learning. Indeed, even as a child, Goitein received a secular education alongside his religious learning; one part of each day was devoted to the study of Bible and Talmud, and another to science and math.

Goitein lived in both worlds as he grew up. On the one hand, he was born into a family deeply steeped in Jewish learning. Goitein's great-great-grandfather was Baruch Benedict Goitein (1779–1842), author of *Kesef Nivchar*, a well-known topically organized compendium of Talmudic law. In his later years, Goitein would often remove his copy of that volume from his shelf and, referring to himself in the third person, remark, "All of the works of Mr. Goitein are as nothing compared to this volume."[11]

On the other hand, growing up in Burgkunstadt, Goitein's exposure to the local non-Jewish community was far more extensive than that of many other Jewish children elsewhere. Once, the local Catholic church needed more singers for its choir. When the church leaders realized that no singers from their own congregation were available, someone mentioned that young Shelomo Goitein had a beautiful soprano voice, and they pressed him into service as an altar boy. Goitein later commented that the experience not only improved his Latin, but also gave him new insights into the nature of communication between man and God.[12]

Goitein continued along this two-track educational system as a young adult, pursuing a doctorate at the University of Frankfurt while also continuing his intensive Talmudic training with a private tutor. In Frankfurt, Goitein majored in Islam and Arabic, studying extensively under the acclaimed Jewish Orientalist Josef Horvitz and Islamic historian Carl Heinrich Becker. Later, as a graduate student, the young scholar of Talmud and Torah wrote his dissertation about prayer in the Qur'an.

The area of specialization Goitein had chosen was just coming into its own. He received his doctorate in 1923, not as a Genizah scholar, but as a historian of Islam. He was a member of the generation of scholars trained by Moritz Steinschneider, Hartwig Hirschfeld, and the other Jewish pioneers of Arabic studies. One of them, in fact, D. H. Baneth, was Goitein's first cousin. As Western European Jewry embraced the modern spirit of science and discovery, its scholars searched for models of culture and enlightenment in Jewish history. Naturally, they were drawn to Judeo-Arabic culture—its poetry, its science, its glorious art. Additionally, early discoveries in the documents of the Cairo Genizah heightened their awareness that medieval Arabic Jewry was worthy of their time and attention.

Goitein—a young man raised at the meeting point of the worlds of the East and the West—entered Western academia and became a scholar of the Jewish Middle East.

Academic pursuits, however, were far from his only interest during these years. As a young man, Goitein became an ardent Zionist, and after receiving his doctorate in 1923, he decided to move to the Land of Israel. He departed on September 12, 1923, sailing on the same ship as another promising young scholar, Gerhard—later, Gershom—Scholem.

When he first arrived in Palestine, Goitein worked as a high school teacher in Haifa. But in 1928, three years after it opened, he joined the faculty of Hebrew University as a professor of Islamic studies. With the security of his university post, he was able to branch out into other areas, as well. From 1938 to 1948, he served the British Mandatory government as senior education inspector and published books about the teaching of Torah and Hebrew. He even published some literary work, including a 1927 play about a Jewish woman in the royal court of France during the Middle Ages, and several Hebrew poems.

Reclaiming Genizah 'Rejects'

As Goitein came of age as a scholar and an educator, Genizah research advanced. Throughout the first half of the twentieth century—first in Europe, and then increasingly in the United States and Israel—scholars quietly forged ahead, unpacking, deciphering, and explaining a massive, jumbled assortment of Genizah texts. For the most part, the scholars who studied the Genizah weren't Genizah scholars per se, but specialists in some other area of the

Jewish literary tradition, lured to the Genizah by the tantalizing hope that its manuscripts might hold priceless treasures relating to their own area of expertise. Jewish liturgists studied Genizah prayer books; literary historians studied its poetry; experts in Rabbinic literature studied its responsa and Talmudic texts; Bible scholars looked at its biblical manuscripts and Torah scrolls. The Genizah was a shopping mall for all scholars of topics that touched in any way upon medieval Jewry in Arab lands. They came to it in droves, and they were not disappointed.

For all of the variety of the texts they studied, however, this generation of scholars, primarily experts in religious literature and history, tended to focus only on the Genizah's literary manuscripts, not its more workaday historical material. They weren't interested in the love letters of a businessman to his wife from a fabric-buying trip to Morocco, or a physician's medical prescriptions, or the doodles of a schoolchild first learning to use a quill. What interested them were Bibles, prayer books, philosophical tracts—the manuscripts written to be read over and over again. These documents represented early versions of many of the foundational texts of Judaism and the Jewish people; to fritter away their time studying Genizah ephemera, they felt, would have been simply foolish. In fact, one catalogue of Genizah documents written in the late 1930s described a document as a "business letter and therefore valueless."[13]

These early generations of Genizah scholars, in other words, were drawn to manuscripts crafted by scribes. They focused on responsa, not memos; on scripture, not scribbles; on Midrash, not medicine. If—at least in its original, untattered form—a document had neat margins, fine handwriting, and high-quality paper or parchment, it was far more likely to be the object of study than the many other, far less "pretty" scraps and scribbles surrounding it in the pile of unstudied Genizah texts.

By the mid-twentieth century, there were tens of thousands of these "Genizah rejects." They remained in their boxes as they had for decades, unstudied and unread. Then, Shelomo Dov Goitein came along and asked to see them.

The Jewish-Arab Symbiosis

The seeds of Goitein's interest in the Genizah were sown in the 1930s when he did field research on the Jewish community of Yemen. Unlike their fellow Jews in Europe and elsewhere, the Jews of Yemen lived deep in Arabia, largely isolated from modern industrialized society, and living in many ways just as they had for centuries. They provided Goitein with a snapshot of a Jewish community that was similar to Arab Jewish communities of the Middle Ages. Goitein traveled to Yemen often for this research, and when most Yemenite Jews later immigrated to Israel, he continued studying their literature and gathering oral histories from them. He described them as "the most Jewish and the most Arab of all Jews."

Goitein's deep rooting in Arabic language and studies put him in an ideal position to study Yemenite Jewry. "My original purpose in all this was linguistic," he wrote. "I wished to study original Arabic dialects uncontaminated as far as feasible by strong foreign influences. But soon I learned that one cannot learn the language of a people without knowing its life."[14] Eventually, Goitein would come to refer to himself as an "interpretive historical sociographer,"[15] a scholar who interprets documents and other evidence to describe societies of ages past.

Out of this work came Goitein's realization of the profound connectedness of Judaism and Islam. The common understanding of the relationship between these two great religions is that Islam is an offshoot of Judaism, which is to say that it shot off from its parent religion and never looked back. But Goitein pointed out that the relationship is far more complex. Yes, Islam does have Jewish roots, but it was only during the Middle Ages that both religions came into their own, and they did so while holding hands.

Goitein wrote of what he called the "Jewish-Arab symbiosis" and described the deep reliance each religion had upon the other. Judaism developed its defining law and philosophies under Islam, he argued; Hebrew only flourished as it did because it developed alongside Arabic. Similarly, Islam borrowed heavily from Jewish thought and practice as it developed during the Middle Ages, too.

The titles of many of the articles Goitein wrote during the 1940s and 1950s reflect these insights: "The Sanctity of Palestine in Moslem Piety," "The Attitude to Authority in Judaism and Islam," "Who Were Mohammad's Teachers?" "Jerusalem in the Arab Period," "The 'Stern Religion' (An Outline of the Portrayal of Judaism in Early Muslim Literature)." Each of these articles described the symbiosis between Jewish and Arab cultures. In 1955, at the request of Salman Schocken, he also wrote a book aimed at a popular reading audience called *Jews and Arabs: Their Contact Through the Ages*, which he updated in 1964, and again in 1974, to reflect changing realities in the Middle East. In that small volume, Goitein gave a sense of the enormous if unheralded influence that medieval Islam exerted over Judaism, much of which he observed in the countless Genizah fragments he studied:

> Under Arab-Muslim influence, Jewish thought and philosophy, and even Jewish law and religious practice were systematized and finally formulated. Even the Hebrew language developed its grammar and vocabulary on the model of the Arab language. The revival of Hebrew in our own times would be entirely unthinkable without the services rendered to it by Arabic in various ways a thousand years ago. Arabic itself became a Jewish language and, unlike Latin in Europe, was employed by Jews for all secular and religious purposes, with the sole exception being the synagogue service.[16]

Of course, the influence between Judaism and Islam was a reciprocal process. Though Judaism has long been known to have been the mother religion of Islam, Goitein's research demonstrated that during the Middle Ages, Judaism and Islam behaved far more like siblings than like parent and child. The siblings sometimes quarreled, of course, but their disputes were those of two deeply connected peoples whose bonds would last through and despite whatever conflicts might arise between them.

Treasures in the Rubbish

Goitein's involvement in Genizah studies began slowly and rather late in his career. In 1948, just after Israel became a state, its fledgling government sent Goitein on a minor diplomatic mission to Budapest. While there, he examined some manuscripts from the collection of David Kaufmann (1852–1899), an Austrian scholar and bibliophile who, coincidentally, had been born in the Moravian city of Kojetein, from which the Goitein family derived its name. Kaufmann had purchased some Genizah fragments during the 1890s, which he donated to the Hungarian Academy in Budapest after his death. Although Kaufmann's collection was catalogued in 1906, over the years it had become disordered and difficult to use. Goitein studied and edited a small selection of the documents and then began to put them back in order.[17] In 1950, Goitein published seven of the Budapest Genizah fragments in an Israeli journal, and soon after, he published two of its letters about the Crusader conquest of Jerusalem and an article about Jewish trade between the Middle East and India.

Goitein couldn't stop thinking about the Genizah. Here were the papers of a Judeo-Arabic society, most from the tenth to thirteenth century, when the encounter between Judaism and Islam was at its peak. And there were so many! Might they contain material he could use in his work? Certainly they were worth a look.

In 1950, Goitein had spent several months in England, shuttling between Cambridge and Oxford to peruse their Genizah collections, when he was approached by a librarian. "Professor Goitein," the librarian said, "we have some materials in our Genizah collection that we would like to discard, but first we would like to show them to you." The librarian walked Goitein to the stacks and directed him to several dozen boxes of documents, the largest of which were labeled "rubbish." Examining them, Goitein later recalled:

I came upon the minutes of a court session that dealt with a business trip to India, made by Joseph Lebdi, a merchant from Tripoli, Libya. Examining other Geniza collections preserved in the same library, and while commuting between Oxford and Cambridge, I was able to piece together the entire dossier of this case, comprising the records of eleven sessions held between November 9, 1097, and August 18, 1098. Four other documents with this lawsuit were also found. This was a startling discovery. For up to that time, only very few and disconnected Geniza fragments dealing with the India trade had been published (including one treated by the present writer). If such precious material about as fascinating a subject as the India trade during the eleventh century had escaped the attention of scholars up to that time, one was entitled to assume that the Geniza contained much more information about it not yet registered. Subsequent visits to the libraries concerned proved that this assumption was more than justified. Slowly, the disjointed fragments became meaningful, and the personalities of the more important merchants and communal leaders took shape.[18]

Goitein saw that he had only skimmed the surface of this material, and already they were yielding great treasures. The Joseph Lebdi letter was only the first. Goitein knew that there were many thousands of documents in these collections that nobody had yet studied. If his brief glance had been so fruitful, then surely this was a veritable gold mine. The possibilities were simply awesome, and disposing of these manuscripts was simply unthinkable. Not only were there letters about the India trade, but correspondence from other lands, too. There were court records, schoolbooks, business receipts, and much more. Experts in Bible and Rabbinic material didn't care at all about this material; Goitein found it fascinating.

Goitein persuaded the library to hold on to these treasures and spent the next two decades overseeing graduate students and research assistants who sorted through them. Eventually, Cambridge would call the material that had been catalogued earlier the "Old Series," and Goitein's historical material became the "New Series." It contains approximately forty-two thousand documents.

By 1954, Goitein had published over a dozen major articles about the Genizah, including a paper about a twelfth-century Jewish messianic movement in Baghdad; another about Obadiah the Convert, the Italian priest who converted to Judaism during the Crusades; and another about Maimonides's son Abraham. Within this short time, Goitein's fascination with the documents of the Cairo Genizah made him the most preeminent Genizah scholar since Solomon Schechter.

Goitein's extensive research created a new dimension of Genizah studies—the analysis not of the literary documents from the Genizah, but of the far more "mundane" papers that documented the daily lives of medieval Jews. For the first time, the Genizah yielded literary truths not only about Judaism, but also historical truths about Jews and non-Jews who lived in medieval Egypt and beyond. Again speaking of himself in the third person, Goitein contrasted his approach with that of his predecessor, saying, "Mr. Schechter's Genizah and Mr. Goitein's Genizah are not the same Genizah."[19]

The Genizah dominated Goitein's professional life from the moment he first encountered it until his death thirty-seven years later, by which time he had published dozens of books and hundreds of articles—more than six hundred works in all—in Hebrew, English, German, and French.

From India to the Mediterranean

In 1957, Goitein moved to the United States to take a position as professor of Arabic at the University of Pennsylvania. In 1971, he retired from teaching and became a member of the Institute for Advanced Studies, in Princeton, New Jersey, where he remained until his death in 1985. His move to the United States puzzled many. He had always been an ardent Zionist and had worked diligently to help build the State of Israel. Why did he leave? Goitein never explained the move, but his student Mark Cohen commented that "he later came to believe he would not have accomplished as much as he did had he remained in Israel. Even those who bore him ill will for (in their words) 'abandoning' Israel would have conceded Goitein's point."[20]

Goitein decided to publish all of the material he had gathered about India in a single volume—his "India Book." But as his work on it progressed, he realized that most of the traders he was studying were on the Mediterranean side of the trade routes, not in India. To really understand what was going on in the correspondence, he needed to understand the lives and motivations of the Mediterranean Jews.[21] What were they importing from India, and why did they choose those items? How long did it take for goods to get from India to Cairo? What currencies did they use? What other economic factors influenced the market?

Using the Genizah texts to answer these questions, however, was going to be difficult. For starters, only a small number of the estimated fifteen thousand historical documents from the Genizah—about 10 percent of them—had been studied, so nobody really knew what they contained. Worse, these manuscripts were scattered in libraries all over the world, making a comprehensive study of them impractical, if not impossible. How could anyone do scholarly work on a Genizah-related topic when some of the documents were in Cambridge, others in New York, still others in St. Petersburg, and maybe even more in who-knows-where? In fact, nobody knew where the pertinent documents could be found, because nobody had even a general sense of what the collections contained.

The India Book was important, but it would have to wait. Goitein realized that he first needed to gather the historical Genizah texts into one place. All of them. Or if not all of them, at least a large enough sample to give scholars and students a general idea of the kinds of information they held.

The idea came to Goitein while he was working at Oxford's Bodleian Library on September 17, 1954. Goitein decided that he would publish a massive collection of the historical documents of the Cairo Genizah—*Living Parchments*, he would call it—and it would be *the* definitive resource for historical Genizah research of all kinds. After all, he realized, to fully appreciate this material, context was crucial. One couldn't really understand *any* of the Genizah documents without some understanding of them *all.* "Only a complete survey of the whole extant Geniza documents," he wrote, "a study of their vocabulary and grammatical usage, their prosopography and legal, as well as historical, aspects, can provide the tools for an exact understanding of each single text."[22] He considered the idea for several months and eventually wrote to his colleague Clemens Heller, of the École Pratique des Hautes Études, in Paris, to share his idea for the book.

As interested as Goitein was in this new project, however, his work on the India Book distracted him. For the time being, his *Living Parchments* was put on ice.

Then, in August 1958, Goitein was working at the Cambridge University Library, an institution he called "the Mecca of Geniza studies," when he received a letter from Dr. G. E. von Grunebaum inviting him to write his proposed book as part of a project jointly sponsored by the University of California and the University of California Press. Goitein didn't hesitate. As of that moment, he later recalled, "I was off India and on the Mediterranean."[23]

And so, at the age of fifty-eight, when most men begin looking toward retirement and relaxation, Shelomo Dov Goitein embarked upon the greatest undertaking of his professional life. He would re-create an entire society based on the jumble of information hidden in the piles of Genizah documents scattered around the world.

Conquering the Genizah

As Goitein commenced his work, he and von Grunebaum estimated that with the Genizah expertise he had already garnered, his concise summary of the historical Genizah material would be complete in short order. After six months, however, Goitein realized the impossibility of simply summarizing a body of work that still remained mostly unstudied.

Shifting gears again, Goitein decided that rather than summarize the relatively small amount of Genizah material he'd already studied, what he really needed to do was look at it all. Only with a sense of what the *entire* corpus of historical Genizah material contained could he write about it with any authority. He might not be able to study *every* manuscript in depth, but he would need to give each one at least a cursory look if he hoped to be able to write authoritatively about the Genizah as a whole.

And so, with quixotic optimism, Shelomo Dov Goitein set off to conquer the Genizah. He traveled to libraries in many countries, consulted photostats, and scanned bibliographies. He visited Cambridge, Oxford, Manchester, London, Paris, Heidelberg, Vienna, Budapest, Leningrad, New York, and Philadelphia. More than a dozen foundations and academic institutions provided funding to cover the costs of his travel and the other expenses associated with his project.

Goitein was meticulous in his research. For each document, he filled out a note card identifying the manuscript, listing the people and families it mentioned, noting the language or languages in which it was written, recording its date, and taking note of other important characteristics. From early on, Goitein knew that his index card file alone would be a valuable tool for future researchers. He took his notes in English, he said, because doing so would allow many to read and understand them, whereas very few people were proficient in the Judeo-Arabic that was the most common language of the texts.[24] In fact, before moving to Philadelphia, Goitein even declined an offer to continue his research in Paris because it would have required him to publish the results of his work in French.[25]

Goitein recorded information about thousands of Genizah documents, each on its own card, each card bearing the distinctive mark of his precise handwriting. Together, they comprise a massive database of Genizah material. The only computer he used was his own mind; his only printer was his pencil point.

Goitein's card files are now at Princeton, with microfilm copies at Cambridge and the Jewish National Library in Jerusalem. Still today, when scholars encounter a Genizah manuscript that stumps them or about which they need more information, they often step away from the flicker of their computer screens and the bright lights of their digital scanning equipment and turn instead to the handwritten notes of this diminutive giant of modern Genizah studies.

At Princeton, Goitein conducted much of his research at home. The living room served as his study, and his graduate assistants often worked in one of the bedrooms. One of his research assistants, Paula Sanders, remembers those years fondly: "Professor Goitein napped from noon until two every day, so I usually arrived at around 2:30. He would greet me at the door with a smile, and always with a line of classic poetry: 'Your dress reminds me of a line from Horace....' We worked for a couple of hours until, promptly at 4:00, Mrs. Goitein served tea." Sanders recalled that Goitein was genuinely interested in her personal life. He was delighted to learn that she was from Kansas City, just like his daughter-in-law; and when Sanders's niece was born, Goitein handed her a twenty-dollar bill, telling her to buy some good candy for her sister, because "a new mother should have sweets."

"Professor Goitein had a personal relationship with the Genizah," Sanders recalls. In a very real sense, he knew the people who wrote the documents and who they were related to, and was intimately familiar with the contours of their daily lives. "Here we have a document from Chalfon ben Netanael," he would say, recognizing a manuscript from its handwriting. "I can think of three possible scenarios for this document," he would note about another that he found more puzzling.

The Genizah permeated Goitein's every moment. Sitting down to study, Goitein could focus his thoughts immediately, and someone could stand beside him for several minutes before he realized he or she was there. Sanders recalls that he often made comments such as, "You know, I was emptying the water pan from my refrigerator today, when I realized that the manuscript I studied yesterday, another that I examined last year in Cambridge, and a third that is in New York were all once part of the same document."

By 1965, eight years after beginning the project, Goitein had not even started to write his report. But his survey had reached a preliminary conclusion. "Preliminary," he noted, "for I do not claim, by any means, to have succeeded in seeing all the relevant manuscripts or to have noted everything of significance. But I do hope that this study ... conveys an idea of the topics and types of information to be found in the Geniza documents."[26]

A World Uncovered

Finally, it was time to write. Goitein spent the remaining years of his life assembling the information on his cards into a coherent profile of Mediterranean life during the time of the Genizah. The result, *A Mediterranean Society: The Jewish Communities of the World as Portrayed in the Documents of the Cairo Genizah,* was originally anticipated to be three volumes long. But he had so much material that it ended up comprising five volumes, plus a sixth for the indices: volume 1, *Economic Foundations* (1967); volume 2, *The Community* (1971); volume 3, *The Family* (1978); volume 4, *Daily Life* (1983); and volume 5, *The Individual* (posthumously, 1988). In 1993, Paula Sanders, now dean of graduate studies at Rice University, edited the sixth and final volume, consisting of cumulative indices of the first five. The margins of *A Mediterranean Society* are narrow; the type is small; it is 3,095 pages long.

A Mediterranean Society uncovers a world. It describes in exacting detail the rich texture of life as Jews lived it during the tenth through thirteenth centuries. We see the personalities, streetscapes, family lives, economic struggles, communal dynamics, and religious yearnings of those Goitein referred to as "the Genizah people." His work explains the economies of the lands in which they lived, the authority and governance of their local communities, the roles and institutions of their family life, how they shopped and ate and built their homes, and how they balanced the needs of individuals with those of the community.

A sampling of the chapter headings and subheadings of *A Mediterranean Society* provides a glimpse of the depth and intricacy of its content: "Piracy, War, and Other Man-Made Dangers"; "Druggists, Pharmacists, Perfumers, Preparers of Potions"; "Interfaith Symbiosis and Cooperation"; "Affection and Conjugal Relations"; "Security and Sanitation"; "Attitudes Toward Clothing and General Appearance"; "Beer"; and "Death."

Because the Genizah people were so thoroughly integrated into the non-Jewish cultures and communities around them, *A Mediterranean Society* teaches a great deal about non-Jews as well. Goitein hoped that Islamists and Arabists would read his work and would learn to appreciate the value of the Genizah for their own work. (One young scholar inspired by Goitein's writing was Indian-born Amitav Ghosh. An Oxford graduate student in social anthropology in 1978, he became fascinated with Goitein's reference to a twelfth-century Jewish merchant named Abraham Ben Yiju and to Bomma, his servant, from Tulunad, a coastal region in southwestern India. Consulting with one of Goitein's students, Mark Cohen of Princeton, Ghosh did his PhD field-work in Egypt and retraced the footsteps of Bomma and Ben Yiju, with help from the latter's handwritten documents found in the Genizah. In 1992, Ghosh published the beautifully crafted *In an Antique Land: History in the Guise of a Traveler's Tale*, telling the story of the two men and of his own search for information about their lives.)

Goitein recalled that from the moment he began working on *A Mediterranean Society*, he was "off India." However, the lure of that Eastern land continued to pull at him, and he often couldn't help but return to the India Book. On September 24, 1979, the almost-octogenarian Goitein wrote to his younger colleague Mordechai

Friedman, saying, "I am eager to return to the India Book, 'my might and first fruit of my vigor' (Genesis 49:3). If I am unable to complete it, I rely on you to undertake the task, because the material and its format are prepared." But there were still two more volumes of *A Mediterranean Society* to polish off. Finally, on December 17, 1984, he mailed the final draft of volume 5 to his publisher. "On the very day I mailed it," he wrote Friedman a few weeks later, "like a 'commencement ceremony'—I began reworking new material for the India Book, this time, 'seriously.' I mean: the book will be completed."[27]

One month after writing that letter—on February 5, 1985—Shelomo Dov Goitein died in Princeton, New Jersey.

Although volume 5 of *A Mediterranean Society* was released three years later, in 1988, the India Book took far longer. Goitein had catalogued, transcribed, and interpreted hundreds of Genizah documents related to the India trade, and in typical Goitein fashion, his work painted a vivid, fully textured portrait of the lives and activities of medieval merchants. Nevertheless, it remained unfinished at the time of his death, and it took Friedman over two decades to complete it. Finally, in 2007, Brill Publishing Company released *India Traders of the Middle Ages: Documents from the Cairo Geniza* (852 pages), listing both Goitein and Friedman as the authors.

Shelomo Dov Goitein never achieved widespread fame; his books never made it to the best-seller lists. But Goitein's work left a priceless legacy. Never one to make the sweeping generalizations of an ideologue, he wrote that "we must strive for great things and concentrate on little ones."[28] Indeed, Goitein's greatness was in the myriad "little things" that he unearthed from the Genizah and in the world he revealed by doing so.

In his epilogue to *A Mediterranean Society*, Goitein evoked the prophet Ezekiel's vision of dry bones coming to life as a metaphor of his Genizah work:

> "The breath entered them; they came to life and stood upon their feet, a very large host" (Ezekiel 37:10). "The dry

bones," the dispersed Geniza fragments, had to be brought together, "bone matching bone," to form skeletons; "sinew, flesh, and skin" grew over these, philological and historical comments making them viable; finally, a breath or "wind," the contact with the other resurrected, let them come to life as members of "a vast multitude," a flourishing society.[29]

9

Sheet Music, Long-Lost Talmud, and a Lame and Decrepit Female Hyena

The Second Half-Century of Genizah Research

Although the breadth and depth of Shelomo Dov Goitein's research permanently redefined the contours of the Genizah landscape, he was far from the only landscaper at work. In fact, both during and after Goitein's illustrious career, Genizah research continued all over the world. Historians, liturgy experts, paleographers, and scholars in other fields continued to discover new treasures in the Genizah, and articles presenting Genizah research continue to appear regularly not only in scholarly journals, but in many popular publications as well.

If collected, these articles could fill a library, and a complete survey of them would be beyond the scope of this book. However, a few highlights of the Genizah discoveries from the late twentieth and early twenty-first centuries will give us a sense of the continued excitement of Genizah research still permeating the field many decades after its documents were first discovered.

A Maimonides Responsum

Late one Friday afternoon in the winter of 2003, Ben Outhwaite sat amid stacks of manuscript albums in the offices of the Taylor-Schechter Genizah Research Unit at Cambridge University. He sat alone. Most of his coworkers back then were Jews, and on Friday afternoons during the winter, they left early to be home by sunset for their Sabbath celebrations.

Outhwaite quickly scanned through the manuscripts—page after page, volume after volume, stack after stack. For several days, he had been in search of Hebrew letters and legal documents, paging through the manuscripts looking for the telltale words or phrases that would indicate he had found one of the documents he was seeking. At that stage of his search, Outhwaite was poring through the manuscripts of what Cambridge calls its "Additional Series," thousands of documents that Schechter and the other early Genizah researchers thought to be of little value. Most of the documents in the Additional Series were fragmentary; many were nothing more than tiny scraps. Nevertheless, scholars had found some textual diamonds in the Additional Series rough, and Outhwaite had to be careful not to lose his concentration in the monotony of the search.

Suddenly, one of the documents caught his eye. It measured about three by five inches, and like many of the documents in the

Fragment of a Maimonides responsum, discovered 2003

Additional Series, it had been reused several times. On one side were several random Arabic letters and some brief excerpts from Jewish liturgy. But then, Outhwaite later recalled, "On the other side of it, I saw, unmistakably, the handwriting of Moses Maimonides."

Maimonides's handwriting was well known to scholars from other documents; he was not only a rabbi, but also a physician, and he had the scrawl to prove it. Many of the documents he penned were responsa—answers to questions Jews asked him about Jewish law. Maimonides's high status meant that his decisions were binding, and like many of today's prominent legal decisors, he put a great deal of effort into crafting his "big" responsa. When Maimonides knew that he was issuing a controversial or historically significant decision, he developed his points carefully and was sure to use language that was precise, correct, and complete. Many of his responsa, however, were more mundane, and for these he was typically very terse: "Question:____; Answer_____; So wrote Moses [Maimonides]." End of responsum.

Ben Outhwaite read the responsum before him and immediately checked the Cambridge Genizah catalogues. Nobody had ever paid much attention to this manuscript, nor was it even identified as a Maimonides responsum. He checked Joshua Blau's four-volume collection of Maimonides responsa. "And sure enough," he remembers, "no one else seemed to have published it."

He knew it was written by Maimonides—not only was it written in the sage's distinctive handwriting, but it also closed with the telltale "So wrote Moses." Maimonides's students had anthologized many of his responsa while he was still alive, but the anthologies omitted those that were briefer and less noteworthy—the one-liners and single-sentence replies to questions about daily life and practice. Most of the responsa that ended up in the Genizah were these "little" ones—those that hadn't made the cut into the anthologies.

And it was one of these responsa that Ben Outhwaite spotted at Cambridge that Friday afternoon—a previously unknown writing by one of the greatest Jewish sages in history.

Years later, he still recalls it as his most exciting Genizah research moment of all. What was frustrating, however, was that everyone else in the office had already left for the day. He had just made the most dramatic discovery of his career, and nobody was there for him to tell.

"Unfortunately," Outhwaite adds, "it's one of those responsa that's not really going to change the world." The upper half of the responsum—the part bearing the vast majority of the question to which Maimonides responded—is missing. Atop the remaining scrap are a couple of errant words from the original question, and beneath it is the only complete sentence on the page: "Answer: He may not enter that house." Then comes Maimonides distinctive sign-off, "So wrote Moses."

What was the question to which Maimonides was responding? Who was the "he" who couldn't enter that house? What "house" was he forbidden to enter? Why was he forbidden to enter it? We have no idea, of course, for unfortunately, the question Maimonides addressed in that responsum has been lost. At least for now.

"He may not enter that house." We don't know what the question was, but trying to imagine what it might have been can yield all kinds of tantalizing possibilities.

A Rabbinic Scroll

The Maimonides responsum that Ben Outhwaite discovered was not the Additional Series' only treasure. The reams of material that Schechter and his Genizah researchers thought worthless turn out to have other hidden nuggets of Genizah-gold, as well.

In 1981, a young scholar named Marc Bregman spent a year in England as a fellow of the Oxford Center for Post-Graduate Hebrew Studies. He was studying *Tanchuma,* a collection of Rabbinic homilies composed during early Talmudic times. The Genizah collections had yielded several significant *Tanchuma* manuscripts, and Bregman was looking for more.[1]

Bregman divided his time that year between the Genizah collections at Cambridge and Oxford. Just as Ben Outhwaite would do years later, Bregman spent many hours searching Genizah albums for manuscripts in his specific area of interest—page after page, volume after volume, stack after stack. At one point while he searched through the Additional Series, Bregman came to a manuscript that looked downright odd. First, unlike most of the other Additional Series manuscripts, this wasn't a tiny scrap, but quite large—12½ by 9½ inches. Second, and more immediately noteworthy to Bregman, the manuscript was almost entirely black and very difficult to read, which is probably why it ended up in the Additional Series to begin with. It was on leather, which was also unusual for a Genizah manuscript, and its dark color indicated that it was very old; later leather and parchments were prepared with treatments designed to avoid such blackening.

Bregman looked closer. The right side of the page had crumbled away, but on the left side were stitch marks, so he realized that the page must have once been part of a scroll. Typically, Jews make scrolls only for their biblical texts—the Torah and occasionally some later books of the Jewish Bible. Which one was this? There was writing on the back of the parchment, too, but that writing seemed to have been added later. Perhaps it was some sort of a mystical text such as *Perek Shirah*, a well-known kabbalistic work mentioned in the Talmud. Returning to the front of the document, Bregman tried to make out the text. The leather had become so dark that most of it was difficult to read.

Then, he came upon two words that he *could* read, and they shocked him: "Rabbi Meir." Rabbi Meir was a *tanna*, a prominent Rabbinic sage from the generation that wrote the Mishnah, the earliest section of the Talmud. Significantly, Rabbi Meir lived *after* biblical times, not during them. This unusual-looking manuscript, Bregman realized, was not a biblical text at all—it was Rabbinic.

But if it was Rabbinic, what was it doing on a scroll? Hebrew codicologists (experts in the history of books as physical objects) had long known that since the ninth century the standard format for Rabbinic literature was the codex, the bound book. There were hints that earlier versions were on scrolls, but there were no surviving manuscripts to prove it. In fact, there are few Jewish manuscripts of any kind dating from the 130s of the Common Era until the ninth century, when the codex became standard. If this was a Rabbinic scroll, Bregman realized, then it was probably a very, very old one.

An early fragment of *Avot D'Rabbi Natan*

Immediately, Bregman wrote an aerogram to his teacher Malachi Beit-Arié. Not only was Beit-Arié widely considered the father of Hebrew codicology, but also years earlier, Beit-Arié had done his doctoral dissertation on *Perek Shirah*, which Bregman suspected was the text on the reverse side of the parchment. Could it be, Bregman asked, that this blackened manuscript was the world's only known antiquarian Rabbinic manuscript in the form of a scroll? Has anyone ever found a scroll of Rabbinic literature before? Beit-Arié was interested and suggested that Bregman get some high-quality images of the piece for further study.

Bregman spoke with the head manuscript photographer at the Cambridge University Library, who doubted that he could get any usable images from such a darkened text. Soon afterward, Bregman left Cambridge and returned to Oxford, interested in the old scroll, but knowing that, lacking photographs, further research would be difficult. Several weeks later, however, a packing tube showed up in the mail containing beautiful eleven-by-fourteen images of the scroll. They were as clear as—if not clearer than—the original.

When he examined the specialized photographs, Bregman was able to decipher nearly every letter of the text and to identify it as an early form of *Avot d'Rabbi Natan*, a commentary on a section of the Talmud called *Pirke Avot* and now considered part of the Talmud itself. "I realized," he recalls, "that this was indeed a very important discovery."[2]

Bregman surveyed the existing research; evidently, this was the only known antiquarian manuscript of Rabbinic literature in scroll form. It was, therefore, not only the oldest known fragment of *Avot d'Rabbi Natan*, but it was also the oldest known manuscript in the entire Cairo Genizah, and the oldest Rabbinic manuscript in the world of any kind! Marc Bregman spent over a year studying the document, and in 1983, he published his findings in a Hebrew journal called *Tarbiz*. Bregman estimates that the *Avot d'Rabbi Natan* manuscript was written sometime in or around the fifth century CE. Coincidentally, it was Solomon Schechter's research into *Avot d'Rabbi Natan* that had first put him onto the scholarly stage back in 1887, almost a century earlier.

Despite the exalted status of Rabbinic literature, it is, nevertheless, Oral Torah and therefore of only secondary importance to the Written Torah, the Five Books of Moses. In a debate over Jewish law, the person who quotes a scriptural passage to support his view typically prevails over a person who quotes only a Rabbinic passage to support his. The words of Torah—so beautifully inscribed in scrolls and stored in synagogue arks—trump the words of the Rabbis.

The physical form that these works now take reflects their relative positions in the Jewish mind. For centuries, Rabbinic teachings have been printed in books; only the Written Torah, the Five Books of Moses, appears in scroll form. Even in this era of word processing and high-speed printing, Jews read their most sacred literature from beautiful parchment scrolls handwritten by scribes using feather quills.

Marc Bregman's find, however, blurs this hierarchy. At least a little. We now know that in the past Rabbinic books also were put into scrolls and that they looked much more like Torah scrolls than they do today. Of course, they *were* Torah—Oral Torah. While that makes a big difference in the way we view these texts today, we now know that there was a time when this wasn't the case, when the words of the Rabbis appeared in a form that looked just like the words of Written Torah.

Jews treasure religious wisdom. Our tradition says that with the Torah, God conveyed that wisdom directly, and with the Talmud and other Rabbinic works God conveyed it through people. The fact that all of these works once appeared in scrolls demonstrates that they are all of one piece, for they share the status of divinely proclaimed wisdom—sacred literature.

A Puzzling Piece of Sheet Music

The story of one of the most fascinating Genizah documents discovered during the past half century begins not long after the first parchments began to fill the synagogue's attic. It was 1082, and a twelve-year-old boy named Giovan had just dreamed a mysterious dream. The visions he had in that dream would eventually transform his life, but not for some time. They would also set off a remarkable chain of events that, nearly a millennium later, would allow not only words but also music to emanate from the Cairo Genizah.

Giovan, also known as Johannes, lived in a small town called Oppido Lucano, just beneath the ankle of Italy's boot, eighty-five miles inland from Naples.[3] He was born into a family of nobility. His older brother, Rogier, studied chivalry and eventually became a baron; Rogier's entourage included four guards and ten servants.

In his autobiography, Giovan described a dream in which Giovan was a priest, serving at the local basilica. At one point, he suddenly "beheld a man standing to his right, opposite the altar, and the man called to him 'Johannes!'"[4]

His account of the remainder of the dream has not survived, but one scholar, Norman Golb, suggests that "the apparition was a saintly or charismatic figure who urged Johannes to perform a religious act."[5] Undoubtedly, Golb argues, the act was connected with the fact that the archbishop of nearby Bari had converted to Judaism a few years earlier, and the conversion had made a deep impression not only on Giovan but also on many of the region's church officials.

Years passed and presumably the images Giovan saw in his dream remained with him the entire time. He became an introspective teenager, and his parents enrolled him in a monastery to be groomed for the priesthood. There he became a serious student of Christian theology and scripture and, presumably, an ordained priest.

In 1096, the First Crusade began, and warriors throughout Europe brandishing crosses on their chests and shoulders began preparing for their journey to Jerusalem. Before they left, Giovan recalled, many crusaders turned to one another and asked, "Why should we [go to a country far away to fight our ene]mies, while in our own countries [and in our own cities there are] our enemies and those who hate [our religion? Why should we lea]ve them here with our wives?"[6] Giovan understood that the Crusade was a war not only for Christian sovereignty over the Holy Land, but also against all "infidels" whom the Crusaders encountered along the way.

Early in the Crusade, an eclipse took place, which Giovan saw as a portent. Had not the prophet Joel written, "The sun shall be turned into darkness, and the moon into blood, before the coming of the great and terrible day of the Lord" (Joel 3:4)?

The Crusaders massacred thousands of Jews throughout Europe—often by sword, sometimes locking entire communities inside their synagogues and burning them alive. Giovan certainly saw some of these horrors, and in 1102—perhaps out of revulsion—he converted to Judaism. When he converted, Giovan took as his Jewish name that of a biblical prophet who also chose to cast his lot with Judaism and the Jewish people. No longer would he be Giovan of Oppido; from now on he would be called Ovadiah Ha-Ger—Obadiah the Convert.

Europe was not a very friendly place for Jews during the Crusades, and it was particularly hostile to those who had converted from Christianity. Conversion to Judaism was a criminal act—often a capital offense. Soon after he converted, therefore, Ovadiah fled Europe and moved to Aleppo, Syria, where he lived for a few years, and around 1110, he moved to Baghdad. When Ovadiah arrived, he was greeted by local Muslims wary of this strange visitor with shaky Arabic, and they immediately tried to kill him. The Jewish community of Baghdad, however, welcomed Ovadiah more warmly, and the head of the local academy invited him to sit in class with the schoolboys to study Hebrew and Torah. During this time, two messianic pretenders wreaked havoc in Baghdad's Jewish community, and Ovadiah's memoirs recall those events in vivid detail. Describing the reaction of the Jewish community when the prophesies of one of these men proved false, Ovadiah wrote:

> When they failed to see anything, their hearts were utterly broken within them, and the Jews became ashamed before all the gentiles. For all the gentiles and the uncircumcised ones heard the rumors which came to the Jews; they would all laugh and mock at the Jews and would say 'Behold the Jews want to fly, yet they have no wings with which to fly to their land.' They continued goading, calumniating and cursing the Jews, and the gentiles would say that everything which the Jews had was false and vain.[7]

Ovadiah's journey continued in 1119, when he moved from Baghdad back to Syria—Damascus, this time—and lived there for two years. From there he traveled to the northern part of Crusader-occupied Palestine, then to Tyre (in Lebanon), and finally, sometime during the early 1120s, to Fustat—Old Cairo.

In 1901, Solomon Wertheimer published a letter of recommendation that Ovadiah had received from a rabbi in Aleppo, which Wertheimer had discovered in a pile of Genizah documents. Since then, several other manuscripts by and about Ovadiah have turned up in other collections. The cover page of a prayer book he wrote was identified in the library of the Hebrew Union College, in Cincinnati; several pages of his memoirs were found at Cambridge, at JTS, and in Budapest.[8] Together, these documents tell the amazing story of Ovadiah Ha-Ger, an Italian priest who converted to Judaism during one of the Jewish people's darkest hours, a man whose journey took him to many lands and who was an eyewitness to important events of Jewish history during the Middle Ages.

This material alone would have made for a wonderful tale of adventure and religious transformation. But then, in late 1964, there was another discovery regarding Ovadiah—one that added an entirely new dimension to his life story.

In November 1964, Norman Golb of the University of Chicago examined a curious document from the JTS Genizah collection. The document was on paper, 5¾ inches long and 4½ inches wide; it was written on both sides, bearing Hebrew block print and neumes—medieval musical notations. Other scholars had studied it before, but it seemed to Golb that none of them had gotten its origin quite right. Some had suggested that it came from the Isle of Wight; others, that it was written in Italy.

It was easy to see why the document had stumped earlier scholars. The paper upon which it was written was typical for the Genizah—the kind that was widely used in twelfth-century Egypt. Its words were a poem that eulogized the death of Moses. Its letters were penned in a Middle Eastern Hebrew script, which, curiously, looked far more Babylonian than Egyptian. Whether it came from Babylonia or Egypt, then, was unclear. What was clear, however, was that this was a Jewish document.

But that wasn't all. If this was a Jewish document, Golb wondered, why were its neumes those of twelfth- or thirteenth-century Lombardy, in northern Italy? And for that matter, how could it be that its "Jewish" music, which musicologists had transcribed into the modern notational system, was clearly Gregorian chant? The JTS manuscript, in other words, was an Egyptian Jewish document, written in Babylonian Hebrew script, bearing Christian sheet music, notated with Italian notes. What was going on?

You can probably guess where this is going. Golb looked at the document more closely and soon realized that the handwriting was remarkably similar to that of the author of another manuscript he had studied in Budapest the previous summer. The music was written by perhaps the only person capable of writing a Hebrew poem in Egypt using Babylonian script and setting it to Gregorian chant with an Italian notational system—Ovadiah Ha-Ger.[9]

Evidently, Ovadiah was not only a religious seeker, world traveler, and memoirist, but also a poet and composer. As a composer, of course, he must have been lonely in Egypt—who else in Jewish

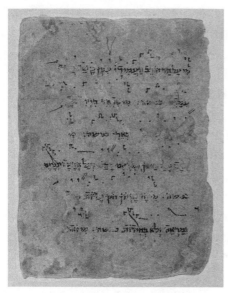

"Mi Al Har Chorev"—sheet music by Ovadiah Ha-Ger

Cairo could read the sheet music of the Gregorian chant of Italy? In all likelihood, this was a document that nobody other than Ovadiah himself could read. Unlike other documents in the Genizah, this was not a letter to another person, a book for other people to read, or a business or legal record for others to consult. This was a document that the author wrote for himself. Ovadiah may have enjoyed sharing his music with others, but his unique set of skills and the unusual path of his life meant that his sheet music was for his use and his use alone.[10]

For many centuries, Jews have often greeted converts with wariness rather than welcome. Although Jewish law forbids reminding converts of their "heathen" past, many Jews, unfortunately, can't help but be suspicious: Is this person really sincere? Why, really, did he choose to convert? Why would anyone? In Ovadiah, however, we see what unique gifts those who do choose to convert can bring to the Jewish people. Ovadiah's music brought the sonorous tones of the Italian monastery together with the cultural idiom of Jewish Cairo and created a form of Jewish expression that only he could have contributed. His work transcended the boundaries of nation and culture, allowing the Gregorian chant of Italy to make its way to the Jews and Judaism of Egypt. Only because his life took the circuitous path that it did was he able to offer this unique and lasting gift.

Yes, lasting. The song is called "Mi Al Har Chorev." Its manuscript is the oldest piece of Jewish sheet music known to exist, its words a majestic tribute to the life of Moses:

WHO stood upon Mount Horeb, heard the order "Stand
with Me!"—as Moses?
WHO to the desert led my flock, fed them manna, drew
from out my well—as Moses?
WHO praised Me with "O merciful and forbearing," whispered "Thou repentest of the evil"—as Moses?
WHO beheld the sight of statute testimonial, witnessed in
full vision, not by parable—as Moses?
WHO is the one who taught and drilled the Torah, mer-
ited to come within the cloud—as Moses?
WHO stayed for forty days in heaven, was sustained with
neither bread nor water—as Moses?

> And the people harked unto the Lord: "My congrega-
> tion, arise, for thy light hath come, and the Glory of
> the Lord on thee doth shine!"
> As it is said, "Arise, O my light, for thy Light hath
> come, and the Glory of the Lord on thee doth shine"
> (Isaiah 60:1).[11]

Musicologists have transposed Ovadiah's composition into modern musical notation, and the music has been recorded and posted
online.[12] Now you can hear it. The tune and its words are haunting
and beautiful—specifically Jewish yet somehow universally human
at the same time.

The music and poetry sat silent in the Genizah for almost
nine hundred years. Now, with help from scholars, musicians, and
the Internet, they sing again. For people the world over.

Stefan Reif and the Taylor-Schechter Genizah Research Unit

In the early twentieth century, the person most commonly associated with the Cairo Genizah and its documents was Solomon
Schechter. By mid-century, Shelomo Dov Goitein had taken the
mantle of Genizah leadership. And by century's end, the world's

leading Genizah scholar and researcher was Professor Stefan Reif.

Born in 1944 in Edinburgh, Scotland, Reif is a short, spry man with a big smile who exudes a palpable enthusiasm for all things Genizah. He began his academic career as a postgraduate researcher at the University of London in the 1960s, later serving posts in Glasgow and Philadelphia before coming to Cambridge University in 1973. The university had hired him to care for the largest and most significant collection of Jewish manuscripts in the world—a task the young scholar found very exciting and highly daunting. When he arrived, Reif was astonished at what he discovered.

The collection was a complete mess.

Walking past the shelves holding boxes of Genizah manuscripts and perusing the library's meager catalogues of its texts, Reif saw that the collection suffered from decades of neglect. Schechter had done the world a great service in discovering the Genizah and, along with his dream team, studying a handful of its manuscripts. As they did their initial research, Cambridge University librarian Francis Jenkinson had done a preliminary sort of the collection and transcribed what documents he could.

But in 1902, just five years after discovering the Genizah, Schechter left for New York, leaving most of the collection heaped in boxes and not much more organized than it had been when he found it. Soon afterward, a young Cambridge librarian named Ernest Worman took charge of the collection, and—with notecard, pencil, and meticulous handwriting—catalogued about five thousand of its historical manuscripts.

Sadly, Ernest Worman died in 1909 at the age of thirty-eight. Afterward, scholars continued to study the texts, but little was done to curate the collection for more than forty years. For much of the first half of the twentieth century, economic constraints, two world wars, and the lack of Solomon Schechter's exuberant energy and charisma all conspired to put the huge Cambridge Genizah collection on the back shelf. In the 1950s, Goitein and his students assembled the New Series, but there still remained dozens of boxes filled with unstudied, unexamined, and uncatalogued Genizah manuscripts. Adding to the chaos was the fact that the processing that had been done was often cursory and of little value—a pile of biblical fragments here, a folder of Rabbinic material there, a box of Arabic documents sitting nearby that nobody had taken the time to read.

Professor Stefan Reif, with Mrs. Elsie Alexander, widow of Solomon Schechter's grandson, and one of her sons, Dr. Ian Alexander, in 1999

The mess that Reif found when he arrived, then, wasn't new—it was centuries-old. Schechter had brought heaps of Genizah material from Cairo seventy-six years earlier, and since then, nobody had gotten around to cleaning it up.

More specifically, the collection that Reif found in 1973 contained the following:

- *The Old Series:* 34,000 documents catalogued in the early days of Genizah research; 1,700 of the documents that the early researchers thought most valuable were encased in glass, 2,000 were in albums, and the rest were collected in 206 boxes. Over the years, librarians had assigned shelf-mark numbers to many of the documents and written the numbers in pencil directly on the old paper or parchment.
- *The New Series:* 44,000 mostly historical documents sorted, but not catalogued, by Goitein and his students.
- *The Additional Series:* 105,000 manuscripts not identified as valuable by either of the two earlier waves of researchers.[13]
- *Several other collections:* From Wertheimer, Henriques, Mrs. Lewis and Mrs. Gibson, etc.

The disarray made studying the Genizah documents difficult, if not impossible. Without knowing what was available and where to find it, researchers were unable to do their work.

There was, of course, no budget for Reif to use as he tackled his enormous task. His predecessors, as well as many of his library colleagues, eschewed fund-raising as an activity beneath their station. Reif, however, had no such qualms and immediately began searching for the money he needed to organize the collection. In February 1974, six months after his arrival, he created a distinct department in the University Library through which he could collect grant money and donations for his work—the Taylor-Schechter Genizah Research Unit.

Reif coaxed and cajoled potential donors, and soon he was able to hire a research staff. During the ensuing thirty-two years, Stefan Reif and the Genizah Research Unit he founded steadily produced an astounding body of work. By 1975, they had sorted the Additional Series into its component subject headings. Soon after, they catalogued forty-five thousand documents and assembled a bibliography of fifty thousand scholarly works related to the Genizah. In 1978 the Genizah Research Unit released the first of its thirteen-volume Genizah Series, a group of bibliographic and scholarly books published one every couple of years by the Cambridge University Press.

The work was contagious. As the Cambridge Genizah collection became more organized, owners of other large collections of Genizah documents realized that it was indeed possible to clean up their heaps of Genizah manuscripts. Libraries in Manchester, New York, Oxford, and elsewhere looked to Cambridge and followed Reif's lead in bringing new order to their Genizah chaos.

In 1999, Reif participated in a project designed to identify and digitize *all* of the documents of the Cairo Genizah, wherever they might be found. Obviously, the Cambridge collection posed the biggest challenge to the project, and in order to begin, a comprehensive inventory of the collection was needed.

Reif's wife, Shulie, headed the effort, cataloguing one hundred manuscripts per hour onto a specially designed spreadsheet. With the help of three assistants, she began her work in 2004, and by April 2006, all of the data had been gathered and compiled. Prior to the inventory, Cambridge thought that its Genizah collection consisted of approximately 140,000 items. The new count, however, revealed that it actually held 193,654 items—225,141 individual folios. For the first time, an accurate picture of the massive Cambridge collection was beginning to emerge.[14]

Stefan Reif's work in Cambridge was not limited to librarianship. During his long career at the helm of the Taylor-Schechter Genizah Research Unit, he also did an enormous amount of research, publishing over three hundred articles and books, including many works on liturgy, bibliographic material, and a book entitled *A Jewish Archive from Old Cairo: The History of Cambridge University's Genizah Collection.*

Reif retired from his post at Cambridge in 2006. However, he continues writing and speaking about the Genizah, spending half of each year in Cambridge and the other in Israel. "Stefan Reif," one of his colleagues suggests, "knows more about the Genizah than God."

Dr. Haskell D. Isaacs and the Genizah's Medical Manuscripts

Toward the end of Reif's first decade running the Genizah Research Unit, he came to realize that the Cambridge collection held a wealth of Middle Eastern medieval medical documents—so much material that it required a researcher charged with the specific task of overseeing the cataloguing and study of the medical manuscripts alone. The first close scrutiny of this documentation had begun twenty years earlier when S. D. Goitein published a major article entitled "The Medical Profession in Light of the Cairo Geniza Documents." Its introductory paragraph gives a good sense of the role of medicine and physicians in Genizah society:

The physicians of our time are certainly better equipped to preserve and restore the health of their patients than were their medieval colleagues. However, they cannot compare with them as far as the latter's unique role of spiritual leadership and honored social position is concerned. The medieval doctors of the Mediterranean were the torchbearers of secular erudition, the professional expounders of philosophy and sciences. While the lawyers studied and applied the sacred laws of various religions and denominations and thus were limited in outlook by their very profession, the physicians were the disciples of the Greeks, heirs to a universal tradition, and as such formed a spiritual brotherhood which transcended the barriers of religion, nations, and countries.[15]

Using the many documents related to medicine and physicians in the Genizah, Goitein described the prominent role that doctors played in medieval Egypt. The doctor was called *tabib*, which means "physician," or *hakim*, "wise man." Sometimes their titles became more flowery: the Sound, the Successful, the Accomplished, the Sun of the Doctors, the Crown, or the Glory of the Physicians. They studied for their profession by attending lectures, immersing themselves in medical literature, serving as apprentices to older physicians, and doing internships at local hospitals. The physicians usually worked long days and were expected to treat needy patients free of charge. Doctors' offices were filled with glass bottles of different colors, scales, and mortars to prepare the medications. Their prescriptions, Goitein notes, were often complex; medicines composed of twenty ingredients or more were not unusual. Often, their prescriptions included expressions of piety: "To be taken with God's blessing" or "In the name of the Merciful, the Compassionate." Genizah society often conflated secular and religious learning, with many physicians also serving as judges.[16]

Goitein expanded on many of these themes in *A Mediterranean Society*, and soon it became evident that the medical documents in the Genizah were of great value, and interest in them grew. Articles appeared in various journals about everything from "The Importance of the Cairo Genizah for the History of Medicine," to one about the nicknames of flowers used in the Genizah's medical prescriptions, to biographies of various physicians whose names appeared in Genizah documents.

In the early 1980s, Stefan Reif began his search for an expert to oversee the collection's medical manuscripts. Clearly, he needed a person who knew both Hebrew and Arabic, was a meticulous scholar, and, ideally, had the scientific and medical expertise that it would take to understand these particular texts.

The man to whom he turned was probably the only person in the world who fit the bill.

Haskell Dawood Isaacs was born in Baghdad in 1913. He attended a school run by the Alliance Israelite Universelle and later received medical training at the Royal College of Medicine, in Baghdad. After moving to Manchester, England, in 1945, Isaacs married and opened his medical practice. For thirty-four years, he worked as a family doctor, and his patients loved him dearly. On the side, Isaacs maintained an active scholarly life, becoming a specialist in medieval Hebrew and Arabic medical literature. He earned a master's degree from the University of Manchester when he was forty-three years old and a PhD when he was fifty-six. By 1983, then, when Stefan Reif needed to find a medical manuscript maven, there was no doubt as to his first choice.

After more than ten years of research, in 1994 Isaacs published *Medical and Para-Medical Manuscripts in the Cambridge Genizah Collections*,[17] a massive assemblage of information regarding more than sixteen hundred different manuscripts

Dr. Haskell D. Isaacs, 1913–93

found at Cambridge—medical treatises, drug recipes, household remedies, letters between doctors and patients, and quasi-medical subjects, such as divination and astrology. He introduces us to individual physicians and details the eye diseases, migraine headaches, and urinary infections that Genizah people frequently confronted. He describes the confidentiality concerns that, then as now, colored much of the doctor-patient relationship. In ways that only a physician could, he describes specific medical cases and the courses of treatment the doctors pursued.

Some of these documents had been previously published; many had not. However, Isaac's book collected the accumulated medical wisdom and described the medical culture of medieval Egypt as nobody had ever done before.

A few months after the publication of his catalogue, Haskell Isaacs died in Cambridge at the age of eighty.

A Medieval Pharmacopoeia

To this day, scholars continue to plumb the Genizah's medical material for its treasures. In 2007, two Israeli scholars, Efraim Lev and Zohar Amar, surveyed all of the medical documents at Cambridge and assembled a comprehensive inventory of their *materia medica*, the ingredients called for in the medicinal prescriptions.

The inventory reads like that of a wizard's workshop:

- 195 plants, listed alphabetically from agaric to yew, including radish for snake bites and lice, galbanum (a Persian gum resin) for liver ailments, and a Mediterranean weed called scammony to be used as medical chewing gum and, interestingly, as both an aphrodisiac and a purgative.
- 27 inorganic substances, from agate to zinc.
- 20 animal products: earthworm for dental treatments, wax for eye problems and as a depilatory for hairy women, and the milk and feces of an ass to stop bleeding and for sore, achy muscles.[18]

Also in 2007, Lev, this time with Leigh Chipman of Ben-Gurion University, published a transcription translation of two manuscripts representing different versions of the world's oldest known Arabic pharmacopoeia, or drug list. Part of the document reads:

> Take a lame and decrepit female hyena, tie its four limbs, place it in a copper cooking pot, sprinkle over it white lupine and dill, of each one handful, add a sufficient amount of sweet water, cover the mouth of the pot, and cook over a gentle fire until the flesh disintegrates. After that, dry and cool it. Strain the broth, remove the skin, bones, and hair, and return the broth to a clean pot. Throw nard oil and balsam oil over it—one *sukurruja* each; and cook over a gentle fire until reduced to one third. Add honey in the quantity of the broth and cook until it is viscous and gains the consistency of thick honey.... Cool and place in a glass vessel, and leave for six months. Use after that, but not before, or else it is lethal.[19]

Taken together, the medical material of the Cairo Genizah has given us an unprecedentedly detailed portrait of medieval medicine, science, and commerce, as well as a reminder of the ongoing effort—then as now—to ease the suffering of human illness, injury, and disease.

New Discoveries, New Inspiration

A full list of the discoveries made in the Genizah collections in recent decades would number well into the hundreds. Other exciting scholarship includes Mordecai Friedman's research into the Genizah's *ketubot* (Jewish marriage certificates), Mark Cohen's work on historical documents from the Genizah, and the work of the late Michael Klein on *Targum* (Aramaic Bible translations). Geoffrey Khan of Cambridge University has studied the Genizah's Karaite documents and also mined the Genizah for linguistic insight, using its documents to reconstruct the Hebrew dialects of medieval Jews. The Genizah has even been a source for fiction writers; A. B. Yehoshua drew on its texts for his novel *A Journey to the End of the Millennium*,[20] and based on some correspondence in the Genizah, Burton Visotzky wrote a novel entitled *A Delightful Compendium of Consolation: A Fabulous Tale of Romance, Adventure and Faith in the Medieval Mediterranean*. Several Muslim historians, such as Hassanein Rabie and Mohamed el-Hawary of Cairo, use Genizah documents in their research as well.

In late 2009, Dr. Renate Smithius of the University of Manchester announced that she had identified a Genizah fragment in the John Rylands University collection as the description of an eighteenth-century Jewish exorcism designed to remove the spirit of a dead man named Nissim ben Bunya from his wife, Qamar bat Rahma. In 2010, David Rozenthal published a catalogue of the Genizah collection in Geneva, which, he explained, contained an entire lost sentence from the Talmud's Tractate *Bikkurim.*

Today, more than a century after its documents came to light, there remains a constant stream of new and important Genizah discoveries. The question that Jacob Saphir asked when he first peeked into the Genizah in 1864 and saw only the top of the massive pile of manuscripts remains pertinent and enticing: "Who knows what lies beneath?"

10

The Genizah Today

On the morning of Tuesday, February 23, 2010, my son Jacob and I walked across Cambridge, England, to visit the largest collection of antiquarian Jewish manuscripts in the world. It was a bitingly cold winter day, and the snow that had been falling when we first awoke had turned to blowing rain by the time we left our hotel. Our route to the library took us through narrow, winding streets. We glimpsed the spires of ornate university chapels. We trekked past the "Old Schools," a group of stately buildings where Solomon Schechter studied the Genizah documents after his return from Egypt. Then we turned down Trinity Lane—a narrow alleyway barely wide enough for a single car—and wound our way toward a bridge that led over the River Cam. A few minutes later, we walked up the front steps of the University Library.

Compared to the august buildings closer to the center of town, the Cambridge University Library is a remarkably plain edifice. When the library outgrew its previous home in the Old Schools in the early 1930s, the university decided to build a new library on West Road in the relatively open university outskirts. That way, it would have room to expand. Its architect, Giles Gilbert Scott, is also known for designing power stations and the red telephone booths that are ubiquitous throughout the United Kingdom. The library is a large, squat, brick building, with a rather plain exterior and a bulky, 157-foot tower rising above the entryway. Rumor has it that at its 1934 dedication, Neville Chamberlain

The Cambridge University Library

referred to the building as "that magnificent erection."

To gain access to the library and its collections, I had to bring a letter of introduction from my publisher and a recent electric bill as a proof of address. Since Jacob was under eighteen, someone from the Genizah Unit needed to personally escort us past the security checkpoint in the lobby. Understandably, the caretakers of the library at Cambridge take every precaution to protect their treasures.

Checking our bags in a nearby locker room, we soon saw the smiling face of Dr. Ben Outhwaite, director of the Taylor-Schechter Genizah Research Unit. He brought us up a flight of stairs, across large rooms of library stacks, and through a complicated maze of hallways. I found myself wishing I had brought breadcrumbs to mark the path for our return trip.

Ben Outhwaite is an affable, boyish-looking man of about forty. He grew up in Cambridge and began as an undergraduate at the university studying Chinese. But then he spent a year in Israel, met and married an Israeli woman—his wife, Smadar—and decided to change course and study Hebrew. Eventually, Outhwaite earned his PhD under Dr. Geoffrey Khan and worked at the Genizah Unit for several years before becoming its director. His terrific sense of humor, his intelligence, and the passion he showed for his work endeared him to both Jacob and me immediately.

Soon we rounded a corner and found ourselves facing a wall-sized version of the famous photo of Solomon Schechter sitting among heaps of Genizah manuscripts. Next to the picture was a wooden door—the Taylor-Schechter Genizah Research Unit. "Well, here we are," Ben said. He opened the door and ushered us in.

Before my visit, I'd expected the Genizah Research Unit to be larger than it actually is. In reality, it consists of just a small reception area surrounded by a few modest offices. And yet, this is where the world's largest collection of Jewish manuscripts is managed and cared for.

Ben took us into his office. On the small conference table occupying half of the workspace sat what looked to be a large photo album. Beside it was a cart holding more albums and several archival boxes. "Here, have a seat," Ben said. "I think I've gotten all of the manuscripts you asked to see."

Dr. Ben Outhwaite, director of the Taylor-Schechter Genizah Research Unit

We all sat down, and Ben opened the album on the table. "This is a volume of children's material," he explained. The documents were all encased in flexible plastic pages, just like a family photo album. These pages, however, were not regular plastic, but rather a special, acid-free archival material called Melinex—known in other forms as Mylar or plastic Coke bottles. Some pages held only a single document, others held several. When a single page held more than one document, machine-sewn stitching often separated the individual manuscripts into separate compartments.

Ben opened the book to a random page, and we immediately saw the document we had requested—a small piece of vellum with bright red, green, and gold lettering. The right side was decorated with a large, seven-branched menorah and two six-pointed stars. The other side was filled with nonsense-syllables in large letters: *ah, ah, eh, ay, ee*.... The manuscript was a children's Hebrew reading primer dating back, scholars believe, to the eleventh century. Its six-pointed stars are among the earliest examples of that symbol's use on a Jewish document.

The page was remarkably similar to those Jacob and I remembered from our own youthful study of Hebrew, though this one was

A children's Hebrew primer, eleventh century

more ornately decorated and made by hand. A thousand years ago, a Jewish child in Cairo sat down at a table to begin learning Hebrew: "*Ah, ah, eh, ay, ee.*" A few dozen years ago, another Jewish child (yours truly) sat at a table in suburban Chicago and began learning Hebrew in much the same way: "*Ah, ah, eh, ay, ee.*" Eight years ago, yet another child—Jacob—sat at *his* table in Washington State and forged one more link in the ancient chain of study. Could the child at his table in Cairo ever have imagined that a millennium after his own studies, a father and son would be looking at his schoolbook in a distant northern land?

"It's so small," I noted, "only about four by six inches. These things look much bigger online."

"There are all kinds of children's documents in here," Ben said, flipping through the pages. "Here's a torn section of another primer that looks similar to the one we just saw. These are some children's writing exercises. And look, this kid here did a sloppy job with his letters and then began to doodle." Jacob and I sat up. In elementary school, Jacob was notorious for zipping through his work so that he could use the extra time for reading. The image of a kid whizzing through his writing exercises in eleventh-century Cairo so as to get on to the fun stuff was strikingly familiar.

Jacob and I both laughed. Some things never change.

Ben closed the book, returned it to the cart, and placed an archival box on the table. "Here's one of the other documents you requested," he said, opening the box.

The moment I saw the document inside, I knew what it was. Ben Sirah! Here was not only a page from an important biblical-era book long thought to have been lost to history, but also the *very same page* that Solomon Schechter saw when he visited the Giblews at Castlebrae in 1896. The page that made him shout to his wife later that day that his name would live on forever. I had told Jacob the story of Schechter's discovery of that page many times; glancing over at him, I could see that he shared my excitement. Also in the box was the letter Schechter wrote to Agnes Lewis from the library later that same day after confirming the identity of the text. The original! *"Dear Mrs. Lewis, I think we have reason to congratulate* ~~ourself~~ *ourselves...."*

The Ben Sirah manuscript was by far the older of the two documents, but I'll confess that coming across the Schechter letter may have been even more exciting. Maybe that was because I hadn't expected to see the letter. Or maybe it was just because it was in English. Or maybe it was because the letter represented such an important link. The 114-year-old note on the table before us, penned in the very institution where we now sat, was handwritten by one of modern Judaism's foremost scholars and rabbis. It referred to a tenth-century manuscript sitting right next to it on the table, which was itself a transcription of a text originally written twelve hundred years before *that.* Across the table was the caretaker of the largest collection of Jewish manuscripts in the world, and next to me was my son, a budding scholar of Judaism who I hope will carry forward the sacred, time-tested wisdom of my people. With all of those pieces in place around the table, that moment became a narrow threshold joining an ancient past to a promising future—the biblical book of Ben Sirah to a distant tomorrow still hidden beyond the horizon.

So maybe that's why I found it exciting.

One by one, the remaining boxes and albums came to the table, each bearing treasures of its own: a Greek-Hebrew palimpsest published by Charles Taylor; a handwritten responsum of Moses Maimonides; the final letter that Maimonides received from his brother, David; the oldest known piece of Jewish sheet music; the Damascus Document; medieval Jewish letters, poetry, Rabbinic commentary, and much more. Each manuscript sent us soaring

Genizah dust

through time and space. Many centuries earlier, these people— some of them are renowned as Jewish history's greatest stars— had sat down and written these documents. And there we were, holding the very same papers in our hands, though touching them only through their pro- tective Melinex coverings. It was a moment of connection that I will never forget.

After the last document was back on the cart, Ben casually turned to us and asked, "Would you like go into the Manuscript Storage Room now?"

Scholars who can demonstrate their credentials can often examine individual Genizah documents or small groups of them in the Manuscript Reading Room. But, for obvious reasons, the stacks themselves are ordinarily closed to visitors. Ben had just invited me to see not only some manuscripts but also the greatest Jewish literary treasure in the world. All of it.

I was there in a professional capacity, so I needed to maintain my cool, professional façade. What I said was, "The Manuscript Storage Room? Why … yes, that would be great." What I thought was, "Would I like to go into the *Manuscript Storage Room*?!?! Oh, boy! Would I *ever*!!! *Woo-hoooo!!!*"

As someone who finds such delight in looking at these texts, I was beginning to feel like I was in the world's biggest candy fac- tory and that Dr. Ben Outhwaite was my very own Willy Wonka.

Using his key card to open the heavy metal door, Ben showed us into the large room where the library keeps its price- less collection of manuscripts. Just inside, he pointed to a tall metal chest with wide, flat drawers. "Here's where we keep some of our larger pieces," he said, "the ones that won't fit on the shelves." Inside the drawers were several oversized documents—Rabbinic texts, marriage certificates, and a brightly colored mystical document that might have been either a family tree or a cemetery map. Nobody knew for certain.

"And this is a box of some tiny pieces of parchment and paper that sifted to the bottom of the crates Schechter brought from Cairo," Ben explained. Inside were thousands, maybe millions of small flakes of Genizah detritus. Some were the size of a quarter, many others had crumbled into fine powder. Genizah dust.

"The main part of our collection is down here," Ben said. He walked us past several aisles of floor-to-ceiling shelves, their contents labeled enticingly at the end of each.

Genizah documents in the Cambridge Manuscripts Storage Room

"Dad," Jacob whispered as he glimpsed one of the tags, "that was the Darwin aisle!" Before our trip, we had heard that the Genizah documents sat near Darwin's diaries from his Beagle voyage in the library stacks.

"Yes," said Ben, "and Isaac Newton's papers are in here too, somewhere."

Finally, Ben stopped and pointed down an aisle. It went down sixty feet or so, and just like the others, its shelves were filled, floor to ceiling, with albums and boxes. "Most of our Genizah collection is in this row and the one next to it," he said.

I quickly scanned the spines of several of the albums. "Bible," "Medical Documents," "Liturgy," "Responsa," "Judeo-Persian," "Elchanan Ben Shemariah" (whoever that was), "Maimonides" (*Maimonides!*), "Poetry" … Each album and each box held the promise of discovery and wonder. And there were thousands of them.

Standing in the dimly lit stacks and looking at the enormous wealth of material that surrounded me, I got a sense of what Solomon Schechter must have felt while poring over the documents in Cairo and later in Cambridge. This agglomeration of literary material was so massive, so rich, so filled with information and knowledge that no single individual could handle it all. Schechter's riches, like those of modern-day billionaires, were so great they would best be bequeathed to posterity. What distinguishes Schechter's wealth from that of the billionaires, of course, is that Schechter's has yielded much more … *interest.*

Jacques Mosseri's Trunk of Manuscripts

The size and scope of the Genizah collection at Cambridge is far from static, and any inventory of its contents must undergo constant adjustments to remain accurate. As recently as 2006, for example, the University Library acquired a brand-new collection— that is, if centuries-old documents could ever be called new.

The "new" manuscripts had spent the past century in a trunk that once belonged to Jacques (Jack) Mosseri (1884–1934). Mosseri was the fifth of thirteen children in the Cairo banking family of Nissim Bey Mosseri and his wife Elena Cattaui Mosseri. Jack was only twelve years old when Solomon Schechter arrived on his Genizah expedition, but as his teenage years progressed, he became keenly aware of the magnitude of the discovery that had taken place in his hometown, and his curiosity grew. Many explorers, scholars, and collectors visited Cairo to examine Egyptian antiquities, and by the time he had reached his mid-twenties, young Jack Mosseri had become part of their social and professional circles.

In 1909, French scholar Israel Levi asked the young Jack Mosseri and archaeologist Raymond Weill to visit the Cairo Genizah. Levi had heard that Schechter may have left some material behind, and he was curious as to whether any of it might be of value or interest. Rumors had reached Mosseri himself that some contents of the Genizah had made their way to the Bassatin (or Bassatine) Cemetery—Cairo's Jewish burial ground—and Schechter had probably left them behind. He also remembered seeing Count d'Hulst and his crew digging for documents in the grounds around the Ben

Ezra Synagogue shortly after Schechter left. Maybe there was more treasure to be found.

Mosseri later recalled his visit:

> We found out that there still existed a few documents in the Gheniza of Old Cairo, which was thought to have been utterly ransacked ... we naturally had them put in a safer place than the Gheniza. In the following years [1910–12] further research work by Prof. Gottheil, Monsieur Weill, Mr. Chapira, and myself led to the complete emptying of the Ghenizot, and to further discoveries both at Bassatine and at Old Cairo, which constitute the new collection.[1]

Mosseri and his friends estimated that they had gathered a total of four thousand manuscripts. Mosseri's friend, Bernard Chapira—a French librarian, scholar, and collector—spent a year during 1912–13 cataloguing the collection and assigning shelf marks to its various items. Immediately, he could see that it was a real treasure, containing, like the rest of the Cairo Genizah, an enormous variety of material.

Jack Mosseri eventually went into the family banking business. With his growing fortune, he hoped to one day open a museum of Egyptian Jewry that would feature the documents in his Genizah collection. The Europeans had ransacked the vast majority of the Genizah papers—often with the active assistance of Cairo's Jews. The museum he hoped to build would allow his manuscripts to remain in Egypt and testify to the glorious history of

Jacques Mosseri

the local Jewish community. In the meantime, he decided, he would store the documents in a large crate and keep them at home.

Throughout the 1920s, Mosseri's social status grew along with his financial wealth. His wife, Rachel, was a beautiful and charming woman, and together she and Jack turned the Mosseri home into a prestigious Cairo salon. Jewish scholars, particularly those from Hebrew University in Jerusalem, repeatedly reached out to the Mosseris, eager to see the precious treasures they knew were somewhere in the house. But Jack held the documents close—no outsiders were going to get access to them. Instead, they would be kept safe until they could be safely ensconced in the museum.

Adding to the scholars' frustration was the fact that Bernard Chapira's 1913 catalogue of the collection had somehow gotten lost. All that remained of it was Mosseri's brief list of its shelf marks from the account he wrote shortly after he gathered the manuscripts. Now, not only were the manuscripts themselves unavailable, but so too was the list detailing just what those manuscripts were.

After moving to France with his family in the early thirties, Jack Mosseri died in 1934 at the age of fifty. Mosseri never saw the fulfillment of his dream of a museum of Egyptian Jewry, and when he died, his Genizah manuscripts remained in the box where he had stashed them twenty years earlier.

Israel Adler Unlocks the Collection

It took a musicologist to unlock the collection. Israel Adler (1925–2009) was born in Berlin, moved with his family to Palestine when he was eleven years old, and after the Israeli War of Independence, studied music in Paris, earning a doctorate from the Sorbonne in 1963. He first became aware of the Mosseri collection in the late 1950s. Researching the notations of ancient Jewish musical manuscripts, Adler came across Mosseri's 1913 article describing his Genizah collection. In it, Mosseri mentioned a beautifully illuminated Hebrew Bible in the collection whose notations to the Song of Songs were pertinent to Adler's research.

Adler was eager to see the Bible, and he asked his teacher George Vajda and other colleagues about it. Nobody had seen the manuscript for years, he learned. And it wasn't for lack of effort. Not only had several Israeli scholars attempted to establish contact with the Mosseri family, but Israel's president, education minister, and an ambassador or two had even tried to make contact, as well. And all of the attempts had failed.

After Adler earned his doctorate, he returned to Israel to head the music department at the Jewish National and University Library in Jerusalem and later to direct the Hebrew University Jewish Music Research Centre. In both contexts, he was again working to catalogue old Jewish musical documents, and he *really* wanted to see that Mosseri Bible. This time, he reached out to the family himself, and this time, he succeeded in making contact.

Rachel Mosseri had remained in France after her husband's death. But in late 1970, she visited Israel, and during her visit she agreed to meet with Israel Adler at the Dead Sea resort where she was staying.

The meeting happened on Saturday, November 28. Adler, of course, was eager to see whether he could examine the Mosseri Bible. But unfortunately, Rachel told him, the Bible had disappeared. Perhaps it had been stolen at some point. Perhaps the Nazis had confiscated it during World War II. In passing, Mrs. Mosseri mentioned that she did have an old crate of her husband's. She had held on to it since Jack died, but she had never opened it. What was inside it? Probably just some old Hebrew documents.

An unopened box that once belonged to Jack Mosseri … presumably containing "some old Hebrew documents"? It must have been the Mosseri Genizah collection! Adler pounced on the opportunity. Mrs. Mosseri was leaving for home a week later; Adler offered to accompany her to France and microfilm the documents on the spot.

Rachel Mosseri was reluctant. "Are you certain that the wooden crate really contains the Mosseri Genizah collection?" she asked.

"Yes, I am."

"And if you are wrong?"

"*Ma'alesh*," Adler shrugged, using an Arabic word best translated as "Well, things like that happen." He hoped it was one of the terms Mrs. Mosseri had retained from Egypt.

"A week later," he wrote, "on Sunday, December 6, I found myself sitting on the plane next to Madame Rachel, on our way to her home to open the wooden crate and microfilm its contents."[2]

Arriving in France, Adler opened the box, and sure enough, it contained several thousand old documents. The papers were loosely bundled according to size and genre, with each group labeled by an index card. Adler noticed that the groupings precisely matched the shelf-mark categories that Mosseri described Bernard Chapira as having used in his preliminary 1913 catalogue. The index cards removed any lingering doubt—this was indeed the Mosseri Genizah collection.

Adler had no time to waste. He had promised Mrs. Mosseri that he would microfilm the entire collection in ten days. In that short a time, there was no way he could get access to a professional microfilming facility, nor was there equipment available for him to rent. Nor, for that matter, could he do the work in the cramped confines of Mrs. Mosseri's home. Immediately, Adler moved the documents to a more spacious apartment owned by the Mosseri's son Gerard, he arranged for special Japanese microfilm cameras to be shipped to France from St. Catherine's Monastery at the foot of Mount Sinai (Mrs. Lewis and Mrs. Gibson would have been delighted), and he rounded up every Israeli he could find in the country willing to spend several days assisting him. Within two days, he began microfilming the documents.

The microfilm images that Adler and his assistants produced were far from perfect. With such little time to do their work, they were unable to be thorough. Some of the images were blurry; others were improperly sized, leaving off large portions of the text. Additionally, the manuscripts had not been conserved. Many were wrinkled, leaving important sections concealed beneath their folds. Others were clumped together in groups—separating them would have taken time that Adler's team didn't have, so instead they simply microfilmed the clump and hoped for the best.

Still, the process yielded great fruit. The microfilms showed that one document bore the personal clay seal of the tenth-century gaon Nehemiah. Another was a hand-written letter of Maimonides. There

Clay seal of Nehemiah Gaon, discovered in the Mosseri Genizah collection

was an early version of Saadya Gaon's *Sefer Hagaluy*, a magical recipe for fending off anger and rage. One document, a Yemenite marriage certificate, was dated 1899. That manuscript, the newest known in the Cairo Genizah, was written two years *after* Solomon Schechter's trip to Egypt.

Adler and his assistants re-counted the manuscripts and realized that there were actually about five thousand of them in the collection, not four thousand as Mosseri had estimated.

And then, the Mosseri Genizah collection disappeared once again. After Adler and his team finished their work, the family thanked them, reboxed the materials, and stored them in a vault. Adler later fell out with the family, and other scholars' repeated requests to examine the documents were all refused.

The Mosseri Collection Finds a Home— Temporarily

Years passed. Rachel Mosseri died in France. Her son Claude came into control of his parents' Genizah manuscripts, and by the early 2000s he realized that the time had come to find a long-term home for the collection. Ideally, the manuscripts would be returned to Egypt to help fulfill his father's Jewish museum dream. But Cairo's Jewish community had shrunk to only a handful of mostly

Assorted fragments from the Mosseri
Genizah collection, as received at
Cambridge

elderly Jews, making it unlikely that his father's dream would come to fruition anytime soon. Perhaps, Claude reasoned, he could at least find a way for the manuscripts to end up in some other Jewish institution.

The natural choice for such an institution was the Jewish National Library, in Israel. But Claude and some of his relatives worried about the fragile Mideast security situation. Would the documents be safe in such a war-torn country?

Claude discussed his dilemma with librarians and conservators, and in 2006, Stefan Reif, director of the Taylor-Schechter Genizah Research Unit at Cambridge University, proposed a solution. The Mosseri family would transfer the collection to Cambridge, where it would be properly conserved, catalogued, and digitized, allowing anyone interested in seeing it to be able to do so over the Internet. The collection would remain at Cambridge for twenty years, when, security permitting, it would be transferred to the Jewish National Library in Jerusalem.

The Mosseri collection was packed into fifty cardboard boxes. As final arrangements were made, the boxes were stored in a garage in Royal Tonbridge Wells, a southeast England spa town. Finally, in 2007, in the back of a library van, the Mosseri Genizah collection arrived at Cambridge. "We opened it up, expecting to find about five thousand items," Ben Outhwaite recalls. "Our conservators went through the whole collection and discovered that there were actually seven thousand."

As of this writing, the Cambridge conservators are working to conserve the collection, processing about four manuscripts each day. At that rate—twenty per week, eighty to one hundred per month, one thousand or so per year—completing the work will demand long-term conservatorial diligence and endurance. Everyone agrees that it's a good thing Cambridge has twenty years to finish its work.

The Science of Document Conservation

One of the reasons that conserving the Mosseri Genizah documents takes so long is that the science of conservation has advanced so extensively during recent years. What was once a matter of simply sliding old documents into plastic sleeves has now become a very elaborate, high-tech process.

Upon receiving a centuries-old, crumbling Genizah manuscript, the conservator's task is to prevent it from crumbling any further and, where possible, to restore it to a condition more closely resembling its original state. The job of the conservator, in other words, is to halt the forces of decay that have been working on the documents for centuries and, if possible, to reverse them.

At Cambridge, I visited the conservation lab—a large room filled with expansive countertops, wide file drawers, and high-resolution computer screens. Around the lab were mysterious machines, some of which looked as if they had come from the nineteenth century, others from the twenty-third. Genizah documents in various stages of preservation lay on several of the countertops.

In the lab, I met Lucy Cheng, a conservator now working on the Mosseri collection. She explained that the work of the conservator can be distilled into three basic steps. The first step is to clean the documents. When she gets the manuscripts, they are often clumped together, and she must carefully remove each one. Many arrive crusted with mud and other Genizah-gunk, often rendering them unreadable, and aging vellum is notorious for leaching out a gluey gelatin that adds many hours to the conservation process. Very gently, she uses scrapers and brushes to remove whatever dirt she can.

This step sometimes poses ethical dilemmas. Paper tends to be highly absorbent, and often the mud that it soaks up becomes irreversibly mixed with the ink of the text. As a result, removing

Dr. Dan Davies, Dr. Ben Outhwaite, and conservator Lucy Cheng, in the Cambridge Conservation Lab

some of the mud would also mean removing the text itself. In these cases, standard conservatorial practice now lets the mud remain. Conservators hope that future technologies will somehow allow them to remove the mud while leaving the ink in place.

The second step involves flattening the documents. Even when cleaned and separated, many documents are wrinkled, if not crumpled up into balls. Under a bright light, Cheng brushes a small amount of deionized water onto each wrinkle, relaxing it enough so that it will lie flat with only a small amount of pressure. Then she puts a small weight over the wrinkle and lets it sit for several minutes until it lies flat on its own.

Once flattened, she moves to the third step—repair. This step demands different processes for different documents. Parchment, for example, is very sensitive to heat and moisture. Newly prepared, it usually lies flat. But when parchment gets warm or moist, it stubbornly wants to curl back into its original sheep-shape. In the process, the parchment often curves away from the ink written upon it, and the letters flake away. To arrest this process, conservators put the parchment under a microscope and, using a fine-tipped instrument, feed a chemical called a consolidant beneath each individual flake of ink. The process locks the ink in place and prevents further erosion of the text. "It's a weird thing that we conservators like to do," Amy Armstrong Gerbracht, conservator at JTS, once told me.

Of course, many Genizah documents are crumbling or torn—their deteriorated condition is often what got them into the Genizah in the first place. The conservators patch these documents with "Japanese paper," a strong, lightweight, translucent film with adhesive on one side and wheat paste on the other. Cheng makes the paper at her workstation, traces the shape she needs, and carefully cuts the paper into that shape. Using a brush, she uses deionized water to dampen the edges of the hole she is patching and gently covers it with the Japanese paper.

When everything on the document is dried and set, she places it in a Melinex sleeve and moves on to her next document. In all, she devotes sixty to ninety minutes to each document, allowing her to conserve about four each day.

On the way out, I met the first conservator to work on the Mosseri collection—a woman from New Zealand named Ngaio Vince-Dewerse. As we chatted, I marveled at how painstaking and meticulous the work of a conservator must be. "Everyone has the patience for something," she replied. "For some, it's raising kids; for others, it's video games. For us conservators, it's working on old documents."

Leaving the lab, I couldn't help but think that she was selling herself and the other conservators short.

The Geneva Collection

In the spring of 2006, Dr. Barbara Roth, of the Bibliothèque Publique et Universitaire, in Geneva, Switzerland, set four cardboard boxes on a table in front of Professor David Rozenthal, of Jerusalem's Hebrew University. "This is our genizah," she said.

Roth had only a vague idea of what the boxes contained. A few years earlier, workers at the library had been searching through some of its storage rooms to find manuscripts for an upcoming research program on Greek papyrus documents, when they came across a metal box that looked as if it hadn't been opened in a long time. It was labeled "Hebrew Texts, parchment and paper fragments (from the 13th Century?), purchased from the Cairo synagogue, in the year 1896–1897, in Cairo, from Philippe by J. Nicole. They were identified in part by Alphonse Nicole in Oxford in 1898, under the supervision of Professor Neubauer."[3]

A box discovered in Geneva in 2006 holding 350 Genizah fragments

Evidently, in the late 1890s, noted Swiss papyrologist Jules Nicole had traveled to Cairo on a papyrus-buying trip. For reasons that are unclear, while he was there he also purchased about 350 Hebrew manuscripts that had just come onto the Cairo manuscript market.

Nicole wasn't very interested in this bunch of medieval Hebrew manuscripts, however—he was, after all, a papyrologist and therefore accustomed to studying documents that were far older. So, when he returned to Geneva, Nicole stashed the manuscripts in a box at the library and never gave them much thought again.

In fact, nobody gave them much thought until they were rediscovered over a century later. Roth was delighted at Rozenthal's interest but also concerned that they might not prove to be of significance or value. "I hope that our material doesn't disappoint you, and that you won't feel that you have come this whole way for nothing," she wrote.

Rozenthal was far from disappointed. From the moment he saw the manuscripts, he knew that he had come upon a great find. His first clue was their size. Early Genizah scholars, he later explained, had occupied themselves mostly with the large and relatively complete Genizah manuscripts. "But as we get further away in time from those first days of the Genizah, we occupy ourselves more and more with torn pages and small fragments." The great majority of the Genizah material, he noted, has been listed and catalogued, so scholars thought they had already mined most of its information. "But then, suddenly, a new collection is discovered."[4]

This new collection held many big documents—complete ones. Unlike the scraps that recent generations of Genizah scholars had relegated themselves to studying, these manuscripts were refreshingly whole, and they held the promise of new and entirely unanticipated information.

The 350 newly discovered documents in the Geneva collection also represented a cross-section of the Genizah as a whole. Among them were a Hebrew/Greek Bible palimpsest, previously unknown variants of the Babylonian Talmud, a Hebrew account of the journeys of Alexander the Great, and a funeral poem eulogizing a man who died the day before his wedding. One manuscript tells the story of a woman named Wuhsha, a female banker who had an extramarital affair through which she bore a child, and was consequently expelled by the local rabbis from the synagogue on Yom Kippur. Evidently, the condemnation failed to turn Wuhsha away forever, for in her will she left money to the Jewish community.[5]

All of these treasures, of course, came from one box in one library in Europe. It begs an obvious question: How many other troves of documents from the Cairo Genizah lay hidden and awaiting our discovery? How many more new discoveries of Cairo's medieval Jewish treasures can we expect to find in the future?

The Challenge of Scattered Collections

There are currently dozens of Genizah collections around the world. Second in size to the Genizah collection at Cambridge is that of The Jewish Theological Seminary in New York. The Seminary purchased most of its thirty to thirty-five thousand documents from Elkan Nathan Adler when he sold his library in the 1920s. There is a large collection in St. Petersburg, Russia, originally acquired by Abraham Firkovitch. Another sits at the Bodleian Library at Oxford University, joined by one at John Rylands University in Manchester and one at the British Library in London. Smaller collections can be found at libraries in Budapest, Strasbourg, Philadelphia, Vienna, Washington, D.C., Jerusalem, Paris, and Oslo. Several other universities and libraries throughout the United States, Europe, and Israel each hold tiny collections of Genizah documents, usually numbering ten or fewer manuscripts.

As S. D. Goitein realized when he traveled to a dozen cities to examine Genizah collections, the scattered nature of the manuscripts has long bedeviled Genizah scholarship. Even studying what the manuscripts could teach about a single topic—say, a certain prayer in the Jewish worship service—could demand that a scholar travel to several cities around the world. Photocopies could help, but at least until recently, the copies were often blurry and of unreliable quality; relying on them tended to be a poor substitute for looking at the originals.

Furthermore, even after more than a century of Genizah research, a comprehensive catalogue of all of the materials from the Cairo Genizah has yet to be written. Individual collections have been catalogued, but some only partially and others not at all.

The diffuse nature of the Genizah collections and the absence of a full catalogue of its contents would have been frustrating enough if it applied to a library or an ordered archive, but the mess and chaos of the Genizah make the situation even worse. As documents sat for centuries in the Genizah pile, occasionally getting shoveled out for synagogue renovations or grabbed by dealers eager to earn a quick profit, many of them fell apart. Sometimes, the bindings of books tore in the press of Genizah papers. Sometimes, pages ripped in half.

In 1920, for example, Jacob Mann came across two letters in Cambridge—one in Hebrew, another in Judeo-Arabic, each on opposite sides of a single sheet. The letters were about an international controversy regarding who would serve as the head of the Palestinian academy, becoming the Palestinian gaon, during the mid-eleventh century. Mann published the document along with his tentative interpretation as to its meaning. Interpreting it was difficult, however, because the top half of the page was missing, and Mann had to gather what information he could from only the remaining bottom half.

Then, in 1976, Dr. Mark Cohen, a student of Goitein's, discovered a similar document at The Jewish Theological Seminary. It, too, looked to be from the eleventh century; it had a Hebrew let-

ter on one side, a Judeo-
Arabic letter on the other,
and it was about an international controversy over
the Palestinian Gaonate.
The document was diffi-
cult to understand, how-
ever, because the bottom
half of it was missing.

Eleventh-century Genizah document, from The
Jewish Theological Seminary, front and back of
the same sheet, published 1976

But Cohen had stud-
ied Mann's work and
suspected that this manu-
script and the one Mann
had published fifty-six
years earlier must some-
how be related. Studying it
further, he soon realized
that they were two pieces
of the same pair of letters.
Looking at photos of the
Cambridge manuscript, he
saw that the two docu-
ments fit together like two
pieces of a jigsaw puzzle.
The two letters had originally been one—one docu-
ment that had somehow
torn in half during the
centuries it had spent in
the Genizah. Mark Cohen

Eleventh-century Genizah document, from
Cambridge University Library, front and back of
the same sheet, published 1920

had discovered what scholars now call a "join."

And all of a sudden, the controversy that the letters described
made perfect sense.[6]

Only because Cohen realized that these two documents fit
together was he able to fully understand them. Scholars have

chanced upon other joins, as well. Some connect only two pieces; others connect more. Some of the pieces remained near their partners in the Genizah and on their subsequent journeys; others, as in the case of this letter, are now separated from their partners by thousands of miles.

In one particularly noteworthy example, in 1979, Dr. Michael Klein of the Hebrew Union College–Jewish Institute of Religion in Jerusalem pieced together nine separate fragments of an Aramaic Bible translation from different parts of the Cambridge collection, adding them to three others that German scholar Paul Kahle had joined in 1930. Printing an image of the reassembled manuscript in the *Hebrew Union College Annual* required a nine-panel centerfold.[7]

We now know of nearly three hundred thousand documents that once sat in the Cairo Genizah. Thanks to the tireless work of generations of scholars, thousands upon thousands of these documents have been catalogued and studied; numerous parchment and paper fragments have been joined to form more complete documents, if not always whole ones. Archives have been created, researchers have hopped between American and European cities, conservation methods have grown more and more sophisticated. A library's worth of books and articles have been written about the Genizah. But even into the twenty-first century, a comprehensive catalogue, a central database, had not been assembled. It was a situation that called out for a remedy.

11

The Friedberg Genizah Project

Scholars have dreamt of cleaning up the Genizah chaos almost since the material first came to light in the 1890s. Ever since Solomon Schechter shared his vision of a unified library that would become the century's "Greatest Historical Work on Jewish lore,"[1] the idea of transforming the heaps of Genizah documents scattered in libraries throughout the world into an organized and accessible collection had become a recurring theme in Genizah literature. In fact, during the very year Schechter revealed his find, David Kaufmann, a scholar and collector from Budapest, envisioned the time "when all the treasures of the Genizah will become revealed."[2]

Over the years, experts in all areas of Genizah studies—Talmud, Geonic literature, historical documents, and so forth—envisioned similar collections of the materials in their own areas of specialization. In 1949, Menahem Zulay echoed Schechter's dream of a single, all-encompassing Genizah collection.[3] With the Genizah material collected and published, the scholars hoped they would no longer need to dig, haggle, finagle, and travel great distances to study it. Instead, they would just need to walk to the library bookshelf.

Albert Friedberg Enters the Picture

In 1999, an erudite and philanthropic Canadian businessman decided that it might be a good idea to transcribe the contents of

Albert D. Friedberg

the Cairo Genizah—particularly its Judeo-Arabic material—a decision that would prove to fulfill the century-old dream of Genizah scholars. Not only would it make the Genizah documents accessible as never before, but it would also usher in a new era in Genizah studies.

The businessman was Albert D. Friedberg, of Toronto, Ontario. Born in 1946 to an Orthodox Jewish family in Lyon, France, Friedberg moved with his family to Montevideo, Uruguay, when he was a small child. There the Friedbergs remained until shortly after Albert became a bar mitzvah, when they moved to Baltimore, and Albert's parents enrolled him in the Ner Yisroel Yeshiva, a prominent Orthodox rabbinic training academy that had been founded in 1933. Albert Friedberg later moved into secular academia, receiving an undergraduate degree from Johns Hopkins University and an MBA from Columbia. He now runs the Friedberg Mercantile Group, a prominent brokerage firm and hedge fund in Toronto.

Albert Friedberg shed the black hat of his yeshiva background when he entered the world of high finance, but he remained an observant Jew and avid student of Jewish texts. For several years during the 1990s, he and his friend James Diamond, an attorney who would later become a professor of Jewish studies at Waterloo University, regularly got together to study Maimonides's philosophical work *The Guide for the Perplexed*. Friedberg's love of Jewish study—particularly for Maimonides, Geonic responsa, and other medieval works—became far more than a passing interest. He was quickly becoming a scholar in his own right.[4]

In December 1997, Friedberg attended the annual meeting of the American Association of Jewish Research, in Boston.[5] The gathering celebrated the centenary of the "discovery" of the Cairo Genizah, and one of the lectures was delivered by Professor Neil Danzig, of The Jewish Theological Seminary. The talk, entitled "Geonic Jurisprudence from the Cairo Genizah: An Appreciation of Early Scholarship," was a broad-based summary of Genizah research beginning in the late nineteenth century. Danzig focused on research into Geonic literature, but he also provided a broad and far-reaching look at Genizah scholarship since the days of Solomon Schechter. His lecture reviewed the research of several leading scholars who had worked on Geonic literature from the Genizah. It described the documents they studied, how they drew from one another's work, and the lasting significance of their research. The picture he painted was of a dynamic and growing field of research—one that expands in each generation as new scholars discover "new" documents and share new insights about them. Along the way, he conveyed a sense of the disorder of the Genizah manuscripts in their current state and the difficulty of researching such a far-flung, disorganized mass of documents. In a footnote to his conclusion, he commented:

> As part of the celebration of the centennial of the "discovery" of the Genizah, together with the accounting of the bounty the Genizah has bestowed upon us, we must note the frustrations that still make Genizah research difficult and thus, the domain of relatively few scholars. Despite complete access to most collections (made greatly easier with the arrival of microfilming after World War II)—now including materials previously hidden behind the "Iron Curtain"—the delays in cataloguing Genizah collections continue to hinder scholars. To a large degree, the clarion call of M. Zulay in 1949 for an international effort to classify and publish Genizah material in all areas fell upon deaf ears.... Only in the very recent past have catalogues of major collections been appearing.... It is my hope that these efforts will continue until all material in all collections

is properly catalogued and the material therein made accessible to scholars.[6]

Danzig's assessment of the situation was accurate. By the late 1990s the terrain of Genizah studies had grown difficult to navigate. In addition to the lack of a comprehensive catalogue, manuscript dispersion, and unstudied documents, there was a parallel chaos created by the 120,000-plus books and articles written in conjunction with the Genizah material.[7] This growing library of Genizah scholarship was just as disorganized as the manuscripts it studied.

In these conditions, it was impossible for a scholar to know whether he or she had examined all available pages of a single manuscript. Though indexes of scholarly articles were widely available, they weren't always complete, and even when they were, actually securing previous research on any Genizah document or topic was often very difficult. To make matters worse, some collection owners had a highly proprietary view of their collections. Many librarians felt that the manuscripts belonged to their institutions. Scholars could study them, of course, but only if they came to the library in person to do so. It was an increasingly intolerable situation.

Several scholars who attended the lecture in Boston that day noticed Friedberg's interest in Danzig's talk. Speaking with him afterward, they realized that this businessman had not attended simply as a back-row spectator; rather, he was eager to become an active participant in the world of Jewish scholarship. Would he be interested, they asked, in helping improve the current state of the Cairo Genizah? If so, several scholars in Israel, the United States, and Europe might want to speak with him further about some ways he could help.

The idea captured Friedberg's imagination. If the manuscripts could be transcribed and a comprehensive catalogue finally assembled, then maybe some order could come to the chaos that had so plagued the Genizah world for the past century.

The Friedberg Genizah Project Takes Shape

The scholars spoke with one another and had further discussions with Friedberg himself. Slowly, out of the conversations an idea began to take shape—the Friedberg Genizah Project (FGP). The new initiative, funded by Friedberg, supported by universities and libraries around the world, and directed by the world's foremost Genizah experts, would assemble once and for all a unified catalogue and digital database of the Cairo Genizah manuscripts. Now, after more than a century of Genizah studies, all of the information would be accessible in a single "place"—albeit a virtual one.

The timing of the idea couldn't have been better. Past generations of Genizah caretakers had to rely on handwritten card files and other primitive methods of cataloguing. Now, however, in the computer age, a host of newly available high-tech tools that previous generations could hardly imagine were available to the FGP. In pursuing their goal, the people working on this new initiative could employ database technology, high-resolution imaging, advanced word processing, Internet communications, and many other new technologies to transform the study of Genizah manuscripts. A new generation of Genizah scholarship was indeed at hand.

Friedberg selected a board consisting of the best of the best in the Genizah world: Professor Neil Danzig, of JTS, whose lecture first sparked Friedberg's interest in the Genizah; New York University's Lawrence Schiffman, one of America's most eminent scholars of Jewish studies; and Yaakov Elman, a prominent Yeshiva University Talmudist. Later, he expanded the board to include Stefan Reif of Cambridge; Menahem Ben-Sasson, Haggai Ben-Shammai, and Menahem Kahana, all of Hebrew University in Jerusalem; and Mordechai Friedman, of Tel Aviv University. Friedberg also hired a friend of his from Toronto to manage the operations of the project out of a Lakewood, New Jersey, office. The scholars in the group were the Genizah giants of the generation. Like Solomon Schechter a century before, Albert Friedberg had assembled a true Genizah dream team.

At the first meeting of the FGP Advisory Board on October 21, 1999, at New York University (NYU), Stefan Reif, director of the Cambridge University's Taylor-Schechter Genizah Research Unit, declared, "Gentlemen, what we should do is just digitize all of the documents." It was an audacious idea. Although the computer age was already in full swing and digital imaging was becoming popular, nobody had ever undertaken a project even remotely approaching the magnitude of what Reif proposed. It was as if he had suggested digitizing the entire public library—an exciting prospect, but daunting in scope.

At the time, digitizing all known Genizah documents would have cost about twenty-four million dollars.[8] Friedberg had decided to be generous in his support of Genizah research, but not *that* generous. Reif's idea would have to wait. For the time being, the FGP would continue to focus on systematically identifying and cataloguing the fragments.

From early on, it was clear that gathering a catalogue would be a very difficult process. Several libraries had already catalogued their collections, but others hadn't. Many of the existing catalogues were inaccurate, others were incomplete, and some, like Bernard Chapira's listing of the documents in the Mosseri collection, had disappeared altogether.

Furthermore, the FGP needed to figure out precisely which collections to include in the catalogue. Sometimes, it was obvious— the large collections, such those at Cambridge and JTS, were shoo-ins. But what about the Firkovitch collection in St. Petersburg? Some of its documents were certainly from the Cairo Genizah, but others came from elsewhere. Firkovitch never provided much

Advisory Board of the Friedberg Genizah Project, founding meeting; left to right, Neil Danzig, Yaakov Elman, Albert Friedberg, Menahem Ben-Sasson, Menahem Kahana, Stefan Reif, Haggai Ben-Shammai, Lawrence Schiffman, Mordechai Friedman, Rabbi Reuven Rubelow

detail about where he obtained his collection, and he was also a bit of a scoundrel, known for forging manuscripts when he couldn't find the genuine ones he wanted. Should his manuscripts be included? What about other collections of doubtful provenance—should they be in the catalogue?

For that matter, where *were* all of the Genizah documents, anyway? The whereabouts of the larger collections were common knowledge, but there were dozens of tiny collections with one hundred or fewer documents. Did anyone have a list of all of these tiny Genizah caches?

And, of course, studying antiquarian manuscripts is notoriously difficult, and so many items in Genizah collections were difficult to identify. How should a shred of paper reading, "... Go ... Moses ... wife for three years ..." be properly catalogued?

Friedberg, his board, and his staff soon realized that even what had seemed the simple task of assembling a catalogue would first demand extensive groundwork. To catalogue the documents, they needed to be able to identify them, and to identify them, they would need to transcribe them and sometimes even translate them. And of course to do any of this, they needed to know where to find the documents in the first place.

Due to these and other difficulties, the work began slowly. Its first academic director was NYU's Lawrence Schiffman, who was succeeded by James Diamond in 2002. The FGP drafted dozens of leading Jewish studies scholars, dividing them into research teams assigned to explore different types of Genizah documents. The list of subjects assigned to the various teams reflects the enormous variety of material they needed to study: Linguistics, Philosophy, Theology and Polemics, Halakhic Midrashim (Legal Bible Commentaries), Bibliography, Judeo-Arabic Halakhic Literature, Judeo-Arabic Biblical Exegesis, Firkovitch Collections, Aggadic Midrashim (Narrative Bible Commentaries), Responsa, Talmud Commentaries and Halakhic Literature (Hebrew), Identification, Liturgy, Late Documentary Material (Hebrew), Princeton Documentary Material (Goitein),

Judeo-Persian, Talmudic Literature, *Yerushalmi, Midrash Eicha Raba* (a commentary on the book of Lamentations), Magic, and Ladino (Judeo-Spanish).

A senior scholar was assigned to lead each team and to assemble several others to help examine the assigned material. For the first time since the days of Solomon Schechter—and in some ways for the first time ever—a serious effort to coordinate Genizah research was under way.

To do the job right, the scholars needed to study not only the manuscripts themselves, but also a century's worth of Genizah research, ancillary information that would help identify the materials, and more. Five years into the massive job, the FGP had barely made a dent in the task it had taken on.

Digitizing the Genizah

By 2004, digital imaging technology had both significantly improved and grown much less expensive than when the FGP began five years earlier. Scanners worked more quickly, produced images of far higher quality, could photograph both large and tiny documents, and did all of this work with considerably less danger of damaging the original manuscripts. Moreover, no longer would digitizing all of the Genizah fragments cost tens of millions of dollars, but only a few hundred thousand. Suddenly, the FGP directors realized, Stefan Reif's bold 1999 suggestion to digitize the entire corpus of Genizah literature had become a very real possibility.

It wouldn't be easy, of course. Digitizing the Genizah would demand an efficient set of protocols, new software and algorithms, and the active cooperation of librarians, scholars, technicians, and countless other stakeholders all over the world.

Clearly, they needed the right person at the helm. Ideally, the leader of such an effort would be an experienced and creative computer scientist who was capable of creating the kind of software and hardware that the job demanded. The person would be well versed in Jewish sacred literature and fluent in both Hebrew and Arabic, appreciate the value of the Cairo Genizah and the role that it could play in Jewish studies, and have the ability to turn to the effort on a full-time basis. In addition, the person would need great people skills—the wisdom to know

Professor Yaacov Choueka

when to use a gentle touch and when to adopt a tougher stance to get things done.

That's when the FGP turned to Professor Yaacov Choueka.

Yaacov Choueka (pronounced *shə-WAY-kah*) was born in Cairo in 1936. His father, Chacham Aharon Choueka, was a leading rabbi in that city, and his great-grandfather had been the chief rabbi of Aleppo, Syria. At the age of twenty, Choueka moved to Israel, where Hebrew University in Jerusalem awarded him a master's degree in 1957 and a PhD in mathematics in 1971. He spent most of his career on the faculty of the department of mathematics and computer science at Bar Ilan University in suburban Tel Aviv, where he became a full professor in 1990. Over the years, Choueka led several innovative data-processing projects in both academia and the business world, and the methodologies he developed to handle large corpuses of information earned him wide acclaim. Before his Genizah work, he was perhaps best known for directing the Bar Ilan Responsa Project—a massive, user-friendly database of tens of thousands of rabbinic responsa dating back to ancient times. His work on this database earned him the prestigious Israel Prize in 2007.

In 2005, FGP board member Menahem Ben-Sasson called Yaacov Choueka, who was then sixty-nine years old. The Friedberg Genizah Project was stuck. They had decided to digitize all of the Genizah manuscripts and had reached out to several computer scientists for help, but nothing had come of their efforts. Ben-Sasson asked whether Professor Choueka would be willing to meet with him and another Friedberg staffer to discuss whether he might be able to help. In short order, the FGP hired Choueka as its chief computerization scientist. A computerization wing called Genazim opened in Jerusalem, and a team of fifteen programmers and consultants were hired as staff.

Choueka got right to work. His first step was to get a full listing of the various Genizah libraries around the world and a count of the number of documents in each collection. The research teams had a general idea as to where the various Genizah manuscript collections were located, but there still was no firm, official listing that accounted for them all.

One reason for the lack of such an inventory is that counting Genizah manuscripts is a notoriously difficult business. For starters, very few libraries that own collections of any size have even bothered to try. Their collections consist of bundles of papers with writing in obscure languages, and many of the documents have disintegrated into so many pieces that it is difficult to determine where one ends and another begins. It was not uncommon for librarians to remove Genizah manuscripts from the box in which they arrived only to find hundreds of little crumbled scraps still lying in the bottom of the box. Were these flakes pieces of the larger documents that the librarian had just removed? Did they represent whole documents that had completely disintegrated? Were they sections of larger manuscripts now housed in other collections? It was hard to tell. Rather than catalogue or even count the manuscripts, most librarians simply stored them unprocessed and waited for interested scholars to come study the collections.

Choueka and his staff conducted a systematic survey of the Genizah world and eventually came up with a list of fifty-six individual manuscript collections. Some of them, such as those in Cambridge, Manchester, and New York, held thousands of documents. Others, in places such as Los Angeles, Ann Arbor, and the Vatican, held twenty or fewer.

Even after this survey, however, the number of Genizah collections and documents remains fluid. In addition to the fifty-six col-

Inventory of Pages of Cairo Genizah Manuscripts[9]

(italicized numbers are estimates)

LIBRARY	IMAGES
Baltimore, Goldsmith Museum, Chizuk Amuno Congregation	1
Birmingham, England[10]	150
Budapest, Hungarian Academy of Sciences	1,348
Cambridge, Cambridge University Library[11]	198,000
Cambridge, Westminster College[12]	2,500
Cincinnati, Hebrew Union College	564
Geneva, Bibliothèque Publique et Universitaire	272
Haifa, University	45
Heidelberg, University	3
Heidelberg, University, Institute of Papyrology	34
Jerusalem, Ben Zvi Institute	3
Jerusalem, Bernard Chapira Collection	2
Jerusalem, Central Archive	1
Jerusalem, Jewish National University Library	585
London, British Library[13]	*10,000*
Los Angeles, Gifford Combs	15
Los Angeles, Steve Weiss	2
Manchester, John Rylands University[14]	*11,000*
New York, Jewish Theological Seminary	30,398
New York, Yeshiva University	2
Oxford, Bodleian Library[15]	*25,000*
Paris, Alliance Israélite Universelle	6,629
Paris, Institut de France	143
Philadelphia, University of Pennsylvania	897
Ramat Gan, Bar Ilan University	6
Strasbourg, Bibliothèque Nationale et Universitaire	1,119
Tel Aviv, University	28
Toronto, University, Friedberg Collection	64
Turin, Biblioteca Nazionale Universitaria	41
Vienna, National Library	392
Washington, D.C., Smithsonian Institution, Freer Gallery	51
Various smaller collections[16]	2,500
Total	*291,793*
Collections in Moscow, Kiev, and St. Petersburg remain uncounted.	

lections listed, the FGP identified twenty-three small collections about which they had little information. Some of them may have sold their fragments; others may have been lost; still others may hold precious Genizah treasures that remain undiscovered. Still, the FGP inventory was the most complete accounting of its kind. At last a comprehensive picture of the whereabouts of the Cairo Genizah documents had begun to emerge.

Once Choueka and his staff had gathered their inventory, their next step was to digitize the documents. Obtaining high-resolution photographs of hundreds of thousands of manuscripts from dozens of different places around the world raised new and difficult challenges. Would librarians agree to have their collections scanned? What kind of machinery would do the scanning? How were the images to be formatted? Since so many different technicians would need to be involved in scanning the manuscripts, how and according to what protocols was the FGP to maintain uniformity among the many images it sought to collect? What image resolution would they use? What should be the color of the background? How should they deal with different fragments that may or may not have been part of the same document? And most of all, how in the world were they ever going to scan such a huge amount of material?

Under Yaacov Choueka's leadership, the FGP confronted all of these questions, established digitization protocols, and moved ahead. The manuscripts would be photographed with high-resolution, 600 dpi cameras, producing images of a far higher quality than the 400 dpi then standard. The manuscripts would be laid out in standardized ways and scanned under specifically predetermined lighting conditions. The images would be in full color, and there would be photographs of each side of every fragment, regardless of its size. Even blank sides were to be imaged; doing so was the best way to confirm that one side of the paper was indeed blank, and sometimes the high-resolution images would allow previously unnoticed writing to become visible. For maximum contrast, the documents would be photographed against a background of a particular shade of royal blue, which Choueka defined with specific numerical coordinates. In time, the staff at the Cambridge University Library gave that color a name—Choueka Blue.

Initially, only a few of the smaller collections signed on. Many of the libraries felt ownership over their collections and were reluctant to open them up to the public. One library was planning to sell their collection, and feared that public access would reduce the monetary value of their holdings. Owners of the larger collections, particularly JTS and Cambridge, faced the added challenge of complexity. Scanning that many manuscripts—tens of thousands at JTS and hundreds of thousands at Cambridge—would take staff, lab space, and an enormous amount of time. Even with Friedberg's financial support, it was not a decision to be made lightly.

More generally, at the time, it was difficult for anyone to imagine undertaking a project of this magnitude. "When we began this activity in 2006," Yaacov Choueka recalls, "digital imaging was really in its infancy. Few professional photographers understood its complexities, and the expensive equipment needed to do the job was not widely available." The Friedberg Genizah Project was pioneering unknown territory in manuscript imaging, and at first it looked as if it might be difficult to persuade anyone to join them in their efforts.

The Jewish Theological Seminary agreed to digitize its images in early 2006, becoming the first of the major Genizah libraries to sign on. Cambridge was not far behind, but arranging for such a gigantic catalogue to be scanned was very difficult, and it took over a year for the FGP and Cambridge to finalize all of the details of their agreement.

Then, one by one, most of the other libraries followed suit.

The moral force of the FGP argument was strong. The documents of the Cairo Genizah were precious treasures, and people everywhere should be able to see them. Scholars around the world had screamed foul when, for decades, a small group of Catholic academicians in Jerusalem had refused to share the Dead Sea Scrolls, and now no self-respecting librarian would ever want to be accused of similar wrongdoing. Furthermore, the FGP was offering to digitize the libraries' collections free of charge. It was a deal that few of them could refuse.

Yaacov Choueka developed an efficient, production-line mechanism by which a single technician could photograph hundreds of images each day. Under his careful supervision and with FGP funding, JTS and Cambridge hired teams to scan images of their documents. The FGP sent technicians and equipment around the world to photograph the documents in the other participating collections.

Although most of the owners of the world's Genizah collections agreed to participate, a few declined. One was John Rylands University in Manchester, which housed eleven thousand manuscripts and had already scanned their collection using their own technology. The Bodleian Library at Oxford (twenty-five thousand manuscripts) and the British Library in London (ten thousand manuscripts) also declined to participate. The FGP staff and directors remain optimistic that these institutions will soon link up with the FGP. There are also collections in the former Soviet Union— in Kiev, Moscow, and St. Petersburg. Most of the St. Petersburg material consists of what Abraham Firkovitch brought there from Cairo, which may or may not have been from the Genizah at the Ben Ezra Synagogue. The FGP has made repeated attempts to reach out to the caretakers of all of the FSU collections, but they have been unable to connect in any meaningful way.

As of this writing, Cambridge University is scanning approximately twenty-five hundred documents each week and hopes to complete the digitization of its entire collection by 2013. The collections at all other participating institutions are fully scanned.

Once FGP had inventoried the Genizah collections and put its imaging processes into place, however, their work was far from over. Step three involved figuring out how to store the data, categorize it, and make it available to users.

The results are now visible on the FGP website, which makes accessible the many thousands of images, countless transcriptions, bibliographies, document identifications, and cataloguing data. It lists each individual collection of documents, indicating the number of images, bibliographical references, identifications, and so on for that collection. The FGP website also allows users to search for manuscripts based on cataloguing data—the author of the document, the date it was written, its size, language, layout, or any of several other attributes.

Thus, if you are interested in seeing all of the Cairo Genizah's twelfth-century Persian palimpsests written in cursive Oriental script, containing text from the Babylonian Talmud, and that have holes, you can perform precisely such a search. When you do, you will learn that the Genizah contains no such documents—and then you can proceed to your next search.

"No other website that deals with manuscripts does so the way we do in terms of breadth of coverage, depth of information, etc.," says Yaacov Choueka. "It is a collection of information, images, and data the likes of which has never been assembled before."[17]

The "New" Cairo Genizah

The work of the Friedberg Genizah Project didn't stop there. The staff went on to address a problem that has plagued everyone who has studied the Genizah since it was discovered: the fragmenting, jumbling, and crumbling of the documents over the centuries. And for more than a century since the discovery, scholars have had to contend with the global scattering of the manuscripts, as individual documents often separated into two or more parts and ended up stored in different libraries located in different countries. It was as if someone had opened many hundreds of jigsaw puzzle boxes, mixed all of the pieces together, and then doled them out to puzzlers around the world.

What does a researcher do if a piece of parchment has been torn in half or into pieces and doesn't fit together with any other fragments in the collection? How are archivists to catalogue a small scrap of paper bearing only a few words? How does that scrap fall into the overall count? If the words are from a biblical text, the manuscript could be part of a Bible, of course, but it could also be part of a book that *quotes* the Bible. How should such a document be identified?

Yaacov Choueka wasn't certain, but he thought that computer technology had advanced to the point where it might be able help. So when the FGP website became fully operational in May 2008, he took on a new challenge—crafting the technology needed to identify "set[s] of manuscript fragments that are known to originate from the same original work." He called them "Genizah joins."[18]

Developing this technology, of course would be a difficult challenge. In the past, scholars who had identified joins had done so from the gut: "Hey, this document looks a little like that other one I saw in Cambridge twelve years ago ..." They usually made those connections based on a host of subtle clues—the size of the document, its content, shape, condition, and color, the handwriting of the scribe who created it, and so on. Most of these criteria are far easier for people to identify than for computers. For example, to recognize someone's handwriting, we look for patterns, similarities, and peculiarities in the way that person forms certain letters. We look at the angle of the letters, the width of the pen strokes, and a host of other factors, many of which are so subtle that we cannot articulate them. "How do I recognize this handwriting?" we might bluster. "Well ... I just do!"

But that's not good enough for a computer. To develop a program to recognize handwriting and all of the other factors needed to join together documents that had been separated for centuries, Choueka would need to teach the computer skills that no machine had ever learned before. He worked with a team of experts, and drew on the latest and most advanced high-tech wizardry—artificial intelligence technology, information retrieval systems, and even the face-recognition software that governments now use to identify terrorists.

In 2009, the team announced that it had developed a system to allow a computer to analyze scanned images of Genizah fragments and to suggest joins with other Genizah fragments in its

Biblical passages (Exodus) from the same volume, now housed in Geneva and New York, "rejoined" by FGP technology

database. Based on complex algorithms, formulas, and programming tools, it involves having the computer describe everything it can about the fragments it analyzes. It looks at whatever previous research has been done on the document that might help with identification, and it analyzes the document's shape, size, color, and other attributes. It also performs a complex analysis of the handwriting, which allows it to suggest not only joins, but also other documents that might have been written by the same scribe.

Before this technology, scholars had identified a total of about four thousand Genizah joins. Now, with the new tools that Yaacov Choueka and his team have developed, one technician working part-time for six months has already identified several hundred more.[19] As they refine the program and run more manuscripts through it, Choueka is confident that he will be able to reconnect thousands of additional manuscripts that have fallen apart in the Genizah crush.

Ultimately, the goal of the new joins technology is simple—to reconstitute the Cairo Genizah in its "original" state. In other words, the FGP is trying to build a computerized version of an imagined Cairo Genizah—one whose every document has been preserved not in the damaged state it probably was in when it first made its way to the Genizah, but even earlier, when it was new and

Server, front and back; the computerization center of the Friedberg Genizah Project, Jerusalem, is the new "home" of the Cairo Genizah

pristine and undamaged. It is a high-tech effort to transform the tattered and torn documents of the Cairo Genizah into a cohesive, organized library and allow them to shine forth more brightly than they have for centuries.

Once housed in a dusty attic in Cairo, the vast majority of all of the manuscripts of the Cairo Genizah will soon rest under a single roof—albeit a virtual one. The new "home" of the Genizah is now a large machine in a high-rise office building in Jerusalem.

The people who amassed the Cairo Genizah wanted to save their documents, even though they probably weren't interested in reading them ever again. Now, with the work of the Friedberg Genizah Project, anyone who wants to read the documents will be able to do so, even when they can't actually touch the documents themselves.

Friedberg's Dream for the Future

Even after all of these great accomplishments, Albert Friedberg is still going strong. In 2008, he earned a PhD from the University of Toronto, with a dissertation entitled "An Evaluation of Maimonides' Enumeration of the 613 Commandments, with Special Emphasis on the Positive Commandments." In May 2010, the FGP website linked to another Friedberg-sponsored initiative—a digital library of about one hundred thousand manuscripts from Yemenite genizahs.

There are also thousands of documents collectively known as the European Genizah—old Jewish papers looted by Christians and recycled as endpapers in Christian books. In time, Friedberg hopes to digitize them, as well.

Albert Friedberg's dream is to digitize and make available all of the world's antiquarian Jewish manuscripts—every single one of them. Speaking of Genizah research and of Jewish manuscript scholarship in general, he says, "I want the world to work on this. I want to democratize it. I don't want there to be only twenty to thirty scholars involved in manuscript research. We can't let the Genizah documents end up like the Dead Sea Scrolls. We must make the Genizah available to everyone."[20]

Albert Friedberg's generosity and devotion to the preservation and dissemination of this priceless trove of Jewish manuscripts is well on its way to doing just that.

The Cairo Genizah in February 2010

Conclusion
Sacred Treasure

Very few people have ever heard of the Cairo Genizah. A handful of scholars study its manuscripts; technicians digitize the collections; librarians conserve and catalogue them; and an assortment of bloggers, collectors, and self-proclaimed manuscript nerds read about them. But with these few exceptions, the massive Genizah collections remain almost as obscure today as they were before Solomon Schechter discovered the Genizah over a century ago. Even many of the people we might expect to know about the Genizah—rabbis, educated Jewish laypeople, medieval historians—have either never heard of it or are only vaguely aware of its existence.

During my research for this book, people who learned that I was writing about the Cairo Genizah usually responded with either a glazed-over look in their eyes or a heartfelt and enthusiastic "Gesundheit!" In fact, one of the only knowledgeable responses I have ever received came when I was at the hospital for some minor knee surgery. As the attendants wheeled me into the operating room and made their final preparations, they asked what I did for a living. "I'm a rabbi," I said, "and I'm also writing a book."

"About what?" they asked, preparing the anesthesia.

"It's about something called the Cairo Genizah."

By that point, the anesthesiologist had my breathing mask in hand and was ready to proceed. His kind face hovered over mine, he smiled, and he spoke in a gentle, soothing voice. "Oh, I know what that is," he said, the gas hissing out of the mask. "It's a repository for damaged and destroyed Jewish documents. The one in Cairo was the largest one of all. Yes … it was very important … very important, indeed."

Then, he placed the mask over my face, and I never saw him again.

Why is it that so few people aside from a few scholars and my anesthesiologist have ever heard of the Cairo Genizah? One factor, of course, is money. Collections of old Jewish documents never command the mega-budgets of King Tut, the Mona Lisa, and other antiquities. As a result, worldwide tours, glitzy documentaries, and other high-profile media appearances are all but unknown in the Genizah world. Antiquities resources usually go to mummies and paintings, not crumbling old synagogue documents.

Related to the lack of money is a lack of personnel. Despite the massive size of the Genizah collections, there are remarkably few people who study and care for them on a full-time basis. In fact, the only library in the world with a full-time Genizah staff is the one at Cambridge, but at any given time it numbers only three to five professionals. The library with the second-largest Genizah collection, JTS, devotes a great deal of staff time to its manuscripts, but nobody works on the Genizah full-time. Its staff, like the staffs of the other major Genizah collections, is charged with caring not only for the Genizah manuscripts but also for other library material as well. Furthermore, most scholars who study the Genizah do so within the context of a broader field of expertise. Maimonides scholars study the Maimonides documents, liturgists study the prayers, and social historians study the letters, court records, and business papers. Thus, even the greatest experts in Genizah studies usually deal with its contents only on a part-time basis.

The Genizah, in short, lacks the worldwide team of full-time scholars and caretakers that it would take to bring its manuscripts into public awareness.

But there must be more to the story. After all, in contrast to the Genizah, *everyone* seems to know about the Dead Sea Scrolls. The Scrolls get world tours, TV documentaries, and worldwide attention. But the Dead Sea Scrolls suffer from budgetary and personnel issues just like the Genizah documents do. Plus, they came on the scene more recently than the Genizah, so there hasn't been much time to research them, and there are far fewer Dead Sea Scrolls than there are Genizah documents. Why do they get so much more attention?

Here too, there are several factors in play. First, the Dead Sea Scrolls are about twice as old as the Genizah documents, and their antiquity is part of their allure. Christianity is also a factor. Many of the Dead Sea Scrolls are thought to have been written during the first century CE, and some scholars suggest that they might reveal important lessons about early Christianity. As a result, the Scrolls draw an enthusiastic and interested audience from among the world's two billion Christians. Genizah manuscripts, on the other hand, come from a medieval Jewish community, so their audience draws from a far smaller pool. They have much to teach about medieval Islam, of course, but very few Muslims are aware of their value.

There is also the mystique factor. For decades after their discovery, the Dead Sea Scrolls remained the exclusive purview of a small group of Catholic scholars in Jerusalem who refused to share them with anyone. Other scholars howled in protest, but it wasn't until the 1990s that the Jerusalem scholars decided to begin releasing the Scrolls. Along the way, many wondered what it was about these old Scrolls that the Catholic Church was hiding. Did they contain some hidden truth that the Church didn't want anyone to know? Was there some dangerous and destructive revelation hidden in their words? By the late twentieth century, conspiracy theories abounded, and the Dead Sea Scrolls had gained a firm footing in public awareness.

The Genizah manuscripts, on the other hand, have always been available to anyone interested in seeing them. Librarians keep a close and protective eye on the manuscripts, of course, but only for security purposes. Nobody has ever tried to keep them from the public eye, and therefore nobody has ever imagined the existence of an international Genizah conspiracy as they have regarding the Scrolls.

The Genizah documents, however, are obscure for a reason that is more fundamental than any of these: the story the Genizah and its contents tell is difficult for people in today's world to understand. The manuscripts paint a picture that clashes with modern sensibilities. Their lessons about Jewish history, Jewish tradition, and Middle East relations, to take the three most important examples, stand in blatant conflict with widely accepted modern perceptions.

For Jews, the Genizah story contradicts much of what we thought we knew about Jewish history. For the most part, the modern Jewish conception of Jewish history follows the viewpoint of modern Zionism. "In ancient days," this view suggests, "the Jewish people thrived in the Land of Israel. But then foreign invaders destroyed the Temple in Jerusalem and expelled the Jewish nation from its land, thus beginning a dark, two-thousand-year period of homelessness and oppression. Throughout that entire time, Jews in exile yearned to return to their homeland, where they could live together in safety and freedom. Now, with the rise of the modern State of Israel, those dreams can finally come true."

It is a powerful national mythos. Like every national mythos, the story is true in some ways, grossly oversimplified in others, and a reflection of its people's deepest values and most heartfelt self-perceptions.

It is also, as we learn from the Genizah, fundamentally incorrect. Reading the Genizah documents, we read of a vibrant, prosperous Jewish community thriving one thousand years ago in Egypt, the very symbol of Jewish suffering and oppression. There, in the very heart of the "two thousand years of darkness," we find enlightenment, security, and success—not the oppression and suffering we have come to expect.

Israel's national anthem, "Hatikvah," speaks of "the hope of two thousand years to be a free people in our land." The Genizah people, on the other hand, were perfectly content to remain in Egypt. Israel's Declaration of Independence opens with these words:

> In the Land of Israel the Jewish people came into being. In this Land was shaped their spiritual, religious, and national character. Here they lived in sovereign independence. Here

they created a culture of national and universal import, and gave to the world the eternal Book of Books.

Exiled by force, still the Jewish people kept faith with their Land in all the countries of their dispersion, steadfast in their prayer and hope to return and here revive their political freedom.

Fired by this attachment of history and tradition, the Jews in every generation strove to renew their roots in the ancient homeland....[1]

To all of this, the overwhelming response of the Genizah would be, "Return to Israel? Us? No, we're doing fine here in Egypt, thank you. Here we feel at home, here we have friends, here we are active in politics and business and most other aspects of daily life. Arabic is our first language; Cairo is our hometown. Yes, we feel a deep bond with the Land of Israel—much more than many of our Jewish neighbors whose connections are with Babylonia—and, yes, we pray for a speedy return to the Land. But when we utter those prayers, we're talking about a distant messianic future. In the meantime, we're perfectly happy to stay here in Cairo."

Here, too, a comparison with the Dead Sea Scrolls can be instructive. Several of the Scrolls are now housed in the Israel Museum's magnificent Shrine of the Book, in Jerusalem—a beautiful building designed to resemble a lid of one of the jars in which they were discovered. The museum's website provides background information about the Scrolls:

The discovery of the Dead Sea Scrolls represents a turning point in the study of the history of the Jewish people in ancient times, *for never before has a literary treasure of such magnitude come to light.* Thanks to these remarkable finds, our knowledge of Jewish society in the Land of Israel during the Hellenistic and Roman periods as well as the origins of rabbinical Judaism and early Christianity has been greatly enriched.[2] [Italics added]

Aside from the questionable veracity of this claim about the magnitude of the Dead Sea Scrolls collection (the Genizah was hundreds of times larger), the statement also reveals part of the Israel Museum's impetus for so prominently featuring the Scrolls. These treasures were discovered in the Land of Israel—they testify to the Jewish people's ancient tie with the Land, and they feature an example of the rich past that Jews have lived and experienced in the Land. Moreover, many of the Scrolls themselves are early fragments of the Bible, the foundational text of the Jewish people. Therefore, not only do they put Jews on center stage in the ancient Land of Israel, but they also establish Israel as the most important staging ground of Jewish history. Were anyone to doubt the antiquity of the Jewish people's claim to the Land of Israel or the centrality and significance to Jewish history of what happened in that land, that person would just need a visit to the Shrine of the Book to set him or her straight.

There are, however, no such shrines for the Genizah documents. For the most part, the Genizah manuscripts—even the several hundred now in Israel—are safely encased in plastic and stored in albums on the shelves of locked rooms rather than housed in beautiful, crowded museums. While the Dead Sea Scrolls testify to a glorious past in the Land of Israel, the Genizah documents paint a vivid picture of Jewish life thriving *outside* the Land—and in *Egypt*, no less!

This is not to say there is any kind of concerted or systematic Israeli attempt to downplay the significance of the Genizah. To the contrary, many Israeli scholars and institutions do important Genizah research, and in recent years Israelis have grown increasingly aware of the Genizah treasures. It does, however, partly explain the obscurity of the Genizah manuscripts in modern Jewish life. The State of Israel has transformed Jewish life, but in the process, it has also defined Jewish history. The Cairo Genizah, on the other hand, tells a very different story—one that doesn't quite fit the narrative.

The Genizah also challenges the ways in which many modern Jews conceive of their religion. To the modern Jew—or at least to the modern Jew who is religiously observant—the central source of religious authority is not God or Torah, as it was in the past. Instead, as Arnold Eisen, now president of JTS, argued in 1997, "In contemporary American Judaism, the most pervasive ground of authority is not 'God' or 'faith,' not 'revelation' or even 'the ancestors,' but 'tradition.'"[3]

Why do you keep kosher? Why do you attend holiday worship services? Why do you mark the anniversaries of your parents' deaths with a memorial prayer? The answer of most Jews today will echo that of *Fiddler on the Roof*'s Tevye—"Tradition!"

What motivates many Jewish decisions today is the desire of Jews to connect themselves with the practices and perspectives of the Jewish past. Part of the reason Jewish worship is meaningful, my congregants tell me, is the knowledge that the words of the prayer book we recite today are the very same ones that Jews have always recited. Similarly, in the synagogue, certain Torah portions are read during certain weeks so that we and our fellow Jews can make our way through the entire Torah over the course of a year, because that's the traditional way to do it. Jewish parents everywhere encourage their children to marry Jews when they grow up; not to do so would be to break an ancient Jewish tradition.

In this view, Jewish tradition is a monolith—a static way of doing, being, and thinking Jewish that has remained unchanged since its inception in ancient times. We inherited the tradition from our parents, who inherited it from their parents, who inherited it from theirs. Yes, God forged the first link of this chain when God spoke to Moses on Mount Sinai, but to the tradition-oriented contemporary Jew, God isn't what's really important. What's really important is the length of the chain.

The Genizah, however, shows us that, at least during the Middle Ages, Jewish tradition was anything but monolithic. In fact, Jewish life back then was just as fractured and contentious as Jewish religious life is today. Cairo itself teemed with all kinds of clashing religious views, practices, and ideas. How long should we take to read through the Torah? What should the Jewish calendar look like? Which prayers should compose the Jewish worship service? Palestinian Jews quoted their rabbis, Babylonian Jews quoted theirs, and the Karaites rejected all rabbis on principle. The Genizah gives voice to all of these views and many more, showing in many of its surviving manuscripts that what we have come to see as the monolith of Jewish tradition was in reality far more complicated.

In time, as we now know, the Karaites faded into obscurity, the Jewish traditions of Palestine were mostly forgotten, and the Babylonian form of Judaism became the standard. But remember, the Ben Ezra Synagogue belonged to the Palestinian community. Although its members had close social and economic ties to their Babylonian counterparts in Cairo and elsewhere, the Genizah collection as a whole exhibits a palpable preference for Palestinian tradition. In this sense, the Cairo Genizah is a special gift, for it expresses not only a great chorus of Jewish voices from the past but also a chorus that has long been silent.

They say that history is written by the winners. The Cairo Genizah, however, gives voice to the losers, as well.

Furthermore, the Cairo Genizah clashes with modern sensibilities in terms of Arab-Jewish relations. While today it may seem that Jews and Arabs have *always* been one another's mortal enemies, the Genizah, of course, paints a different picture. The Genizah people usually got along with their Egyptian neighbors. Sometimes they were friends. Sometimes they were business associates. And sometimes, they were even lovers and spouses. In fact, as the Genizah research of S. D. Goitein, Mark Cohen, and others has repeatedly shown, for centuries Jews and Judaism thrived far more under Islam than it did under Christianity. There are exceptions, of course— Jews did sometimes experience persecution under Islam. But these incidents tended to be the exception rather than the rule.

Looking at the broad span of Jewish history, in fact, we find that Judeo-Arabic culture remained hugely significant among the Jewish people until recently. Before the creation of the State of Israel, more Jews lived in Arab lands than anywhere else, with Arabic the most widely spoken language among Jews for centuries.

Again we mustn't oversimplify—Jews did face oppression in these lands from time to time. But even though Judeo-Arabic life wasn't *all* great, a lot of it was.

There's one more factor to note about the Genizah. The very idea that a community would create a genizah is not something everyone immediately grasps. *The Genizah people saved all this paper, these dusty scraps—why?* The Cairo Genizah was not an archive, a place to safeguard documents in an orderly way for study, nor was it merely a tall, room-sized trash receptacle. *So what was it exactly?* The material placed in the Genizah was unneeded, but at the same time indispensable. Literally. The documents simply could not be thrown away.

The people of the Genizah acted out of a shared understanding of what God wanted of them. They didn't save everything, just written words. At first they saved just the names of God, then the words of Torah, then all written words. They viewed word-bearing papers and parchments as sacred. And in accordance with divine command, they gave their texts a proper burial.

I believe that if we try, if we take a moment—even in this age of document shredders, instant deletes of text on computer screens, and the "paperless" office—if we pause to think of the Genizah people, we can begin to understand them. There is something awesome about the power of writing, isn't there? Pen touches paper and moves across the surface, leaving a trail of ink behind it. Just so. The shape of that trail forms letters; the letters form words; the words form thoughts, ideas, and images, sometimes of indescribable splendor. The written word can convey the evanescent content of one mind or heart to another. God knew this; that's why God's greatest gift to the Jewish people is Torah—a magnificent collection of written words. And even those of us who don't use genizahs know it, too. Why else would we cherish our old letters, flowery certificates, and tattered children's books? To save these papers is to connect ourselves to our past, retain long-ago experiences, and bind ourselves, if only fleetingly, to the souls of others.

If that's not holy, then what is?

The Cairo Genizah, then, was much more than a pile of old scraps. It was a collection of countless lives and stories, a massive, messy heap of humanity stored in an attic for centuries. Its every document brought a bit of immortality to the people and thoughts it preserved. Studying any one of them is to resurrect something of times long past, often in ways that can help us make things better for the future.

The Cairo Genizah was—and is—a sacred treasure.

Acknowledgments

During the many months it took me to write this book, I was continually amazed and touched by the generosity of time, spirit, wisdom, and resources that I received from so many people. My name is the one on the cover, but this volume would not have been possible without the contributions of many others.

I am grateful to Michael Strong, whose early enthusiasm and ongoing wisdom were essential to its development. Mike began his involvement with this project as my agent, ended it as my advisor and friend, and this book's every word bears the mark of his devotion and support.

I also thank Phil Hanrahan, whose editorial insight and long hours of work were of inestimable value in helping lift the manuscript out of its original Genizah-like chaos.

For their assistance in planning my Genizah expedition, I am grateful to Rabbi Andrew Baker of the American Jewish Committee, Eliot Levy of JIMENA, Yves Fedida, Dr. Donald P. Ryan, Dr. Salima Karim, Sara Kemp, Lucette Lagnado, Aaron Kiviat, and Levana Zamir.

In Cairo, thanks to Dr. Zahi Hawass of the Supreme Council of Antiquities for his permission to visit the Genizah and for his support of my visit; Dr. Janice Kamrin for helping shepherd through my request; and Mr. Gamal Moustafa and the other staff members of the Supreme Council and at the Ben Ezra Synagogue for their enthusiastic support. I am also grateful to Jere Bacharach and Barbara Fudge for their wisdom and advice, and to Mrs. Carmen Weinstein, head of the Jewish Community of Cairo.

At The Jewish Theological Seminary of America, I thank Dr. David Kraemer, Rabbi Jerry Schwarzbard, Dr. Burton Visotzky, Dr.

Raymond Scheindlin, Dr. Menahem Schmelzer, Dr. Jay Rovner, Amy Armstrong Gerbracht, Ellen Kastel, and Michala Biondi.

Many current and former members of the Cambridge University staff and faculty were of great help. Thanks to Dr. Ben Outhwaite for his time and warm welcome at the Genizah Unit and for his invaluable assistance in procuring Genizah information, images, and insight throughout the process of writing this book. Thanks also to Professor Stefan Reif, Sarah Sykes, Dr. Janet Soskice, Dr. Dan Davies, Elizabeth Stratton, Dr. Geoffrey Khan, Dr. Rebecca Jefferson, Anne Hughes, Christine Patel, and Charlie Hampton.

From the Friedberg Genizah Project, I thank Albert Dov Friedberg, Professor Yaacov Choueka, Dr. Roni Shweka, and Dr. James Diamond.

From the Hebrew Union College–Jewish Institute of Religion, I am grateful to Dr. Reuven Firestone, Dr. Lawrence Hoffman, Dr. Richard Sarason, and Dr. Joshua Holo.

Special thanks to Gifford Combs, Dr. Marc Bregman, Dr. Mohamed el-Hawary, Dr. Hassanein Rabie, Dr. David M. Levy, and Rabbi John S. Schechter, all of whom agreed to be interviewed for this book and whose insights I appreciate very much.

For their assistance in various elements of my research and preparation of my manuscript, I thank Benjamin Heimfeld, Dr. Ron Wolfson, Matthew Zerwekh, Peggy Barnett, Sue Pearl, H. Bondar, and Larry Glickman. I also thank Rabbi Hara Person for her encouragement, and her entire family for their hospitality during my first Genizah trip to New York.

I thank the many individuals whose generous financial support enabled me to conduct my research for this book. In particular, I am grateful to the Fritz and Adelaide Kauffmann Foundation for its generous grant to Congregation Kol Shalom in support of my work, and to Rob Hershberg for making the match.

Special thanks to Stuart M. Matlins, publisher of Jewish Lights, for immediately understanding the importance of the project and for bringing it to a broader audience. Thanks also to Emily Wichland, vice president of Editorial and Production, and the rest of the editorial staff for their many invaluable contributions to this book.

I am especially grateful to the members of Congregation Kol Ami in Woodinville, Washington, and Congregation Kol Shalom on Bainbridge Island, Washington, for their ongoing support and enthusiasm for this project. Not only did they tolerate the investment of time and energy that this project demanded, but they also seemed downright excited about it. Their enthusiasm energized me; their support encouraged me; I feel blessed and honored to serve as their rabbi.

I am also blessed with a terrific family. I thank my parents—Ron and Sharon Glickman, Harriet and Joel Katz, and Vicki Nelson. I thank my kids—Taylor, Kyleigh, Jacob, and Shoshana. I am particularly grateful to Jacob—photographer, critic, Genizah lover, and travel buddy extraordinaire. His companionship on the Genizah expedition and throughout my research has been an unexpected and wonderful joy.

My wife, Caron, has been my strength through this entire process, showing patience at my long absences, faith in my ability, and a willingness to assume a far greater share of the family workload than was fair. My love and appreciation for her go beyond words, and it is to her that I dedicate this book.

Notes

Prologue

1. Maimonides, Mishneh Torah, *Hilkhot Yesodei Hatorah* 8:1.

Introduction: Treasures in the Synagogue Attic

1. Simon Hopkins, "The Oldest Dated Document in the Genizah?" in *Studies in Judaism and Islam,* ed. Shelomo Morag, Issachar Ben-Ami, and Norman A. Stillman (Jerusalem: Magnes Press, Hebrew University, 1981); S. D. Goitein, *Mediterranean Society: The Jewish Communities of the World as Portrayed in the Documents of the Cairo Genizah,* vol. 1, *Economic Foundations* (Berkeley: University of California Press, 1967), 398–99, n43. I thank Ben Outhwaite for making me aware of this document.
2. Babylonian Talmud, *Baba Batra* 14b.
3. *Genesis Rabbah* 98:19; Babylonian Talmud, *Megillah* 26b. My translation.
4. Babylonian Talmud, *Shabbat* 115a.
5. Solomon Schechter, "A Hoard of Hebrew Manuscripts," in *Studies in Judaism: Second Series* (Philadelphia: Jewish Publication Society, 1908), 1.

Chapter 1: The Genizah Moment

1. Daniel Elazar, "Can Sephardic Judaism be Reconstructed?" *Judaism* 41, no. 3 (1992): 217–28. Elazar specifies that, in 1931, Ashkenazic Jews constituted 92 percent of world Jewry.
2. Ismar Schorsch, "The Myth of Sephardic Supremacy," in *From Text to Context: The Turn to History in Modern Judaism* (Hanover, NH: Brandeis University Press, 1994), 72.
3. Ibid. Schorsch argues that the architecture of these synagogues evoked Spain rather than the Middle East but acknowledges that there is no scholarly consensus in this regard.
4. "Steinschneider, Moritz," *Encyclopaedia Judaica* 2nd ed., ed. Michael Berenbaum and Fred Skolnik (Detroit: Macmillan Reference USA, 2007), 19:197–99.

5. Solomon Schechter, "Moritz Steinschneider" [Necrology], Publications *American Jewish Historical Society,* Vol. 17 (Baltimore: Lord Baltimore Press, 1909), 229.

6. Heinrich Heine, *The Memoirs of Heinrich Heine and Some Newly Discovered Fragments of His Writings* (London: George Bell and Sons, 1887), 168.

7. *Jewish Encyclopedia* (Funk and Wagnalls: New York, 1902), 5:612. *Encyclopaedia Judaica* (Jerusalem: Keter, 1972), 7:405.

8. Based on a quotation in Stefan Reif, *A Jewish Archive in Old Cairo: The History of Cambridge University's Genizah Collection* (Surrey: Curzon, 2000), 15.

9. For this and other information on Firkovitch, see "Firkovitch, Abraham," *Encyclopaedia Judaica* (Jerusalem: Keter, 1972), 6:1305–6.

10. Reif, *A Jewish Archive,* 15–16; Menahem Ben Sasson, "Firkovitch's Second Collection: Notes on Historical and Halakhic Material," *Jewish Studies* 31 (1991): 47–67 (in Hebrew).

11. Ben Sasson, ibid.

12. Reif, *A Jewish Archive,* 70–72.

13. Rebecca Jefferson, "The Cairo Genizah Unearthed: The Excavations Conducted by the Count d'Hulst on Behalf of the Bodleian Library and Their Significance for Genizah History," in *"A Sacred Source": Genizah Studies in Honour of Professor Stefan C. Reif,* ed. S. Bhayro and B. M. Outhwaite, Cambridge Genizah Studies 1 (Leiden: Brill, 2010), 16.

14. Adolf Neubauer, "Egyptian Fragments: Megillot, Scrolls Analogous to That of Purim, with an Appendix on the First Negidim," *Jewish Quarterly Review* 8, no. 4 (July 1896): 559, 560.

15. Neil Danzig, "Geonic Jurisprudence from the Cairo Genizah: An Appreciation of Early Scholarship," *Proceedings of the American Academy for Jewish Research* 63 (1997–2001): 1–47.

16. My translation. Quoted in ibid., p. 27. The final sentence refers to Ecclesiastes 9:15: "Now, there was found [in the city] a poor wise man, and he by his wisdom saved the city; yet no man remembered that same poor man."

17. E. N. Adler, "An Eleventh-Century Introduction to the Hebrew Bible: Being a Fragment from the Sepher ha-Ittim of Rabbi Judah ben Barzilai of Barcelona," *Jewish Quarterly Review* 9, no. 4 (July 1897): 672.

18. Danzig, 27.

19. Ibid., 672–73.

20. Neubauer to Archibald Sayce, November 29, 1896. Quoted in Jefferson, "The Cairo Genizah Unearthed," 9.

21. Jefferson, "The Cairo Genizah Unearthed," 9.

Chapter 2: Solomon Schechter

1. Schechter's precise birthdate is unclear. Norman Bentwich suggests that he was born in 1849 (*Solomon Schechter: A Biography* [Philadelphia: Jewish Publication Society, 1938], 24), whereas Cyrus Adler ("Solomon Schechter: A Biographical Sketch," *American Jewish Yearbook*, 1916) and Schechter's own tombstone put the date at 1850. Private e-mail, David Golinkin to Daniel Schechter, December 20, 2006. I thank Rabbi John S. Schechter for sharing this information with me.
2. Bentwich, *Soloman Schechter*, 30.
3. Ibid., 31. Given that the two towns are more than 160 miles from one another, we can safely assume that the story is apocryphal.
4. Adler, "Solomon Schechter," 28.
5. Alexander Marx, *Essays in Jewish Biography* (Philadelphia: Jewish Publication Society, 1947), 230
6. Bentwich, 47.
7. Mel Scult, "The Baale Boste Reconsidererd: The Life of Mathilde Roth Schechter (M.R.S.)," *Modern Judaism* 7, no. 1 (February, 1987).
8. Adler, "Solomon Schechter," 30–31.
9. Bentwich, *Solomon Schechter*, 64.
10. Ibid., 84.

Chapter 3: "The Giblews"

1. Except where otherwise indicated, information for this chapter comes from A. Whigham Price, *The Ladies of Castlebrae: A Story of Nineteenth-Century Travel and Research* (Gloucester: Alan Sutton, 1985); and Janet Soskice, *The Sisters of Sinai: How Two Lady Adventurers Discovered the Hidden Gospels* (New York: Alfred A. Knopf, 2009).
2. Whigham Price, *Ladies of Castlebrae*, 13–14.
3. Agnes Smith Lewis and Margaret Dunlop Gibson, *In the Shadow of Sinai: Stories of Travel and Biblical Research* (Brighton: Alpha Press, 1999 [1893, 1898]), 73–74.
4. Ibid., 74.
5. Private e-mail from Janet Soskice to author, October 5, 2009.
6. Soskice, *Sisters of Sinai*, 96, 220. Personal conversation, Clare College, Cambridge, February 25, 2010. The Schechter request is recounted by Mathilde Schechter, quoted from her papers in the JTS archives, in Rebecca Jefferson, "A Genizah Secret: The Count d'Hulst and Letters Revealing the Race to Discover the Lost Leaves of the Original Ecclesiasticus," 15, n94.
7. Lewis and Gibson, *Shadow of Sinai*, 143.
8. Ibid., 152–54.

Chapter 4: May 13, 1896

1. Mrs. Lewis's and Mrs. Gibson's accounts of this meeting, though mostly in agreement, vary slightly in the details. This quotation and what follows is a composite of their memories of the event years after it occurred. For the Gibson version, see Margaret Dunlop Gibson, "Dr. Solomon Schechter," *Weekday*, January 15, 1916, quoted in Bentwich, *Solomon Schechter*, 140. For the Lewis account, see Lewis and Gibson, *Shadow of Sinai*, 155.

2. *The New Oxford Annotated Bible with the Apocrypha, Expanded Edition—Revised Standard Version*, ed. Merbert G. May and Bruce M. Metzger (Oxford: Oxford University Press, 1999).

3. Solomon Schechter, *Studies in Judaism: Second Series* (Philadelphia: Jewish Publication Society, 1938), 45.

4. Reif, *A Jewish Archive*, 73.

5. Reif, Stefan C. "The Discovery of the Cambridge Genizah Fragments of Ben Sira: Scholars and Texts," in *The Book of Ben Sira in Modern Research: Proceedings of the First International Ben Sira Conference, 28–31 July 1996*, ed. Pancratius Cornelis Beentjes (Soesterberg, Netherlands: Walter De Gruyter, 1997), 5.

6. D. S. Margoliouth, *An Essay on the Place of Ecclesiasticus in Semitic Literature* (Oxford: Clarendon Press, 1890), 22.

7. Solomon Schechter, "The Quotations from Ecclesiasticus in Rabbinic Literature," *Jewish Quarterly Review* 3, no. 4 (July, 1891): 686.

8. www.lib.cam.ac.uk/Taylor-Schechter/GF/31/letter.html (retrieved on May 22, 2008).

9. Lewis and Gibson, *Shadow of Sinai*, 156.

10. Bentwich, *Solomon Schechter*, 140.

11. Lewis and Gibson, *Shadow of Sinai*, 155–56.

12. Ibid., 157–58.

13. Reif, *A Jewish Archive*, 76; Bentwich, *Solomon Schechter*, 142.

14. Alexander Marx, "The Importance of the Geniza for Jewish History," *Proceedings of the American Academy for Jewish Research* 16 (1946–1947): 184.

15. Sayce to Neubauer, March 26, 1895. On the roles of d'Hulst and Sayce, see Jefferson, "A Genizah Secret," and "The Cairo Genizah Unearthed." Unless otherwise indicated, all citations regarding this story are quoted in these articles.

16. Sayce to E. W. B. Nicholson, February 6, 1896.

17. D'Hulst to Reginald Stuart Poole, February 16, 1890.

18. Jefferson, "The Cairo Genizah Unearthed."

Chapter 5: A Battlefield of Books

1. Elkan Nathan Adler, "Notes of a Journey to the East," *Jewish Chronicle*, December 21, 1888, 8, quoted in Phyllis Lambert, ed., *Fortifications and the Synagogue: The Fortress of Babylon and the Ben Ezra Synagogue, Cairo* (London: Weidenfield and Nicholson, 1994), 246.

2. Lewis and Gibson, *Shadow of Sinai*, 161.

3. Bentwich, *Solomon Schechter*, 127.

4. Ibid.

5. Karl Baedeker, ed., *Egypt: A Handbook for Travellers, Fifth Remodelled Edition* (Leipsic: Karl Baedeker, 1902). Baedeker indicates that express train was the primary mode of conveyance for Europeans traveling between Alexandria and Cairo.

6. Andre Raymond, *Cairo* (Cambridge: Harvard University Press, 2000), 315.

7. *The Times*, London, August 3, 1897, quoted in Schechter, *Studies in Judaism*, 4–5. *Encyclopaedia Judaica* (Jerusalem: Keter, 1972), 5: 255–56, indicates that the president of Cairo's Jewish community at this time was Moses Cattaui. The account I provide here comes from Schechter's recollections written soon after his return to Cambridge.

8. Charles Le Quesne, "Legend and Tradition at the Ben Ezra Synagogue," in Lambert, *Fortifications and the Synagogue*, 197–99.

9. Marcus Nathan Adler, ed., *The Itinerary of Benjamin of Tudela: Critical Text, Translation, and Commentary* (London: Henry Frowde, Oxford University Press, Amen Corner, E.C., 1907), 69–70.

10. Ibid., 93 and throughout.

11. Schechter, *Studies in Judaism*, 6–7.

12. Reif, *A Jewish Archive*, 43; *The Jewish Encyclopedia* (New York: Funk and Wagnalls, 1902), 3:283.

13. *The Jewish Chronicle*, London, October 15, 1897, and April 1, 1898. Quoted in Schechter, *Studies in Judaism*, 12–30.

14. Rebecca Jefferson, "The Historical Significance of the Cambridge Genizah Inventory Project," in *Language, Culture, Computation: Essays in Honour of Yaacov Choueka*, ed. N. Dershowitz and E. Nissan (Berlin: Springer Verlag, 2010), 11.

15. Schechter, *Studies in Judaism*, 6.

16. Ibid., 9ff.

17. T. Carmi, ed., *The Penguin Book of Hebrew Verse* (London: Penguin, 1981), 87.

18. Schechter, *Studies in Judaism*, 3; Paul E. Kahle, *The Cairo Genizah* (New York: Frederick A. Praeger, 1959), 10.

19. Schechter, *Studies in Judaism*, 8.

20. Ibid.
21. Agnes Lewis to Mathilde Schechter, February 7, 1897.
22. Quoted in A. Lufti al-Sayyid, *Egypt and Cromer: A Study in Anglo-Egyptian Relations* (London: John Murray, 1868), 62. Quote taken from Amitav Ghosh, *In an Antique Land: History in the Guise of a Traveler's Tale* (New York: Vintage Books, 1994), 91.
23. Lambert, *Fortifications and the Synagogue*, 239.
24. He was the leader of Cairo's Karaites in 1905.
25. Bentwich, *Solomon Schechter*, 129.
26. Ibid.
27. Ibid.
28. Agnes Lewis to Mathilde Schechter, January 21, 1897, in Solomon Schechter papers, Archives of The Jewish Theological Seminary, New York, 2/33.
29. Ibid.
30. Stefan C. Reif, "Giblews and Genizah Views," *Journal of Jewish Studies* 55, No. 2 (Autumn 2004), 342.
31. Lewis to Mathilde Schechter, February 7, 1897.
32. Lewis and Gibson, *Shadow of Sinai*, 160.
33. Ibid.
34. Ibid., 161.
35. Ibid., 9.
36. Reif, *A Jewish Archive*, 81.
37. Lewis and Gibson, *Shadow of Sinai*, 161–62.
38. Bentwich, *Solomon Schechter*, 130.
39. Jefferson, "Historical Significance," 11.
40. Schechter to Jenkinson, January 12, 1897, quoted in "Genizah Fragments," #32, www.lib.cam.ac.uk/Taylor-Schechter/GF/32/ #Art07.
41. Jefferson, "Historical Significance," 26–27
42. Bentwich, *Solomon Schechter*, 133; Jefferson, "Genizah Secret," 9.
43. Jefferson, "Unearthing the Genizah," 13.
44. Rebecca Jefferson, personal e-mail to the author, September 20, 2010.
45. March 18–19, 1898, quoted in Jefferson, "Unearthing the Genizah," n69.
46. Ibid.
47. Ibid., 9ff.
48. Sayce to Laura d'Hulst, May 26, 1923, quoted in ibid., 11.
49. Schechter, *Studies in Judaism*, 30.

Chapter 6: Unpacking the Boxes

1. Meir Ben Horin, "Solomon Schechter to Judge Mayer Sulzberger: Part I. Letters from the Pre-Seminary Period (1895–1901)," *Jewish Social Studies* 25, no. 1 (October 1963): 261.

2. Solomon Schechter, "The Lewis-Gibson Hebrew Collection. I," *Jewish Quarterly Review* 9, no. 1 (October 1896): 115.

3. Arthur Ernest Cowley and Adolf Neubauer, *The Original Hebrew of a Portion of Ecclesiasticus, XXIX.15 to XLIX.11* (Oxford: Clarendon Press, 1897), xii.

4. Alexander Marx, "The Importance of the Geniza for Jewish History," *Proceedings of the American Academy for Jewish Research* 16 (1946–1947): 184.

5. Reif, *A Jewish Archive,* 85.

6. Schechter to Sulzberger, August 30, 1897.

7. Schechter to Sulzberger, January 14, 1898.

8. Schechter to Sulzberger, August 5, 1897.

9. D. S. Margoliouth, *The Origin of the "Original Hebrew" of the Book of Ecclesiasticus* (London: James Parker and Co., 1899), 19–20.

10. Referenced in Charles Taylor and Solomon Schechter, *The Wisdom of Ben Sirah: Portions of the Book of Ecclesiasticus* (Cambridge: Cambridge University Press, 1899), v–vi.

11. George Margoliouth, "The Original Hebrew of Ecclesiasticus XXXI.12–31, and XXXVI.22–XXXVII.26," *Jewish Quarterly Review* 12, no. 1 (October 1899): 2.

12. Taylor and Schechter, *Wisdom of Ben Sirah,* lxx.

13. Ibid., lxxff.

14. Shulamit Elitzur, "A New Fragment from the Hebrew Version of the Book of Ben Sirah," *Tarbiz* 76 (2008) (Hebrew).

15. Israel Abrahams, "Some Egyptian Fragments of the Passover Hagada," *Jewish Quarterly Review* 10, no. 1 (October 1897): 41–51.

16. Ibid., 41.

17. Agnes Smith Lewis and Margaret Dunlop Gibson, *Palestinian Syriac Texts from Palimpsest Fragments in the Taylor-Schechter Collection* (London: CJ Clay and Sons, 1900), vii–viii.

18. Ibid., ix.

19. Ibid.

20. Ibid., x.

21. Charles Taylor, *Hebrew-Greek Cairo Genizah Palimpsests from the Taylor-Schechter Collection, Including a Fragment of the Twenty-Second Psalm According to Origen's Hexapla, Edited for the Syndics of the University Press* (Cambridge: University Press, 1900).

22. Ibid., v.

23. David Werner Amram, in *The Green Bag: An Entertaining Magazine for Lawyers*, 13 (1901): 115–20, 339–43.

24. Schechter to Sulzberger, March 5, 1900. For Schechter's description of the Damascus Document, see "Documents of Jewish Sectaries, Volume I: Edited from Hebrew Manuscripts in the Cairo Genizah Collection Now in the Possession of the University Library, Cambridge" (Cambridge: Cambridge University Press, 1910).

25. Schechter, "Documents of Jewish Sectaries," x.

26. Paul Kahle, *The Cairo Genizah*, 2nd ed. (New York: Frederick A. Praeger Publishers, 1959), 15–17.

27. For details on these negotiations, see Reif, *A Jewish Archive*, 90–94.

Chapter 7: More Treasures Come to Light

1. Schechter to Mayer Sulzberger, August 5, 1897.

2. Schechter, *Seminary Addresses*, 17–18.

3. *New York Times*, November 21, 1902.

4. Goiten, *A Medieval Society*, 1:7.

5. Quoted in Bentwich, *Solomon Schechter*, 162.

6. On Jacob Mann, see Stanley Brav, *Telling Tales Out of School* (Cincinnati: Alumni Association of Hebrew Union College–Jewish Institute of Religion, 1965), 145; and Michael A. Meyer, *Hebrew Union College–Jewish Institute of Religion: At One Hundred Years* (Cincinnati: Hebrew Union College Press, 1976), 91–92.

7. Jacob Mann, *The Jews in Egypt and in Palestine under the Fatimid Caliphs: A Contribution to Their Political and Communal History Eased Chiefly on Genizah Material Hitherto Unpublished Caliphs* (London: Oxford University Press, 1920), 1:5.

8. Ibid., 1:7.

9. Goitein, *A Mediterranean Society*, 1:25.

10. Shelomo Dov Goitein, "What Would Jewish and General History Benefit by a Systematic Publication of the Documentary Geniza Papers?" *Proceedings of the American Academy for Jewish Research* 23 (1954): 29–39.

11. For the following discussion, interview with Lawrence Hoffman, December 23, 2009.

12. Solomon Schechter, *Seminary Addresses and Other Papers*, 35.

13. "Balfour Day Service," Hebrew Union College–Jewish Institute of Religion, November 2, 1972. I thank Richard Sarason for sharing the service packet with me.

14. Chaim Stern, ed., *Gates of Repentance: The New Union Prayerbook for the Days of Awe* (New York: Central Conference of American Rabbis, 1978), 87.

15. *Mishkan T'filah: A Reform Siddur* (New York: Central Conference of American Rabbis, 2007), 227.

Chapter 8: Professor Genizah

1. Goitein, "What Would Jewish and General History Benefit?"
2. S. D. Goitein, *Letters of Medieval Jewish Traders* (Princeton: Princeton University Press, 1974), 208, 209 n3.
3. Jefferson, "Historical Significance."
4. Goitein, *Letters of Medieval Jewish Traders*, 209.
5. Ibid., 209.
6. Ibid., 209.
7. Ibid., 211.
8. Ibid., 211.
9. Ibid., 212.
10. Quoted in ibid., 207.
11. Paula Sanders, author's interview, April 29, 2010.
12. Abraham L. Udovitch, "Memorial Comments for S. D. Goitein," Princeton, NJ, March 1985, 5.
13. Goitein, *Mediterranean Society*, 26.
14. Goitein, *Mediterranean Society*, vol. 5, *The Individual* (Berkeley: University of California press, 1988), 498.
15. Ibid., 501.
16. S. D. Goitein, *Jews and Arabs: Their Contacts Through the Ages*, 3rd ed. (New York: Schocken Books, 1974), 7–8.
17. Moshe Gil, "Shlomo Dov Goitein, 1900–1985: A Mediterranean Scholar," *Mediterranean Historical Review* 1:1, 9–12.
18. S. D. Goitein and Mordechai A. Friedman, *India Traders of the Middle Ages: Documents from the Cairo Geniza* (Leiden: Brill, 2007), 4.
19. Sanders interview.
20. Mark R. Cohen, "Goitein, the Geniza, and Muslim History," 2001, available at www.dayan.org/mel/cohen.pdf.
21. Goitein, *Mediterranean Society*, 1:vii.
22. S. D. Goitein, "From the Mediterranean to India: Documents on the Trade to India, South Arabia, and East Africa from the Eleventh and Twelfth Centuries," *Speculum* 29, no. 2, pt. 1 (April 1954): 181–97.
23. Goitein, *Mediterranean Society*, 1:vii–viii.
24. Author's interview with Dr. Jere Bacharach, October 20, 2009.
25. Udovitch, "Memorial Comments," 7.
26. Goitein, *Mediterranean Society*, 1:viii.
27. Goitein and Friedman, *India Traders*, xxiii.
28. Quoted in Gideon Libson, "Hidden Worlds and Open Shutters: S. D. Goitein Between Judaism and Islam," in *The Jewish Past Revisited: Reflections on Modern Jewish Historians*, ed. David N. Myers and David B. Ruderman (New Haven: Yale University Press, 1998), 169.
29. S. D. Goitein, *Mediterranean Society*, 5:501.

Chapter 9: Sheet Music, Long-Lost Talmud, and a Lame and Decrepit Female Hyena

1. For this and the ensuing description, author's interview with Marc Bregman, April 7, 2010.
2. Marc Bregman, personal e-mail to author, May 29, 2010.
3. Except where otherwise indicated, information on Ovadiah/Giovan/Johannes is from Norman Golb, "The Autograph Memoirs of Obadiah the Proselyte of Oppido Lucano, and the Epistle of Barukh B. Isaac of Aleppo," prepared for the Convegno Internazionale di Studi, Giovanni-Obadiah do Oppido: Proselito, Viaggiatore, e Muscista Dell'eta Normanna, Oppido Lucana (Basilicata), March 28–30, 2004.
4. Ibid., iii.
5. Ibid.
6. Ibid., iv, translation attributed to S. D. Goitein.
7. Ibid., 9.
8. I am grateful to Dr. Joshua Holo, of HUC-JIR, for providing me with a bibliography of this material.
9. Norman Golb, "The Music of Obadiah the Proselyte and His Conversion," *Journal of Jewish Studies* 18 (1967): 46–47.
10. I thank Rabbi Jerry Schwartzbard of JTS for this insight.
11. Golb, "Autograph Memoirs of Obadiah," 33–34.
12. jewish-music-research.blogspot.com/2008/07/mi-al-har-horev-from-manuscripts-of.html.
13. Author's interview with Stefan Reif, April 19, 2010; Jefferson, "Historical Significance."
14. Jefferson, ibid.
15. S. D. Goitein, "The Medical Profession in Light of the Cairo Geniza Documents," *Hebrew Union College Annual* 34 (1963): 177.
16. Ibid., 177–94.
17. Haskell Isaacs and Colin F. Baker, *Medical and Para-Medical Manuscripts in the Cambridge Genizah Collections* (Cambridge: Cambridge University Press, 1994).
18. Efraim Lev and Zohar Amar, "Reconstruction of the Inventory of *Materia Medica* used by members of the Jewish Community of Medieval Cairo According to Prescriptions Found in the Taylor-Schechter Genizah Collection, Cambridge," *Journal of Ethnopharmacology* 108 (2006): 428–444.
19. Leigh N. Chipman and Efraim Lev, "*Take a Lame and Decrepit Female Hyena* ...: A Genizah Study of Two Additional Fragments of Sābūr Ibn Ibn Sahl's *al-Aqrābādhīn al-çaghīr,*" *Early Science and Medicine* 13 (2008): 361–83. The passage is an adapted combination of the two different versions of the text that the article presents.

20. Steven Wasserstrom, "Apology for S. D. Goitein: An Essay," in *A Faithful Sea: The Religious Cultures of the Mediterranean, 1200–1700*, ed. Andan A. Husain and K. E. Fleming (Oxford: Oneworld Publications, 2007), 190.

Chapter 10: The Genizah Today

1. J. Mosseri, "A Hoard of Jewish MSS. in Cairo," *Jewish Review* 4, no. 21 (September 1913); 208–16, quoted in Israel Adler's preface to *Catalogue of the Jack Mosseri Collection* (Jerusalem: Jewish National and University Library, 1989).
2. Ibid. Also, Dr. Ben Outhwaite, personal interview, February 25, 2010.
3. David Rozenthal, "Who Has Created Wine, Juice, and Good New Vintage," *Ha'aretz* (Hebrew), May 2006.
4. Ibid. (author's translation).
5. Stefan C. Reif, "A Fresh Set of Genizah Texts," *SBL Forum*, n.p. [cited August 2006].
6. Mark R. Cohen, "New Light on the Conflict over the Palestinian Gaonate, 1038–1042, and on Daniel b. 'Azarya: A Pair of Letters to the Nagid of Qayrawan," *AJS Review* 1 (1976): 1–39.
7. Michael L. Klein, "Nine Fragments of Palestinian Targum to the Pentateuch from the Cairo Genizah (Additions to MS A)," *Hebrew Union College Annual* 50 (1979): 149–64. I am grateful to Dr. Marc Bregman for making me aware of this article.

Chapter 11: The Friedberg Genizah Project

1. See chapter 7 (at note 5).
2. Quoted in Menahem Schmelzer, "The Contribution of the Genizah to the Study of Liturgy and Poetry," *Proceedings of the American Academy for Jewish Research* 63 (1997–2001): 163.
3. On Menahem Zulay, see ibid., 178.
4. Author's interview with James Diamond, March 28, 2010.
5. For location of meeting, see Stefan C. Reif and Shulamit Reif, *The Cambridge Genizah Collections: Their Contents and Significance* (Cambridge: Cambridge University Press, 2002), 75.
6. Neil Danzig, "Geonic Jurisprudence from the Cairo Genizah: An Appreciation of Early Scholarship," *Proceedings of the American Academy for Jewish Research* 63 (1997–2001): 1–47.
7. www.genizah.org/about-SoA-Research_Platform.htm.
8. Author's interview with Albert Friedberg, February 9, 2010; author's interview with Reuven Rubelow, March 25, 2010.
9. Except where otherwise indicated, this information is based on "FGP List of Images, 2010." The chart lists the number of images in each collection.

Since images are taken of both sides of each document, I have divided the numbers in half to reflect the number of leaves in each collection. Due to certain imaging anomalies, four of the collections list odd numbers of images. In these cases, I have rounded up, but I also decreased the total count of manuscripts at the bottom of the chart by half.

10. Reuven Rubelow, author's interviews and personal e-mails to author, March 2010.

11. Total documents at the Cambridge University Library, two sides for each.

12. Various reviews of Elazar Hurvitz, *Catalogue of the Cairo Geniza Fragments in the Westminster College Library*, describe the collection as containing 2,500 manuscripts.

13. Rubelow and Bodleian Library website.

14. John Rylands University website.

15. Estimate per Reuven Rubelow. Oxford's Bodleian website makes a remarkably offhanded comment referring to their collection containing 5,000 manuscripts.

16. Rubelow.

17. Yaacov Choueka, author's interview, March 16, 2010.

18. Lior Wolf, Rotem Littman, Naama Mayer, Nachum Dershowitz, R. Shweka, and Y. Choueka, "Automatically Identifying Join Candidates in the Cairo Genizah" (paper presented at the 12th IEEE International Conference on Computer Vision, 2009).

19. Choueka interview.

20. Friedberg interview.

Conclusion: Sacred Treasure

1. Reprinted in Daniel Shimshoni, *Israeli Democracy: The Middle of the Journey* (New York: The Free Press, 1982), 475.

2. www.english.imjnet.org.il/HTMLs/article_392.aspx?c0=13657& bsp=13246&bss=13657&bscp=12940.

3. Arnold Eisen, *Rethinking Modern Judaism: Ritual, Commandment, Community* (Chicago: University of Chicago Press, 1997), 216.

Photo Credits

Grateful acknowledgment is given for permission to use the following:

Page 5. Reprinted courtesy of the Library at the Herbert D. Katz Center for Advanced Judaic Studies, University of Pennsylvania.

Page 18: Isidore Singer, "Steinschneider, Moritz," *Jewish Encyclopedia*, vol. XI. New York: Funk and Wagnalls, 1905.

Page 20: Schulim Ochser, "Saphir, Jacob," *Jewish Encyclopedia*, vol. XI. New York: Funk and Wagnalls, 1905.

Page 22: Peter Wiernik, "Firkovich, Abraham b. Samuel," *Jewish Encyclopedia*, vol. v. New York: Funk and Wagnalls, 1903.

Page 24: Copyright K'TAV Yad Ve'sefer Institute, Jerusalem.

Page 28: Copyright The Jewish Historical Society of England. Used by permission.

Page 38: Reprinted from *Solomon Schechter: A Biography*, © 2010, by Norman Bentwich, published by The Jewish Publication Society, with the permission of the publisher.

Pages 43 and 47: Reproduced by permission of Westminster College, Cambridge.

Page 44, 220: Photographs by Jacob Glickman, copyright Mark Glickman.

Pages v, x, 59, 60, 76, 79, 95, 106, 111, 136, 158, 162, 171, 175, 180, 181, 182, 184, 185, 187, 191, 192, 194, 199, 206: Copyright University of Cambridge, reproduced by kind permission of the Syndics of Cambridge University Library.

Page 65: Copyright Beit Hatfutsot, photo archive, Tel Aviv. Used by permission.

Pages 66, 67: John L. Stoddard, *John L. Stoddard's Lectures*. Boston: Balch Brothers, 1915.

Page 68: Reprinted from *Jews in 19th Century Egypt*, © 1969 by Jacob M. Landau, published by New York University Press, with the permission of the publisher.

Index

Notes

Notes

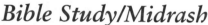
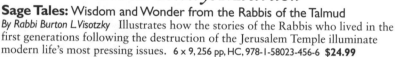

Congregation Resources

Empowered Judaism: What Independent Minyanim Can Teach Us about Building Vibrant Jewish Communities
By Rabbi Elie Kaunfer; Foreword by Prof. Jonathan D. Sarna
Examines the independent minyan movement and the lessons these grassroots communities can provide. 6 x 9, 224 pp, Quality PB, 978-1-58023-412-2 **$18.99**

Spiritual Boredom: Rediscovering the Wonder of Judaism *By Dr. Erica Brown*
Breaks through the surface of spiritual boredom to find the reservoir of meaning within. 6 x 9, 208 pp, HC, 978-1-58023-405-4 **$21.99**

Building a Successful Volunteer Culture
Finding Meaning in Service in the Jewish Community
By Rabbi Charles Simon; Foreword by Shelley Lindauer; Preface by Dr. Ron Wolfson
Shows you how to develop and maintain the volunteers who are essential to the vitality of your organization and community. 6 x 9, 192 pp, Quality PB, 978-1-58023-408-5 **$16.99**

The Case for Jewish Peoplehood: Can We Be One?
By Dr. Erica Brown and Dr. Misha Galperin; Foreword by Rabbi Joseph Telushkin
6 x 9, 224 pp, HC, 978-1-58023-401-6 **$21.99**

Inspired Jewish Leadership: Practical Approaches to Building Strong Communities
By Dr. Erica Brown 6 x 9, 256 pp, HC, 978-1-58023-361-3 **$24.99**

Jewish Pastoral Care, 2nd Edition: A Practical Handbook from Traditional & Contemporary Sources *Edited by Rabbi Dayle A. Friedman, MSW, MAJCS, BCC*
6 x 9, 528 pp, Quality PB, 978-1-58023-427-6 **$30.00**

Rethinking Synagogues: A New Vocabulary for Congregational Life
By Rabbi Lawrence A. Hoffman, PhD 6 x 9, 240 pp, Quality PB, 978-1-58023-248-7 **$19.99**

The Spirituality of Welcoming: How to Transform Your Congregation into a Sacred Community *By Dr. Ron Wolfson* 6 x 9, 224 pp, Quality PB, 978-1-58023-244-9 **$19.99**

Children's Books

Around the World in One Shabbat
Jewish People Celebrate the Sabbath Together
By Durga Yael Bernhard
Takes your child on a colorful adventure to share the many ways Jewish people celebrate Shabbat around the world.
11 x 8½, 32 pp, HC, 978-1-58023-433-7 **$18.99** *For ages 3–6*

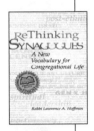

What You Will See Inside a Synagogue
By Rabbi Lawrence A. Hoffman, PhD, and Dr. Ron Wolfson; Full-color photos by Bill Aron
A colorful, fun-to-read introduction that explains the ways and whys of Jewish worship and religious life.
8½ x 10½, 32 pp, Full-color photos, Quality PB, 978-1-59473-256-0 **$8.99** *For ages 6 & up*
(A book from SkyLight Paths, Jewish Lights' sister imprint)

Because Nothing Looks Like God
By Lawrence Kushner and Karen Kushner Introduces children to the possibilities of spiritual life. 11 x 8½, 32 pp, Full-color illus., HC, 978-1-58023-092-6 **$17.99** *For ages 4 & up*

The Book of Miracles: A Young Person's Guide to Jewish Spiritual Awareness
Written and illus. by Lawrence Kushner
6 x 9, 96 pp, 2-color illus., HC, 978-1-879045-78-1 **$16.95** *For ages 9–13*

In God's Hands *By Lawrence Kushner and Gary Schmidt* 9 x 12, 32 pp, Full-color illus., HC, 978-1-58023-224-1 **$16.99** *For ages 5 & up*

In Our Image: God's First Creatures *By Nancy Sohn Swartz*
9 x 12, 32 pp, Full-color illus., HC, 978-1-879045-99-6 **$16.95** *For ages 4 & up*

The Kids' Fun Book of Jewish Time
By Emily Sper 9 x 7½, 24 pp, Full-color illus., HC, 978-1-58023-311-8 **$16.99** *For ages 3–6*

What Makes Someone a Jew? *By Lauren Seidman*
Reflects the changing face of American Judaism.
10 x 8½, 32 pp, Full-color photos, Quality PB, 978-1-58023-321-7 **$8.99** *For ages 3–6*

Children's Books by Sandy Eisenberg Sasso

Adam & Eve's First Sunset: God's New Day
Explores fear and hope, faith and gratitude in ways that will delight kids and adults—inspiring us to bless each of God's days and nights.
9 x 12, 32 pp, Full-color illus., HC, 978-1-58023-177-0 **$17.95** *For ages 4 & up*

Also Available as a Board Book: **Adam and Eve's New Day**
5 x 5, 24 pp, Full-color illus., Board Book, 978-1-59473-205-8 **$7.99** *For ages 0–4*
(A book from SkyLight Paths, Jewish Lights' sister imprint)

But God Remembered: Stories of Women from Creation to the Promised Land
Four different stories of women—Lilith, Serach, Bityah and the Daughters of Z—teach us important values through their faith and actions.
9 x 12, 32 pp, Full-color illus., Quality PB, 978-1-58023-372-9 **$8.99** *For ages 8 & up*

Cain & Abel: Finding the Fruits of Peace
Shows children that we have the power to deal with anger in positive ways. Provides questions for kids and adults to explore together.
9 x 12, 32 pp, Full-color illus., HC, 978-1-58023-123-7 **$16.95** *For ages 5 & up*

For Heaven's Sake
Heaven is often found where you least expect it.
9 x 12, 32 pp, Full-color illus., HC, 978-1-58023-054-4 **$16.95** *For ages 4 & up*

God in Between
If you wanted to find God, where would you look? This magical, mythical tale teaches that God can be found where we are: within all of us and the relationships between us. 9 x 12, 32 pp, Full-color illus., HC, 978-1-879045-86-6 **$16.95** *For ages 4 & up*

God Said Amen
An inspiring story about hearing the answers to our prayers.
9 x 12, 32 pp, Full-color illus., HC, 978-1-58023-080-3 **$16.95** *For ages 4 & up*

God's Paintbrush: Special 10th Anniversary Edition
Wonderfully interactive, invites children of all faiths and backgrounds to encounter God through moments in their own lives. Provides questions adult and child can explore together. 11 x 8½, 32 pp, Full-color illus., HC, 978-1-58023-195-4 **$17.95** *For ages 4 & up*

Also Available as a Board Book: **I Am God's Paintbrush**
5 x 5, 24 pp, Full-color illus., Board Book, 978-1-59473-265-2 **$7.99** *For ages 0–4*
(A book from SkyLight Paths, Jewish Lights' sister imprint)

Also Available: **God's Paintbrush Teacher's Guide**
8½ x 11, 32 pp, PB, 978-1-879045-57-6 **$8.95**

God's Paintbrush Celebration Kit
A Spiritual Activity Kit for Teachers and Students of All Faiths, All Backgrounds
9½ x 12, 40 Full-color Activity Sheets & Teacher Folder w/ complete instructions
HC, 978-1-58023-050-6 **$21.95**
8-Student Activity Sheet Pack (40 sheets/5 sessions), 978-1-58023-058-2 **$19.95**

In God's Name
Like an ancient myth in its poetic text and vibrant illustrations, this award-winning modern fable about the search for God's name celebrates the diversity and, at the same time, the unity of all people.
9 x 12, 32 pp, Full-color illus., HC, 978-1-879045-26-2 **$16.99** *For ages 4 & up*

Also Available as a Board Book: **What Is God's Name?**
5 x 5, 24 pp, Full-color illus., Board Book, 978-1-893361-10-2 **$7.99** *For ages 0–4*
(A book from SkyLight Paths, Jewish Lights' sister imprint)

Also Available in Spanish: **El nombre de Dios**
9 x 12, 32 pp, Full-color illus., HC, 978-1-893361-63-8 **$16.95** *For ages 4 & up*

Noah's Wife: The Story of Naamah
When God tells Noah to bring the animals of the world onto the ark, God also calls on Naamah, Noah's wife, to save each plant on Earth. Based on an ancient text.
9 x 12, 32 pp, Full-color illus., HC, 978-1-58023-134-3 **$16.95** *For ages 4 & up*

Also Available as a Board Book: **Naamah, Noah's Wife**
5 x 5, 24 pp, Full-color illus., Board Book, 978-1-893361-56-0 **$7.95** *For ages 0–4*
(A book from SkyLight Paths, Jewish Lights' sister imprint)

Ecology/Environment

A Wild Faith: Jewish Ways into Wilderness, Wilderness Ways into Judaism
By Rabbi Mike Comins; Foreword by Nigel Savage 6 x 9, 240 pp, Quality PB, 978-1-58023-316-3 **$16.99**

Ecology & the Jewish Spirit: Where Nature & the Sacred Meet
Edited by Ellen Bernstein 6 x 9, 288 pp, Quality PB, 978-1-58023-082-7 **$18.99**

Torah of the Earth: Exploring 4,000 Years of Ecology in Jewish Thought
Vol. 1: Biblical Israel & Rabbinic Judaism; Vol. 2: Zionism & Eco-Judaism
Edited by Rabbi Arthur Waskow Vol. 1: 6 x 9, 272 pp, Quality PB, 978-1-58023-086-5 **$19.95**
Vol. 2: 6 x 9, 336 pp, Quality PB, 978-1-58023-087-2 **$19.95**

The Way Into Judaism and the Environment *By Jeremy Benstein, PhD*
6 x 9, 288 pp, Quality PB, 978-1-58023-368-2 **$18.99**; HC, 978-1-58023-268-5 **$24.99**

Graphic Novels/History

The Adventures of Rabbi Harvey: A Graphic Novel of Jewish Wisdom and Wit in the
Wild West *By Steve Sheinkin* 6 x 9, 144 pp, Full-color illus., Quality PB, 978-1-58023-310-1 **$16.99**

Rabbi Harvey Rides Again: A Graphic Novel of Jewish Folktales Let Loose in the
Wild West *By Steve Sheinkin* 6 x 9, 144 pp, Full-color illus., Quality PB, 978-1-58023-347-7 **$16.99**

Rabbi Harvey vs. the Wisdom Kid: A Graphic Novel of Dueling
Jewish Folktales in the Wild West *By Steve Sheinkin*
Rabbi Harvey's first book-length adventure—and toughest challenge.
6 x 9, 144 pp, Full-color illus., Quality PB, 978-1-58023-422-1 **$16.99**

The Story of the Jews: A 4,000-Year Adventure—A Graphic History Book
By Stan Mack 6 x 9, 288 pp, Illus., Quality PB, 978-1-58023-155-8 **$16.99**

Grief/Healing

Facing Illness, Finding God: How Judaism Can Help You and Caregivers
Cope When Body or Spirit Fails *By Rabbi Joseph B. Meszler*
Will help you find spiritual strength for healing amid the fear, pain and chaos of
illness. 6 x 9, 208 pp, Quality PB, 978-1-58023-423-8 **$16.99**

Midrash & Medicine: Healing Body and Soul in the Jewish Interpretive
Tradition *Edited by Rabbi William Cutter, PhD; Foreword by Michele F. Prince, LCSW, MAJCS*
Explores how midrash can help you see beyond the physical aspects of healing to
tune in to your spiritual source. 6 x 9, 352 pp, HC, 978-1-58023-428-3 **$29.99**

Healing from Despair: Choosing Wholeness in a Broken World
By Rabbi Elie Kaplan Spitz with Erica Shapiro Taylor; Foreword by Abraham J. Twerski, MD
5½ x 8½, 208 pp, Quality PB, 978-1-58023-436-8 **$16.99**

Healing and the Jewish Imagination: Spiritual and Practical Perspectives on
Judaism and Health *Edited by Rabbi William Cutter, PhD*
6 x 9, 240 pp, Quality PB, 978-1-58023-373-6 **$19.99**

Grief in Our Seasons: A Mourner's Kaddish Companion *By Rabbi Kerry M. Olitzky*
4½ x 6½, 448 pp, Quality PB, 978-1-879045-55-2 **$15.95**

Healing of Soul, Healing of Body: Spiritual Leaders Unfold the Strength & Solace
in Psalms *Edited by Rabbi Simkha Y. Weintraub, LCSW*
6 x 9, 128 pp, 2-color illus. text, Quality PB, 978-1-879045-31-6 **$16.99**

Mourning & Mitzvah, 2nd Edition: A Guided Journal for Walking the Mourner's
Path through Grief to Healing *By Rabbi Anne Brener, LCSW*
7½ x 9, 304 pp, Quality PB, 978-1-58023-113-8 **$19.99**

Tears of Sorrow, Seeds of Hope, 2nd Edition: A Jewish Spiritual Companion for
Infertility and Pregnancy Loss *By Rabbi Nina Beth Cardin*
6 x 9, 208 pp, Quality PB, 978-1-58023-233-3 **$18.99**

A Time to Mourn, a Time to Comfort, 2nd Edition: A Guide to Jewish
Bereavement *By Dr. Ron Wolfson; Foreword by Rabbi David J. Wolpe*
7 x 9, 384 pp, Quality PB, 978-1-58023-253-1 **$19.99**

When a Grandparent Dies: A Kid's Own Remembering Workbook for Dealing
with Shiva and the Year Beyond *By Nechama Liss-Levinson, PhD*
8 x 10, 48 pp, 2-color text, HC, 978-1-879045-44-6 **$15.95** *For ages 7–13*

Holidays/Holy Days

Who by Fire, Who by Water—Un'taneh Tokef
Edited by Rabbi Lawrence A. Hoffman, PhD
Examines the prayer's theology, authorship and poetry through a set of lively essays, all written in accessible language.
6 x 9, 272 pp, HC, 978-1-58023-424-5 **$24.99**

All These Vows—Kol Nidre
Edited by Rabbi Lawrence A. Hoffman, PhD
The most memorable prayer of the Jewish New Year—what it means, why we sing it, and the secret of its magical appeal.
6 x 9, 300 pp (est), HC, 978-1-58023-430-6 **$24.99**

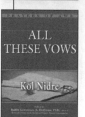

Rosh Hashanah Readings: Inspiration, Information and Contemplation
Yom Kippur Readings: Inspiration, Information and Contemplation
Edited by Rabbi Dov Peretz Elkins; Section Introductions from Arthur Green's These Are the Words
Rosh Hashanah: 6 x 9, 400 pp, Quality PB, 978-1-58023-437-5 **$19.99**; HC, 978-1-58023-239-5 **$24.99**
Yom Kippur: 6 x 9, 368 pp, Quality PB, 978-1-58023-438-2 **$19.99**; HC, 978-1-58023-271-5 **$24.99**

Jewish Holidays: A Brief Introduction for Christians
By Rabbi Kerry M. Olitzky and Rabbi Daniel Judson
5½ x 8½, 176 pp, Quality PB, 978-1-58023-302-6 **$16.99**

Reclaiming Judaism as a Spiritual Practice: Holy Days and Shabbat
By Rabbi Goldie Milgram 7 x 9, 272 pp, Quality PB, 978-1-58023-205-0 **$19.99**

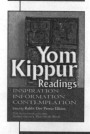

Shabbat, 2nd Edition: The Family Guide to Preparing for and Celebrating the Sabbath
By Dr. Ron Wolfson 7 x 9, 320 pp, Illus., Quality PB, 978-1-58023-164-0 **$19.99**

Hanukkah, 2nd Edition: The Family Guide to Spiritual Celebration
By Dr. Ron Wolfson 7 x 9, 240 pp, Illus., Quality PB, 978-1-58023-122-0 **$18.95**

The Jewish Family Fun Book, 2nd Edition
Holiday Projects, Everyday Activities, and Travel Ideas with Jewish Themes
By Danielle Dardashti and Roni Sarig; Illus. by Avi Katz
6 x 9, 304 pp, 70+ b/w illus. & diagrams, Quality PB, 978-1-58023-333-0 **$18.99**

Passover

My People's Passover Haggadah
Traditional Texts, Modern Commentaries
Edited by Rabbi Lawrence A. Hoffman, PhD, and David Arnow, PhD
A diverse and exciting collection of commentaries on the traditional Passover Haggadah—in two volumes!
Vol. 1: 7 x 10, 304 pp, HC, 978-1-58023-354-5 **$24.99**
Vol. 2: 7 x 10, 320 pp, HC, 978-1-58023-346-0 **$24.99**

Freedom Journeys: The Tale of Exodus and Wilderness across Millennia
By Rabbi Arthur O. Waskow and Rabbi Phyllis O. Berman
Explores how the story of Exodus echoes in our own time, calling us to relearn and rethink the Passover story through social-justice, ecological, feminist and interfaith perspectives. 6 x 9, 288 pp, HC, 978-1-58023-445-0 **$24.99**

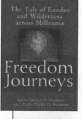

Leading the Passover Journey: The Seder's Meaning Revealed, the Haggadah's Story Retold *By Rabbi Nathan Laufer*
Uncovers the hidden meaning of the Seder's rituals and customs.
6 x 9, 224 pp, Quality PB, 978-1-58023-399-6 **$18.99**; HC, 978-1-58023-211-1 **$24.99**

Creating Lively Passover Seders, 2nd Edition: A Sourcebook of Engaging Tales, Texts & Activities *By David Arnow, PhD* 7 x 9, 464 pp, Quality PB, 978-1-58023-444-3 **$24.99**

Passover, 2nd Edition: The Family Guide to Spiritual Celebration
By Dr. Ron Wolfson with Joel Lurie Grishaver 7 x 9, 416 pp, Quality PB, 978-1-58023-174-9 **$19.95**

The Women's Passover Companion: Women's Reflections on the Festival of Freedom
Edited by Rabbi Sharon Cohen Anisfeld, Tara Mohr and Catherine Spector; Foreword by Paula E. Hyman
6 x 9, 352 pp, Quality PB, 978-1-58023-231-9 **$19.99**; HC, 978-1-58023-128-2 **$24.95**

The Women's Seder Sourcebook: Rituals & Readings for Use at the Passover Seder
Edited by Rabbi Sharon Cohen Anisfeld, Tara Mohr and Catherine Spector
6 x 9, 384 pp, Quality PB, 978-1-58023-232-6 **$19.99**

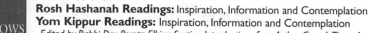

Life Cycle
Marriage/Parenting/Family/Aging

The New Jewish Baby Album: Creating and Celebrating the Beginning of a Spiritual Life—A Jewish Lights Companion
By the Editors at Jewish Lights; Foreword by Anita Diamant; Preface by Rabbi Sandy Eisenberg Sasso
A spiritual keepsake that will be treasured for generations. More than just a memory book, *shows you how—and why it's important*—to create a Jewish home and a Jewish life. 8 x 10, 64 pp, Deluxe Padded HC, Full-color illus., 978-1-58023-138-1 **$19.95**

The Jewish Pregnancy Book: A Resource for the Soul, Body & Mind during Pregnancy, Birth & the First Three Months *By Sandy Falk, MD, and Rabbi Daniel Judson, with Steven A. Rapp* Medical information, prayers and rituals for each stage of pregnancy. 7 x 10, 208 pp, b/w photos, Quality PB, 978-1-58023-178-7 **$16.95**

Celebrating Your New Jewish Daughter: Creating Jewish Ways to Welcome Baby Girls into the Covenant—New and Traditional Ceremonies *By Debra Nussbaum Cohen; Foreword by Rabbi Sandy Eisenberg Sasso* 6 x 9, 272 pp, Quality PB, 978-1-58023-090-2 **$18.95**

The New Jewish Baby Book, 2nd Edition: Names, Ceremonies & Customs—A Guide for Today's Families *By Anita Diamant* 6 x 9, 320 pp, Quality PB, 978-1-58023-251-7 **$19.99**

Parenting as a Spiritual Journey: Deepening Ordinary and Extraordinary Events into Sacred Occasions *By Rabbi Nancy Fuchs-Kreimer, PhD*
6 x 9, 224 pp, Quality PB, 978-1-58023-016-2 **$17.99**

Parenting Jewish Teens: A Guide for the Perplexed
By Joanne Doades Explores the questions and issues that shape the world in which today's Jewish teenagers live and offers constructive advice to parents.
6 x 9, 176 pp, Quality PB, 978-1-58023-305-7 **$16.99**

Judaism for Two: A Spiritual Guide for Strengthening and Celebrating Your Loving Relationship *By Rabbi Nancy Fuchs-Kreimer, PhD, and Rabbi Nancy H. Wiener, DMin; Foreword by Rabbi Elliot N. Dorff, PhD*
Addresses the ways Jewish teachings can enhance and strengthen committed relationships. 6 x 9, 224 pp, Quality PB, 978-1-58023-254-8 **$16.99**

The Creative Jewish Wedding Book, 2nd Edition: A Hands-On Guide to New & Old Traditions, Ceremonies & Celebrations *By Gabrielle Kaplan-Mayer*
9 x 9, 288 pp, b/w photos, Quality PB, 978-1-58023-398-9 **$19.99**

Divorce Is a Mitzvah: A Practical Guide to Finding Wholeness and Holiness When Your Marriage Dies *By Rabbi Perry Netter; Afterword by Rabbi Laura Geller*
6 x 9, 224 pp, Quality PB, 978-1-58023-172-5 **$16.95**

Embracing the Covenant: Converts to Judaism Talk About Why & How
By Rabbi Allan Berkowitz and Patti Moskovitz 6 x 9, 192 pp, Quality PB, 978-1-879045-50-7 **$16.95**

The Guide to Jewish Interfaith Family Life: An InterfaithFamily.com Handbook
Edited by Ronnie Friedland and Edmund Case
6 x 9, 384 pp, Quality PB, 978-1-58023-153-4 **$18.95**

A Heart of Wisdom: Making the Jewish Journey from Midlife through the Elder Years
Edited by Susan Berrin; Foreword by Rabbi Harold Kushner
6 x 9, 384 pp, Quality PB, 978-1-58023-051-3 **$18.95**

Introducing My Faith and My Community: The Jewish Outreach Institute Guide for the Christian in a Jewish Interfaith Relationship
By Rabbi Kerry M. Olitzky 6 x 9, 176 pp, Quality PB, 978-1-58023-192-3 **$16.99**

Making a Successful Jewish Interfaith Marriage: The Jewish Outreach Institute Guide to Opportunities, Challenges and Resources *By Rabbi Kerry M. Olitzky with Joan Peterson Littman*
6 x 9, 176 pp, Quality PB, 978-1-58023-170-1 **$16.95**

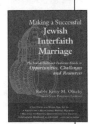

A Man's Responsibility: A Jewish Guide to Being a Son, a Partner in Marriage, a Father and a Community Leader *By Rabbi Joseph B. Meszler*
6 x 9, 192 pp, Quality PB, 978-1-58023-435-1 **$16.99**; HC, 978-1-58023-362-0 **$21.99**

So That Your Values Live On: Ethical Wills and How to Prepare Them
Edited by Rabbi Jack Riemer and Rabbi Nathaniel Stampfer
6 x 9, 272 pp, Quality PB, 978-1-879045-34-7 **$18.99**

Meditation

Jewish Meditation Practices for Everyday Life
Awakening Your Heart, Connecting with God
By Rabbi Jeff Roth
Offers a fresh take on meditation that draws on life experience and living life with greater clarity as opposed to the traditional method of rigorous study.
6 x 9, 224 pp, Quality PB, 978-1-58023-397-2 **$18.99**

The Handbook of Jewish Meditation Practices
A Guide for Enriching the Sabbath and Other Days of Your Life
By Rabbi David A. Cooper Easy-to-learn meditation techniques.
6 x 9, 208 pp, Quality PB, 978-1-58023-102-2 **$16.95**

Discovering Jewish Meditation: Instruction & Guidance for Learning an Ancient Spiritual Practice *By Nan Fink Gefen, PhD* 6 x 9, 208 pp, Quality PB, 978-1-58023-067-4 **$16.95**

Meditation from the Heart of Judaism: Today's Teachers Share Their Practices, Techniques, and Faith *Edited by Avram Davis*
6 x 9, 256 pp, Quality PB, 978-1-58023-049-0 **$16.95**

Ritual/Sacred Practices

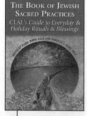

The Jewish Dream Book: The Key to Opening the Inner Meaning of Your Dreams *By Vanessa L. Ochs, PhD, with Elizabeth Ochs; Illus. by Kristina Swarner*
Instructions for how modern people can perform ancient Jewish dream practices and dream interpretations drawn from the Jewish wisdom tradition.
8 x 8, 128 pp, Full-color illus., Deluxe PB w/ flaps, 978-1-58023-132-9 **$16.95**

God in Your Body: Kabbalah, Mindfulness and Embodied Spiritual Practice
By Jay Michaelson
The first comprehensive treatment of the body in Jewish spiritual practice and an essential guide to the sacred.
6 x 9, 272 pp, Quality PB, 978-1-58023-304-0 **$18.99**

The Book of Jewish Sacred Practices: CLAL's Guide to Everyday & Holiday Rituals & Blessings *Edited by Rabbi Irwin Kula and Vanessa L. Ochs, PhD*
6 x 9, 368 pp, Quality PB, 978-1-58023-152-7 **$18.95**

Jewish Ritual: A Brief Introduction for Christians
By Rabbi Kerry M. Olitzky and Rabbi Daniel Judson
5½ x 8½, 144 pp, Quality PB, 978-1-58023-210-4 **$14.99**

The Rituals & Practices of a Jewish Life: A Handbook for Personal Spiritual Renewal *Edited by Rabbi Kerry M. Olitzky and Rabbi Daniel Judson*
6 x 9, 272 pp, Illus., Quality PB, 978-1-58023-169-5 **$18.95**

The Sacred Art of Lovingkindness: Preparing to Practice
By Rabbi Rami Shapiro 5½ x 8½, 176 pp, Quality PB, 978-1-59473-151-8 **$16.99**
(A book from SkyLight Paths, Jewish Lights' sister imprint)

Science Fiction/Mystery & Detective Fiction

Criminal Kabbalah: An Intriguing Anthology of Jewish Mystery & Detective Fiction *Edited by Lawrence W. Raphael; Foreword by Laurie R. King*
All-new stories from twelve of today's masters of mystery and detective fiction—sure to delight mystery buffs of all faith traditions.
6 x 9, 256 pp, Quality PB, 978-1-58023-109-1 **$16.95**

Mystery Midrash: An Anthology of Jewish Mystery & Detective Fiction
Edited by Lawrence W. Raphael; Preface by Joel Siegel
6 x 9, 304 pp, Quality PB, 978-1-58023-055-1 **$16.95**

Wandering Stars: An Anthology of Jewish Fantasy & Science Fiction
Edited by Jack Dann; Introduction by Isaac Asimov
6 x 9, 272 pp, Quality PB, 978-1-58023-005-6 **$18.99**

More Wandering Stars: An Anthology of Outstanding Stories of Jewish Fantasy and Science Fiction *Edited by Jack Dann; Introduction by Isaac Asimov*
6 x 9, 192 pp, Quality PB, 978-1-58023-063-6 **$16.95**

Spirituality/Prayer

Making Prayer Real: Leading Jewish Spiritual Voices on Why Prayer Is Difficult and What to Do about It *By Rabbi Mike Comins*
A new and different response to the challenges of Jewish prayer, with "best prayer practices" from Jewish spiritual leaders of all denominations.
6 x 9, 320 pp, Quality PB, 978-1-58023-417-7 **$18.99**

Witnesses to the One: The Spiritual History of the *Sh'ma*
By Rabbi Joseph B. Meszler; Foreword by Rabbi Elyse Goldstein
6 x 9, 176 pp, Quality PB, 978-1-58023-400-9 **$16.99**; HC, 978-1-58023-309-5 **$19.99**

My People's Prayer Book Series: Traditional Prayers, Modern Commentaries *Edited by Rabbi Lawrence A. Hoffman, PhD*
Provides diverse and exciting commentary to the traditional liturgy. Will help you find new wisdom in Jewish prayer, and bring liturgy into your life. Each book includes Hebrew text, modern translations and commentaries from all perspectives of the Jewish world.

Vol. 1—The *Sh'ma* and Its Blessings
7 x 10, 168 pp, HC, 978-1-879045-79-8 **$29.99**
Vol. 2—The *Amidah* 7 x 10, 240 pp, HC, 978-1-879045-80-4 **$24.95**
Vol. 3—*P'sukei D'zimrah* (Morning Psalms)
7 x 10, 240 pp, HC, 978-1-879045-81-1 **$29.99**
Vol. 4—*Seder K'riat Hatorah* (The Torah Service)
7 x 10, 264 pp, HC, 978-1-879045-82-8 **$29.99**
Vol. 5—*Birkhot Hashachar* (Morning Blessings)
7 x 10, 240 pp, HC, 978-1-879045-83-5 **$24.95**
Vol. 6—*Tachanun* and Concluding Prayers
7 x 10, 240 pp, HC, 978-1-879045 84-2 **$24.95**
Vol. 7—Shabbat at Home 7 x 10, 240 pp, HC, 978-1-879045-85-9 **$24.95**
Vol. 8—*Kabbalat Shabbat* (Welcoming Shabbat in the Synagogue)
7 x 10, 240 pp, HC, 978-1-58023-121-3 **$24.99**
Vol. 9—Welcoming the Night: *Minchah* and *Ma'ariv* (Afternoon and Evening Prayer) 7 x 10, 272 pp, HC, 978-1-58023-262-3 **$24.99**
Vol. 10—Shabbat Morning: *Shacharit* and *Musaf* (Morning and Additional Services) 7 x 10, 240 pp, HC, 978-1-58023-240-1 **$29.99**

Spirituality/Lawrence Kushner

I'm God; You're Not: Observations on Organized Religion & Other Disguises of the Ego
6 x 9, 256 pp, HC, 978-1-58023-441-2 **$21.99**

The Book of Letters: A Mystical Hebrew Alphabet
Popular HC Edition, 6 x 9, 80 pp, 2-color text, 978-1-879045-00-2 **$24.95**
Collector's Limited Edition, 9 x 12, 80 pp, gold-foil-embossed pages, w/ limited-edition silkscreened print, 978-1-879045-04-0 **$349.00**

The Book of Miracles: A Young Person's Guide to Jewish Spiritual Awareness
6 x 9, 96 pp, 2-color illus., HC, 978-1-879045-78-1 **$16.95** *For ages 9–13*

The Book of Words: Talking Spiritual Life, Living Spiritual Talk
6 x 9, 160 pp, Quality PB, 978-1-58023-020-9 **$18.99**

Eyes Remade for Wonder: A Lawrence Kushner Reader *Introduction by Thomas Moore*
6 x 9, 240 pp, Quality PB, 978-1-58023-042-1 **$18.95**

God Was in This Place & I, i Did Not Know: Finding Self, Spirituality and Ultimate Meaning 6 x 9, 192 pp, Quality PB, 978-1-879045-33-0 **$16.95**

Honey from the Rock: An Introduction to Jewish Mysticism
6 x 9, 176 pp, Quality PB, 978-1-58023-073-5 **$16.95**

Invisible Lines of Connection: Sacred Stories of the Ordinary
5½ x 8½, 160 pp, Quality PB, 978-1-879045-98-9 **$15.95**

Jewish Spirituality: A Brief Introduction for Christians
5½ x 8½, 112 pp, Quality PB, 978-1-58023-150-3 **$12.95**

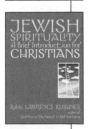

The River of Light: Jewish Mystical Awareness
6 x 9, 192 pp, Quality PB, 978-1-58023-096-4 **$16.95**

The Way Into Jewish Mystical Tradition
6 x 9, 224 pp, Quality PB, 978-1-58023-200-5 **$18.99**; HC, 978-1-58023-029-2 **$21.95**

Theology/Philosophy/The Way Into... Series

The Way Into... series offers an accessible and highly usable "guided tour" of the Jewish faith, people, history and beliefs—in total, an introduction to Judaism that will enable you to understand and interact with the sacred texts of the Jewish tradition. Each volume is written by a leading contemporary scholar and teacher, and explores one key aspect of Judaism. The Way Into... series enables all readers to achieve a real sense of Jewish cultural literacy through guided study.

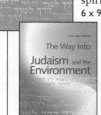

The Way Into Encountering God in Judaism
By Rabbi Neil Gillman, PhD
For everyone who wants to understand how Jews have encountered God throughout history and today.
6 x 9, 240 pp, Quality PB, 978-1-58023-199-2 **$18.99**; HC, 978-1-58023-025-4 **$21.95**
Also Available: **The Jewish Approach to God:** A Brief Introduction for Christians
By Rabbi Neil Gillman, PhD
5½ x 8¼, 192 pp, Quality PB, 978-1-58023-190-9 **$16.95**

The Way Into Jewish Mystical Tradition
By Rabbi Lawrence Kushner
Allows readers to interact directly with the sacred mystical texts of the Jewish tradition. An accessible introduction to the concepts of Jewish mysticism, their religious and spiritual significance, and how they relate to life today.
6 x 9, 224 pp, Quality PB, 978-1-58023-200-5 **$18.99**; HC, 978-1-58023-029-2 **$21.95**

The Way Into Jewish Prayer
By Rabbi Lawrence A. Hoffman, PhD
Opens the door to 3,000 years of Jewish prayer, making anyone feel at home in the Jewish way of communicating with God.
6 x 9, 208 pp, Quality PB, 978-1-58023-201-2 **$18.99**

The Way Into Jewish Prayer Teacher's Guide
By Rabbi Jennifer Ossakow Goldsmith
8½ x 11, 42 pp, PB, 978-1-58023-345-3 **$8.99**
Download a free copy at www.jewishlights.com.

The Way Into Judaism and the Environment
By Jeremy Benstein, PhD
Explores the ways in which Judaism contributes to contemporary social-environmental issues, the extent to which Judaism is part of the problem and how it can be part of the solution.
6 x 9, 288 pp, Quality PB, 978-1-58023-368-2 **$18.99**

The Way Into *Tikkun Olam* (Repairing the World)
By Rabbi Elliot N. Dorff, PhD
An accessible introduction to the Jewish concept of the individual's responsibility to care for others and repair the world.
6 x 9, 304 pp, Quality PB, 978-1-58023-328-6 **$18.99**

The Way Into Torah
By Rabbi Norman J. Cohen, PhD
Helps guide you in the exploration of the origins and development of Torah, explains why it should be studied and how to do it.
6 x 9, 176 pp, Quality PB, 978-1-58023-198-5 **$16.99**

The Way Into the Varieties of Jewishness
By Sylvia Barack Fishman, PhD
Explores the religious and historical understanding of what it has meant to be Jewish from ancient times to the present controversy over "Who is a Jew?"
6 x 9, 288 pp, Quality PB, 978-1-58023-367-5 **$18.99**; HC, 978-1-58023-030-8 **$24.99**

Theology/Philosophy

The God Who Hates Lies: Confronting and Rethinking Jewish Tradition
By Dr. David Hartman with Charlie Buckholtz
The world's leading Modern Orthodox Jewish theologian probes the deepest questions at the heart of what it means to be a human being and a Jew.
6 x 9, 208 pp, HC, 978-1-58023-455-9 **$24.99**

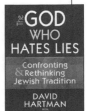

Jewish Theology in Our Time: A New Generation Explores the Foundations and Future of Jewish Belief *Edited by Rabbi Elliot J. Cosgrove, PhD; Foreword by Rabbi David J. Wolpe; Preface by Rabbi Carole B. Balin, PhD*
A powerful and challenging examination of what Jews can believe—by a new generation's most dynamic and innovative thinkers.
6 x 9, 240 pp, HC, 978-1-58023-413-9 **$24.99**

Maimonides, Spinoza and Us: Toward an Intellectually Vibrant Judaism
By Rabbi Marc D. Angel, PhD A challenging look at two great Jewish philosophers and what their thinking means to our understanding of God, truth, revelation and reason. 6 x 9, 224 pp, HC, 978-1-58023-411-5 **$24.99**

The Death of Death: Resurrection and Immortality in Jewish Thought
By Rabbi Neil Gillman, PhD 6 x 9, 336 pp, Quality PB, 978-1-58023-081-0 **$18.95**

Doing Jewish Theology: God, Torah & Israel in Modern Judaism *By Rabbi Neil Gillman, PhD*
6 x 9, 304 pp, Quality PB, 978-1-58023-439-9 **$18.99**

Hasidic Tales: Annotated & Explained *Translation & Annotation by Rabbi Rami Shapiro*
5½ x 8½, 240 pp, Quality PB, 978-1-893361-86-7 **$16.95***

A Heart of Many Rooms: Celebrating the Many Voices within Judaism
By Dr. David Hartman 6 x 9, 352 pp, Quality PB, 978-1-58023-156-5 **$19.95**

The Hebrew Prophets: Selections Annotated & Explained
Translation & Annotation by Rabbi Rami Shapiro; Foreword by Rabbi Zalman M. Schachter-Shalomi
5½ x 8½, 224 pp, Quality PB, 978-1-59473-037-5 **$16.99***

A Jewish Understanding of the New Testament *By Rabbi Samuel Sandmel; Preface by Rabbi David Sandmel* 5½ x 8½, 368 pp, Quality PB, 978-1-59473-048-1 **$19.99***

Jews and Judaism in the 21st Century: Human Responsibility, the Presence of God and the Future of the Covenant *Edited by Rabbi Edward Feinstein; Foreword by Paula E. Hyman*
6 x 9, 192 pp, Quality PB, 978-1-58023-374-3 **$19.99**

A Living Covenant: The Innovative Spirit in Traditional Judaism
By Dr. David Hartman 6 x 9, 368 pp, Quality PB, 978-1-58023-011-7 **$25.00**

Love and Terror in the God Encounter: The Theological Legacy of Rabbi Joseph B. Soloveitchik *By Dr. David Hartman* 6 x 9, 240 pp, Quality PB, 978-1-58023-176-3 **$19.95**

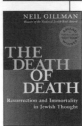

A Touch of the Sacred: A Theologian's Informal Guide to Jewish Belief
By Dr. Eugene B. Borowitz and Frances W. Schwartz
6 x 9, 256 pp, Quality PB, 978-1-58023-416-0 **$16.99**; HC, 978-1-58023-337-8 **$21.99**

Traces of God: Seeing God in Torah, History and Everyday Life *By Rabbi Neil Gillman, PhD*
6 x 9, 240 pp, Quality PB, 978-1-58023-369-9 **$16.99**

Your Word Is Fire: The Hasidic Masters on Contemplative Prayer
Edited and translated by Rabbi Arthur Green, PhD, and Barry W. Holtz
6 x 9, 160 pp, Quality PB, 978-1-879045-25-5 **$15.95**

I Am Jewish
Personal Reflections Inspired by the Last Words of Daniel Pearl
Almost 150 Jews—both famous and not—from all walks of life, from all around the world, write about many aspects of their Judaism.
Edited by Judea and Ruth Pearl 6 x 9, 304 pp, Deluxe PB w/ flaps, 978-1-58023-259-3 **$18.99**
Download a free copy of the *I Am Jewish Teacher's Guide* at www.jewishlights.com.

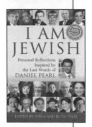

Hannah Senesh: Her Life and Diary, The First Complete Edition
By Hannah Senesh; Foreword by Marge Piercy; Preface by Eitan Senesh; Afterword by Roberta Grossman
6 x 9, 368 pp, b/w photos, Quality PB, 978-1-58023-342-2 **$19.99**

---

*A book from SkyLight Paths, Jewish Lights' sister imprint

Social Justice

Confronting Scandal
How Jews Can Respond When Jews Do Bad Things
By Dr. Erica Brown
A framework to transform our sense of shame over reports of Jews committing crime into actions that inspire and sustain a moral culture.
6 x 9, 192 pp, HC, 978-1-58023-440-5 **$24.99**

There Shall Be No Needy
Pursuing Social Justice through Jewish Law and Tradition
By Rabbi Jill Jacobs; Foreword by Rabbi Elliot N. Dorff, PhD; Preface by Simon Greer
Confronts the most pressing issues of twenty-first-century America from a deeply Jewish perspective. 6 x 9, 288 pp, Quality PB, 978-1-58023-425-2 **$16.99**
There Shall Be No Needy Teacher's Guide 8½ x 11, 56 pp, PB, 978-1-58023-429-0 **$8.99**

Conscience
The Duty to Obey and the Duty to Disobey
By Rabbi Harold M. Schulweis
Examines the idea of conscience and the role conscience plays in our relationships to government, law, ethics, religion, human nature, God—and to each other.
6 x 9, 160 pp, Quality PB, 978-1-58023-419-1 **$16.99**; HC, 978-1-58023-375-0 **$19.99**

Judaism and Justice
The Jewish Passion to Repair the World
By Rabbi Sidney Schwarz; Foreword by Ruth Messinger
Explores the relationship between Judaism, social justice and the Jewish identity of American Jews. 6 x 9, 352 pp, Quality PB, 978-1-58023-353-8 **$19.99**

Spirituality/Women's Interest

New Jewish Feminism
Probing the Past, Forging the Future
Edited by Rabbi Elyse Goldstein; Foreword by Anita Diamant
Looks at the growth and accomplishments of Jewish feminism and what they mean for Jewish women today and tomorrow.
6 x 9, 480 pp, Quality PB, 978-1-58023-448-1 **$19.99**; HC, 978-1-58023-359-0 **$24.99**

The Divine Feminine in Biblical Wisdom Literature
Selections Annotated & Explained
Translation & Annotation by Rabbi Rami Shapiro
5½ x 8½, 240 pp, Quality PB, 978-1-59473-109-9 **$16.99**
(A book from SkyLight Paths, Jewish Lights' sister imprint)

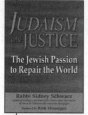

The Quotable Jewish Woman
Wisdom, Inspiration & Humor from the Mind & Heart
Edited by Elaine Bernstein Partnow
6 x 9, 496 pp, Quality PB, 978-1-58023-236-4 **$19.99**

The Women's Haftarah Commentary
New Insights from Women Rabbis on the 54 Weekly Haftarah Portions, the 5 Megillot & Special Shabbatot
Edited by Rabbi Elyse Goldstein
Illuminates the historical significance of female portrayals in the Haftarah and the Five Megillot. 6 x 9, 560 pp, Quality PB, 978-1-58023-371-2 **$19.99**

The Women's Torah Commentary
New Insights from Women Rabbis on the 54 Weekly Torah Portions
Edited by Rabbi Elyse Goldstein
Over fifty women rabbis offer inspiring insights on the Torah, in a week-by-week format.
6 x 9, 496 pp, Quality PB, 978-1-58023-370-5 **$19.99**; HC, 978-1-58023-076-6 **$34.95**

See Passover for *The Women's Passover Companion: Women's Reflections on the Festival of Freedom* and *The Women's Seder Sourcebook: Rituals & Readings for Use at the Passover Seder.*

Inspiration

God of Me: Imagining God throughout Your Lifetime
By Rabbi David Lyon Helps you cut through preconceived ideas of God and dogmas that stifle your creativity when thinking about your personal relationship with God. 6 x 9, 176 pp, Quality PB, 978-1-58023-452-8 **$16.99**

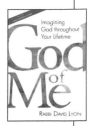

The God Upgrade: Finding Your 21st-Century Spirituality in Judaism's 5,000-Year-Old Tradition *By Rabbi Jamie Korngold; Foreword by Rabbi Harold M. Schulweis* A provocative look at how our changing God concepts have shaped every aspect of Judaism. 6 x 9, 176 pp, Quality PB, 978-1-58023-443-6 **$15.99**

The Seven Questions You're Asked in Heaven: Reviewing and Renewing Your Life on Earth *By Dr. Ron Wolfson* An intriguing and entertaining resource for living a life that matters. 6 x 9, 176 pp, Quality PB, 978-1-58023-407-8 **$16.99**

Happiness and the Human Spirit: The Spirituality of Becoming the Best You Can Be *By Rabbi Abraham J. Twerski, MD*
Shows you that true happiness is attainable once you stop looking outside yourself for the source. 6 x 9, 176 pp, Quality PB, 978-1-58023-404-7 **$16.99**; HC, 978-1-58023-343-9 **$19.99**

A Formula for Proper Living: Practical Lessons from Life and Torah
By Rabbi Abraham J. Twerski, MD 6 x 9, 144 pp, HC, 978-1-58023-402-3 **$19.99**

The Bridge to Forgiveness: Stories and Prayers for Finding God and Restoring Wholeness *By Rabbi Karyn D. Kedar* 6 x 9, 176 pp, Quality PB, 978-1-58023-451-1 **$16.99**

The Empty Chair: Finding Hope and Joy—Timeless Wisdom from a Hasidic Master, Rebbe Nachman of Breslov *Adapted by Moshe Mykoff and the Breslov Research Institute* 4 x 6, 128 pp, Deluxe PB w/ flaps, 978-1-879045-67-5 **$9.99**

The Gentle Weapon: Prayers for Everyday and Not-So-Everyday Moments— Timeless Wisdom from the Teachings of the Hasidic Master, Rebbe Nachman of Breslov *Adapted by Moshe Mykoff and S. C. Mizrahi, together with the Breslov Research Institute* 4 x 6, 144 pp, Deluxe PB w/ flaps, 978-1-58023-022-3 **$9.99**

God Whispers: Stories of the Soul, Lessons of the Heart *By Rabbi Karyn D. Kedar* 6 x 9, 176 pp, Quality PB, 978-1-58023-088-9 **$15.95**

God's To-Do List: 103 Ways to Be an Angel and Do God's Work on Earth *By Dr. Ron Wolfson* 6 x 9, 144 pp, Quality PB, 978-1-58023-301-9 **$16.99**

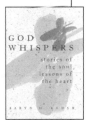

Jewish Stories from Heaven and Earth: Inspiring Tales to Nourish the Heart and Soul *Edited by Rabbi Dov Peretz Elkins* 6 x 9, 304 pp, Quality PB, 978-1-58023-363-7 **$16.99**

Life's Daily Blessings: Inspiring Reflections on Gratitude and Joy for Every Day, Based on Jewish Wisdom *By Rabbi Kerry M. Olitzky* 4½ x 6½, 368 pp, Quality PB, 978-1-58023-396-5 **$16.99**

Restful Reflections: Nighttime Inspiration to Calm the Soul, Based on Jewish Wisdom *By Rabbi Kerry M. Olitzky and Rabbi Lori Forman* 4½ x 6½, 448 pp, Quality PB, 978-1-58023-091-9 **$15.95**

Sacred Intentions: Morning Inspiration to Strengthen the Spirit, Based on Jewish Wisdom *By Rabbi Kerry M. Olitzky and Rabbi Lori Forman* 4½ x 6½, 448 pp, Quality PB, 978-1-58023-061-2 **$16.99**

Kabbalah/Mysticism

Jewish Mysticism and the Spiritual Life: Classical Texts, Contemporary Reflections *Edited by Dr. Lawrence Fine, Dr. Eitan Fishbane and Rabbi Or N. Rose* Inspirational and thought-provoking materials for contemplation, discussion and action. 6 x 9, 256 pp, HC, 978-1-58023-434-4 **$24.99**

Ehyeh: A Kabbalah for Tomorrow
By Rabbi Arthur Green, PhD 6 x 9, 224 pp, Quality PB, 978-1-58023-213-5 **$18.99**

The Gift of Kabbalah: Discovering the Secrets of Heaven, Renewing Your Life on Earth
By Tamar Frankiel, PhD 6 x 9, 256 pp, Quality PB, 978-1-58023-141-1 **$16.95**

Seek My Face: A Jewish Mystical Theology *By Rabbi Arthur Green, PhD*
6 x 9, 304 pp, Quality PB, 978-1-58023-130-5 **$19.95**

Zohar: Annotated & Explained *Translation & Annotation by Dr. Daniel C. Matt; Foreword by Andrew Harvey* 5½ x 8½, 176 pp, Quality PB, 978-1-893361-51-5 **$15.99**
(A book from SkyLight Paths, Jewish Lights' sister imprint)

See also *The Way Into Jewish Mystical Tradition* in The Way Into... Series.

Spirituality

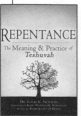

Repentance: The Meaning and Practice of *Teshuvah*
By Dr. Louis E. Newman; Foreword by Rabbi Harold M. Schulweis; Preface by Rabbi Karyn D. Kedar
Examines both the practical and philosophical dimensions of *teshuvah*, Judaism's core religious-moral teaching on repentance, and its value for us—Jews and non-Jews alike—today. 6 x 9, 256 pp, HC, 978-1-58023-426-9 **$24.99**

Tanya, the Masterpiece of Hasidic Wisdom
Selections Annotated & Explained
Translation & Annotation by Rabbi Rami Shapiro; Foreword by Rabbi Zalman M. Schachter-Shalomi
Brings the genius of *Tanya*, one of the most powerful books of Jewish wisdom, to anyone seeking to deepen their understanding of the soul.
5½ x 8½, 240 pp, Quality PB, 978-1-59473-275-1 **$16.99**
(A book from SkyLight Paths, Jewish Lights' sister imprint)

Aleph-Bet Yoga: Embodying the Hebrew Letters for Physical and Spiritual Well-Being
By Steven A. Rapp; Foreword by Tamar Frankiel, PhD, and Judy Greenfeld; Preface by Hart Lazer
7 x 10, 128 pp, b/w photos, Quality PB, Lay-flat binding, 978-1-58023-162-6 **$16.95**

A Book of Life: Embracing Judaism as a Spiritual Practice
By Rabbi Michael Strassfeld 6 x 9, 544 pp, Quality PB, 978-1-58023-247-0 **$19.99**

Bringing the Psalms to Life: How to Understand and Use the Book of Psalms
By Rabbi Daniel F. Polish, PhD 6 x 9, 208 pp, Quality PB, 978-1-58023-157-2 **$16.95**

Does the Soul Survive? A Jewish Journey to Belief in Afterlife, Past Lives & Living with Purpose *By Rabbi Elie Kaplan Spitz; Foreword by Brian L. Weiss, MD*
6 x 9, 288 pp, Quality PB, 978-1-58023-165-7 **$16.99**

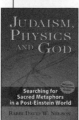

First Steps to a New Jewish Spirit: Reb Zalman's Guide to Recapturing the Intimacy & Ecstasy in Your Relationship with God *By Rabbi Zalman M. Schachter-Shalomi with Donald Gropman* 6 x 9, 144 pp, Quality PB, 978-1-58023-182-4 **$16.95**

Foundations of Sephardic Spirituality: The Inner Life of Jews of the Ottoman Empire
By Rabbi Marc D. Angel, PhD 6 x 9, 224 pp, Quality PB, 978-1-58023-341-5 **$18.99**

God & the Big Bang: Discovering Harmony between Science & Spirituality
By Dr. Daniel C. Matt 6 x 9, 216 pp, Quality PB, 978-1-879045-89-7 **$16.99**

God in Our Relationships: Spirituality between People from the Teachings of Martin Buber *By Rabbi Dennis S. Ross* 5½ x 8½, 160 pp, Quality PB, 978-1-58023-147-3 **$16.95**

The Jewish Lights Spirituality Handbook: A Guide to Understanding, Exploring & Living a Spiritual Life *Edited by Stuart M. Matlins*
What exactly is "Jewish" about spirituality? How do I make it a part of my life? Fifty of today's foremost spiritual leaders share their ideas and experience with us.
6 x 9, 456 pp, Quality PB, 978-1-58023-093-3 **$19.99**

Judaism, Physics and God: Searching for Sacred Metaphors in a Post-Einstein World
By Rabbi David W. Nelson 6 x 9, 352 pp, Quality PB, inc. reader's discussion guide,
978-1-58023-306-4 **$18.99**; HC, 352 pp, 978-1-58023-252-4 **$24.99**

Meaning & Mitzvah: Daily Practices for Reclaiming Judaism through Prayer, God, Torah, Hebrew, Mitzvot and Peoplehood *By Rabbi Goldie Milgram*
7 x 9, 336 pp, Quality PB, 978-1-58023-256-2 **$19.99**

Minding the Temple of the Soul: Balancing Body, Mind, and Spirit through Traditional Jewish Prayer, Movement, and Meditation *By Tamar Frankiel, PhD, and Judy Greenfeld*
7 x 10, 184 pp, Illus., Quality PB, 978-1-879045-64-4 **$18.99**

One God Clapping: The Spiritual Path of a Zen Rabbi *By Rabbi Alan Lew with Sherril Jaffe*
5½ x 8½, 336 pp, Quality PB, 978-1-58023-115-2 **$16.95**

The Soul of the Story: Meetings with Remarkable People
By Rabbi David Zeller 6 x 9, 288 pp, HC, 978-1-58023-272-2 **$21.99**

There Is No Messiah … and You're It: The Stunning Transformation of Judaism's Most Provocative Idea *By Rabbi Robert N. Levine, DD*
6 x 9, 192 pp, Quality PB, 978-1-58023-255-5 **$16.99**

These Are the Words: A Vocabulary of Jewish Spiritual Life
By Rabbi Arthur Green, PhD 6 x 9, 304 pp, Quality PB, 978-1-58023-107-7 **$18.95**

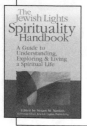

Judaism / Christianity / Interfaith

Christians & Jews—Faith to Faith: Tragic History, Promising Present, Fragile Future *By Rabbi James Rudin*
A probing examination of Christian-Jewish relations that looks at the major issues facing both faith communities.   6 x 9, 288 pp, HC, 978-1-58023-432-0 **$24.99**

How to Do Good & Avoid Evil: A Global Ethic from the Sources of Judaism   *By Hans Küng and Rabbi Walter Homolka* Explores how the principles of Judaism provide the ethical norms for all religions to work together toward a more peaceful humankind.   6 x 9, 224 pp, HC, 978-1-59473-255-3 **$19.99***

Getting to the Heart of Interfaith: The Eye-Opening, Hope-Filled Friendship of a Pastor, a Rabbi and a Sheikh
By Rabbi Ted Falcon, Pastor Don Mackenzie and Imam Jamal Rahman
Presents ways we can work together to transcend the differences that have divided us historically.   6 x 9, 192 pp, Quality PB, 978-1-59473-263-8 **$16.99***

Claiming Earth as Common Ground: The Ecological Crisis through the Lens of Faith   *By Rabbi Andrea Cohen-Kiener*   6 x 9, 192 pp, Quality PB, 978-1-59473-261-4 **$16.99***

Modern Jews Engage the New Testament: Enhancing Jewish Well-Being in a Christian Environment *By Rabbi Michael J. Cook, PhD*   6 x 9, 416 pp, HC, 978-1-58023-313-2 **$29.99**

The Changing Christian World: A Brief Introduction for Jews
By Rabbi Leonard A. Schoolman   5½ x 8½, 176 pp, Quality PB, 978-1-58023-344-6 **$16.99**

Christians & Jews in Dialogue: Learning in the Presence of the Other
By Mary C. Boys and Sara S. Lee
6 x 9, 240 pp, Quality PB, 978-1-59473-254-6 **$18.99**; HC, 978-1-59473-144-0 **21.99***

Disaster Spiritual Care: Practical Clergy Responses to Community, Regional and National Tragedy *Edited by Rabbi Stephen B. Roberts, BCJC, and Rev. Willard W. C. Ashley Sr., DMin, DH*
6 x 9, 384 pp, HC, 978-1-59473-240-9 **$40.00***

Healing the Jewish-Christian Rift: Growing Beyond Our Wounded History
By Ron Miller and Laura Bernstein 6 x 9, 288 pp, Quality PB, 978-1-59473-139-6 **$18.99***

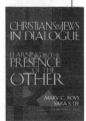

How to Be a Perfect Stranger, 5th Edition: The Essential Religious Etiquette Handbook   *Edited by Stuart M. Matlins and Arthur J. Magida*
6 x 9, 432 pp, Quality PB, 978-1-59473-294-2 **$19.99***

InterActive Faith: The Essential Interreligious Community-Building Handbook
Edited by Rev. Bud Heckman with Rori Picker Neiss
6 x 9, 304 pp, Quality PB, 978-1-59473-273-7 **$16.99**; HC, 978-1-59473-237-9 **$29.99***

Introducing My Faith and My Community
The Jewish Outreach Institute Guide for the Christian in a Jewish Interfaith Relationship
By Rabbi Kerry M. Olitzky 6 x 9, 176 pp, Quality PB, 978-1-58023-192-3 **$16.99**

The Jewish Approach to Repairing the World (*Tikkun Olam*)
A Brief Introduction for Christians *By Rabbi Elliot N. Dorff, PhD, with Rev. Cory Willson*
5½ x 8½, 256 pp, Quality PB, 978-1-58023-349-1 **$16.99**

The Jewish Connection to Israel, the Promised Land: A Brief Introduction for Christians   *By Rabbi Eugene Korn, PhD* 5½ x 8½, 192 pp, Quality PB, 978-1-58023-318-7 **$14.99**

Jewish Holidays: A Brief Introduction for Christians *By Rabbi Kerry M. Olitzky and Rabbi Daniel Judson* 5½ x 8½, 176 pp, Quality PB, 978-1-58023-302-6 **$16.99**

Jewish Ritual: A Brief Introduction for Christians *By Rabbi Kerry M. Olitzky and Rabbi Daniel Judson* 5½ x 8½, 144 pp, Quality PB, 978-1-58023-210-4 **$14.99**

A Jewish Understanding of the New Testament *By Rabbi Samuel Sandmel;
Preface by Rabbi David Sandmel* 5½ x 8½, 368 pp, Quality PB, 978-1-59473-048-1 **$19.99***

Righteous Gentiles in the Hebrew Bible: Ancient Role Models for Sacred Relationships *By Rabbi Jeffrey K. Salkin; Foreword by Rabbi Harold M. Schulweis; Preface by Phyllis Tickle*
6 x 9, 192 pp, Quality PB, 978-1-58023-364-4 **$18.99**

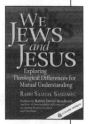

Talking about God: Exploring the Meaning of Religious Life with Kierkegaard, Buber, Tillich and Heschel *By Rabbi Daniel F. Polish, PhD* 6 x 9, 160 pp, Quality PB, 978-1-59473-272-0 **$16.99***

We Jews and Jesus: Exploring Theological Differences for Mutual Understanding
By Rabbi Samuel Sandmel; Preface by Rabbi David Sandmel
6 x 9, 192 pp, Quality PB, 978-1-59473-208-9 **$16.99**

*A book from SkyLight Paths, Jewish Lights' sister imprint

About Jewish Lights

People of all faiths and backgrounds yearn for books that attract, engage, educate, and spiritually inspire.

Our principal goal is to stimulate thought and help all people learn about who the Jewish People are, where they come from, and what the future can be made to hold. While people of our diverse Jewish heritage are the primary audience, our books speak to people in the Christian world as well and will broaden their understanding of Judaism and the roots of their own faith.

We bring to you authors who are at the forefront of spiritual thought and experience. While each has something different to say, they all say it in a voice that you can hear.

Our books are designed to welcome you and then to engage, stimulate, and inspire. We judge our success not only by whether or not our books are beautiful and commercially successful, but by whether or not they make a difference in your life.

For your information and convenience, at the back of this book we have provided a list of other Jewish Lights books you might find interesting and useful. They cover all the categories of your life:

Bar/Bat Mitzvah	Life Cycle
Bible Study / Midrash	Meditation
Children's Books	Men's Interest
Congregation Resources	Parenting
Current Events / History	Prayer / Ritual / Sacred Practice
Ecology / Environment	Social Justice
Fiction: Mystery, Science Fiction	Spirituality
Grief / Healing	Theology / Philosophy
Holidays / Holy Days	Travel
Inspiration	Twelve Steps
Kabbalah / Mysticism / Enneagram	Women's Interest

Stuart M. Matlins, Publisher

Or phone, fax, mail or e-mail to: **JEWISH LIGHTS Publishing**
Sunset Farm Offices, Route 4 • P.O. Box 237 • Woodstock, Vermont 05091
Tel: (802) 457-4000 • Fax: (802) 457-4004 • www.jewishlights.com
Credit card orders: **(800) 962-4544** (8:30AM–5:30PM ET Monday–Friday)
Generous discounts on quantity orders. SATISFACTION GUARANTEED. Prices subject to change.